# The Turkish–Israeli Relationship

# The Turkish–Israeli Relationship

## Changing Ties of Middle Eastern Outsiders

*Ofra Bengio*

First published in hardcover in 2004 by PALGRAVE MACMILLAN® in the United States—a division of St. Martin's Press LLC, 175 Fifth Avenue, New York, NY 10010.

Where this book is distributed in the UK, Europe and the rest of the world, this is by Palgrave Macmillan, a division of Macmillan Publishers Limited, registered in England, company number 785998, of Houndmills, Basingstoke, Hampshire RG21 6XS.

Palgrave Macmillan is the global academic imprint of the above companies and has companies and representatives throughout the world.

Palgrave® and Macmillan® are registered trademarks in the United States, the United Kingdom, Europe and other countries.

ISBN: 978–0–230–62033–9

Library of Congress Cataloging-in-Publication Data

Bengio, Ofra
    The Turkish-Israeli relationship : changing ties of Middle Eastern outsiders / by Ofra Bengio.
        p. cm.
    Includes bibliographical references (p.) and index.
    ISBN 1–4039–6589–7
        1. Turkey-Foreign relations—Israel. 2. Israel-Foreign relations—Turkey. I. Title.

DR479.I78B46 2004
327.56105694—dc22                                                    2003063227

A catalogue record for this book is available from the British Library.

Design by Newgen Imaging Systems (P) Ltd., Chennai, India.

First PALGRAVE MACMILLAN paperback edition: January 2010

10 9 8 7 6 5 4 3 2 1

Printed in the United States of America.

Transferred to Digital Printing in 2009.

*In memory of my beloved parents*
*Adina and Avraham Bassoul*

# Contents

# Preface

The idea for this book was born during an international seminar held in 1996, at Ann Arbor, Michigan, attended by a large number of scholars from all over the world, including myself, from Israel, and Prof. Gencer Özcan, of Yıldız University in Istanbul. It so happened that at that very time the strategic partnership between Turkey and Israel was being forged. After considering several other ideas, we decided to undertake a joint project that would deal with the deeper roots of this partnership. Since that time, we have continuously exchanged ideas, thoughts, and research materials, resulting in a number of coauthored articles on the subject. At some point, we each decided to write our own books on the subject, while continuing to benefit from ongoing exchanges and cooperation. Apart from the intellectual enrichment derived from our brainstorming marathons, my greatest joy has been the lasting friendship that has developed between us, for which I am deeply grateful to Gencer, his wife Hatice, and daughter Idil. My long night together with the Özcan family in earthquake-stricken Istanbul only cemented the relationship that much more.

This book is about encounters in different points of time between two cultures, societies, and nations, the Muslim Ottoman/Turkish and the Jewish–Israeli ones. These encounters were, on the whole, quite positive, and as such they were unique in the conflict-ridden Middle East. In weaving the story of those relations I have used a variety of Turkish, Israeli, and Arab source materials, as well as extensive interviews with people who were actively involved in forging Turkish–Israeli ties. For the period of the 1950s and 1960s, I have also made extensive use of Israeli diplomatic archives. Unfortunately, I had no such access to parallel Turkish documentation, while the British and the American archival sources were quite disappointing. Therefore, until such time as the Turkish archives are open, the story of the unfolding of relations will remain incomplete.

Working on this book turned out to be a very special experience for me. In excavating the deeper layers of the Turkish–Israeli relationship,

I discovered how my own personal family story fits in with the larger history of Jews and Turks. My parents, Adina and Avraham Bassoul, of Blessed Memory, and to whom this book is dedicated, were born in the Ottoman Empire, near Aleppo. They thus shared the fate of the multitude of Jews who found refuge in the Ottoman Empire after their expulsion from Spain in 1492. The ceremonies held in Turkey in 1992 to commemorate the five-hundredth anniversary of the Jews' arrival to the empire signified, as it were, the continuity in this special relationship. In later years, when Syria and the new State of Israel were in conflict, and the Syrian Jewish community became hostage to the whims of Syria's rulers, Turkey became the secret escape route for many Jews, including my family, through which they could pass to Israel. The strained relations between Turkey and Syria throughout the latter half of the twentieth century, and the conflict between Syria and Israel, would serve in time as an important glue for the Turkish–Israeli strategic partnership. Would it be too optimistic to hope that Turkey will one day fill the opposite role: that of a model for other Muslim states and even of a bridge to peace between Israel and Muslim Arab countries?

Writing a novel, I am told, is a solitary endeavor, but not a book of historical research, which requires the support, encouragement, and cooperation of many individuals and institutions. Indeed, I was fortunate to have plenty of all of these. The Moshe Dayan Center, my professional home, granted me all possible backing. Martin Kramer, the Center's former director, encouraged me to tread down an unknown path, and Asher Susser, the current director, helped me to reach its end. Aryeh Shmuelevitz provided constructive comments on the entire manuscript and made available to me his deep knowledge and insight concerning Turkey and the Ottoman Empire. Bruce Maddy-Weitzman accompanied the research and the writing of the book in its various phases, and his contribution to the final product was invaluable. I doubt whether it could have seen the light of day without his help. Other members of the Dayan Center who contributed in different ways to the book's completion were Roslyn Loon, Aryeh Ezra, Lydia Gareh, Elena Lesnick, Ilana Greenberg, Amira Margalith, Liat Kozma, and Ayelet Baruch. Haim Gal, head of the Center's Documentation Unit, and Marion Gliksberg and Dorit Porat, the Center's librarians, were also extremely helpful. I thank them all for their patience and their friendly assistance.

The research and writing of the book was assisted by grants from Süleyman Demirel Program at the Moshe Dayan Center, the Begin-Sadat Center for Strategic Studies at Bar-Ilan University, and the

Leonard Davis Institute of International Affairs at The Hebrew University. Yıldız University in Istanbul hosted me during various phases of my research, and the friendship of its staff has made me feel at home there. The staff of the Israeli National Archives was also most helpful. I would like to thank my Turkish and Israeli interviewees, most of whom must remain anonymous, for their time and insights. In the final stages of the work on the book, I benefited from the important suggestions made by two anonymous readers as well as from the linguistic editing and styling of Virginia Myers. David Pervin and the Palgrave team were most helpful in bringing the manuscript to publication. Last but not least, my husband Shmuel, and my sons Lavi and Adi, took active part in the endeavor, contributing ideas, observations, and insights, joining me in the great adventure of becoming better acquainted with another country, its people, language, and culture.

# Introduction

Shortly after the coup d'état of May 1960 in Turkey, an Israeli diplomat approached General Cemal Gürsel, the head of the new government in Ankara, to inquire about the prospect of upgrading relations with Israel. The General answered frankly: "We want you to know that we wish to befriend the Arabs," adding that: "our situation resembles that of a man in love with a woman who is surrounded [being courted] by many men. If I declare that I am in love with the woman, I will only annoy the other men with no benefit [to her]."[1] The analogy is, of course, false, since Israel was patently not being courted by the surrounding Arab countries, and was indeed a complete outcast. Nevertheless, it is helpful in illustrating the triangle of relations that shaped and reshaped itself over some four decades, from the establishment of the state of Israel in 1948 up to the early 1990s, when they were fundamentally transformed.

The heart of this book is the story of the Turkish–Israeli relationship over the past half century, which began in the shadows and eventually faded to insignificance, only to reemerge during the 1990s, this time in the full light of day, constituting a tectonic shift in the Middle Eastern strategic equation. But the story is not explored narrowly, rather as a lens for viewing the Middle Eastern strategic landscape, both past and present. With this new perspective, the received wisdom about the inter-Arab and Arab–Israeli conflicts and rivalries that characterized the 1950s must now be reexamined and revised. No longer can events such as the Suez Crisis and War, and the Egyptian–Iraqi struggle for regional hegemony, be viewed without regard to Turkey's crucial strategic role. It goes without saying that this is also true for the yet-to-be written history of the tumultuous 1990s.

Unlike most accounts that place overwhelming emphasis on American and British perspectives, this study analyzes modern Middle Eastern History from within the region, based on Turkish, Israeli, and Arab sources. It demonstrates how regional parties are far from passive "clients" of great powers, and in fact often act as the proverbial tail wagging the dog. Simultaneously, they vigorously pursue their own regional foreign policies *vis-à-vis* their immediate neighbors. It is this simultaneity that is often lost in the literature of the foreign policies of Middle East states. Turkey provides ample proof of foreign policy activism in both these directions: in contrast to accepted notions, Ankara was neither a mere follower of Washington in foreign policy matters, nor did the legacy of Kemalism result in Turkey's refraining from active engagement with its Arab neighbors in order to pursue its interests. In fact, profound geostrategic forces compelled Turkey to adopt policies that were not always in line with the desires of its Great Power patron, and to orient its foreign policies not just westward but also toward the Middle East. Hence, the account developed here provides the proper historical context for the full-fledged Turkish–Israeli alignment that began to emerge in 1993.

The major players in the Middle East—Israel, the Arab states, and Turkey—all acted according to certain basic assumptions or beliefs that conditioned their relations throughout this period, even when some of these proved to be mistaken or irrelevant.

Turkey's stance toward the Arab states can best be described as a duality. On the one hand, the memory of the Arabs as having "stabbed the Turks in the back" during the World War I continued to shape their image in Turkish eyes and to arouse suspicions and reservations about Arab intentions. On the other, considerations of *realpolitik* in the economic, political, and diplomatic spheres dictated close relations with Arab regimes. Although Turkey considered Israel to be a strategic asset in the region and a potential counterweight to the radical states in its immediate vicinity, it did not wish to endanger its relations with Arab countries for the sake of friendship with Jerusalem. As a consequence, four interrelated rules guided Turkey's behavior throughout the period: the need to adopt a balanced position *vis-à-vis* Israel and the Arab states; an assumption that the quality of relations with Arab countries was almost entirely determined by the type of relations with Israel; the view that friendly relations with Israel could only be detrimental to relations with the Arabs; and that Turkey should maintain its ties with Israel, but keep them as discreet as possible.

Israel's view of Turkey was conditioned by the fact that Ankara had for years been the only Muslim country in the region—and indeed the world—to have recognized Israel both de facto and de jure. Relations with Turkey were therefore of crucial strategic, political, and diplomatic importance. In other words, Turkey was a strategic asset, a pivotal country for Jerusalem in the years of its total isolation in the region. This drove Israel to do everything possible to strengthen relations with Ankara. Thus, almost all the initiatives for improving or upgrading relations came from Israel's side. In a sense, the Jewish state was completely dependent on Turkey's goodwill. It had to tread cautiously on any subject that was sensitive for Turkey, or could cause annoyance, and its room for maneuver between Turkey and the Arab states was almost nonexistent.

The Arab world's view of Turkey was shaped by the Ottoman legacy and by lingering fears that Turkey might one day encroach again on their sphere of influence. Suspicions were increased significantly by Turkey's recognition of Israel, which was perceived as a stab in the back, because it undermined Arab attempts to deny Jerusalem any legitimacy. Hence the endeavors by Arab states to turn the clock back, making their point of reference Turkey, rather than Israel—a country over which they had no leverage at all. The assumption was that the Arab states could, and should, exploit their numerical superiority to pressure Turkey to sever—or at least reduce to the minimum—its relations with Israel. Different levers were used at different times, including the oil weapon, Islamic solidarity, the Palestinian cause, and the issue of Cyprus.

The effect of all these contradictory interests, inhibitions, fears, and pressures was that relations between Turkey and Israel up to the 1990s developed along two tracks: a secret strategic track, which, when it existed, was quite intense and intimate, and a public track, which for most of the period was generally low-key and unimpressive. However, the Gulf crisis of 1990 and its aftermath eroded this duality, and little by little the two tracks drew closer together, and by 1996 they had openly converged. The key to this change lay in Turkey, and not Israel, which had always been eager to develop strong and open relations with Ankara. Indeed, the shift in Turkish policy was intimately linked to the far-reaching changes that engulfed the region after the Gulf crisis. As a result of that war, the Arab states lost much of their influence over Turkey, although this had been eroding for many years; the Israeli–Arab peace process granted legitimacy to Israel; and Turkey's own basic assumptions underwent some important transformations. All this persuaded Ankara to overcome the fear barrier and approach Israel openly, both politically and strategically.

Because the 1991 Gulf War was crucial to the various processes in the Middle East, this book begins with a panoramic view, analyzing the role of the various actors in the conflict: the United States, Iraq, and the

Arab world, Turkey, and Israel. The Gulf War and its consequences thus provide a framework for the regional developments of the 1990s, one aspect of which was the close alignment between Turkey and Israel. Chapter 2 is a flashback to the secret peripheral alliance between Turkey and Israel of the 1950s, which laid the foundations for the rapprochement of the 1990s. The historical context enables a better understanding of the forces at work during that time and allows comparisons to be drawn between the two periods. The background to the new alignment of the 1990s, and its different motives and motivators, are discussed in chapter 3. Placing the alignment in a domestic context illustrates the particular developments, pressures, dilemmas, and interests that were at play in both countries and helped shape their special relationship. This chapter also discusses the dual role of the United States in the alignment. Chapter 4 analyzes the content of the alignment and its strategic, military, political, and economic ramifications. The emphasis is less on the dry details of strategic agreements than on presenting a wider picture of the type of relations that developed between the two countries and their peoples. The reactions of states in the region, which have sometimes confounded scholars and analysts, are the focus of chapter 5: to what extent did neighbouring states actively oppose the Turkish–Israeli alignment, and to what extent did they accomodate it; and what was the overall effect on the balance of relations in the region. The conclusion tries to answer the two basic questions of this study: to what extent did the alignment form a new regional order? And did Turkish–Israeli relations cross a point of no return after the Gulf War?

On the whole, the book is not written chronologically, but rather in a "Rashomon style," in which each chapter provides a different perspective and emphasis on the relationship. They can therefore be read separately, but for the sake of clarity certain details are occasionally repeated. Although the general time frame is the 12-year period between the 1991 Gulf War and the 2003 American *coup de grace* against Saddam Hussein's regime, relevant historical contexts and factors are discussed in all chapters.

# Chapter 1

# After the 1991 Gulf War Earthquake

We are a nation of rock-solid realism and clear-eyed idealism. We are Americans: we are the nation that believes in the future. We are the nation that can shape the future.

(President George Bush, *State of the Union address*, January 30, 1991)[1]

Shortly after the Iraqi invasion of Kuwait, when President Bush began to develop his vision of the "New World Order," he had no clear idea of its shape and guiding principles. Although the Cold War was over, the Soviet Union was not yet defunct and the Gulf War not yet won. Bush therefore outlined a rather vague mission of achieving "the universal aspirations of mankind: peace and security, freedom and the rule of law."[2] This was reminiscent of President Woodrow Wilson's famous Fourteen Points and similar declarations made 72 years earlier, which had called for "self-determination" for all people, including the "unmolested opportunity of autonomous development" for nationalities under Turkish [Ottoman] rule in particular.[3] It is instructive to compare the two declarations in terms of their vision for the Middle East and America's standing in it. While the Wilson doctrine envisaged a drastic change from the *status quo ante* by allowing self-determination to the nations of the region that of Bush planned to return to the *status quo ante* by freeing Kuwait from Iraqi occupation. Second, both sought to shape the future of the Middle East, but Wilson let others—Britain and France—decide the fate of the region, while Bush himself was the moving force behind his vision. Third, Wilson's doctrine was followed by an era of America's near-aloofness from the Middle East, which lasted until World War II, while that of Bush ushered in a period of unprecedented American presence in the region.

## America's Moment in the Middle East

In a speech on the New World Order delivered in the middle of the Gulf War, President Bush spoke about America's "indispensable" leadership of the world and depicted the coming century as "the next American century."[4] While this has yet to prove its validity, one can certainly speak of an "American decade" in the Middle East during the 1990s. The U.S. position in the region has undergone a sweeping change, not only in comparison to its relative aloofness during the first part of the twentieth century, but also with its much more activist stance of the 1950s and beyond. The questions that need concern us, therefore, are as follows. What is the impact of the New World Order on the American position in the region, and what made it possible? To what extent was the U.S. reactive, or proactive, in its Middle East policies? To what extent did it manage to shape the region according to its own vision, and how much did the competing visions of the regional players dictate the agenda? More particularly, what place, if any, did the alignment between Turkey and Israel have in this American vision?

President Bush's idealistic articulation of the New World Order was ridiculed by leftist intellectuals, who depicted his vision as "clichés," "lovely phrases," and a "cracking facade of high principles," all of which were but a cover for "old goals of world domination," for "supporting the most reactionary regimes going and assisting them in controlling the third world populations, and for maintaining America's near monopoly of force with no likely contestant for that role."[5] Yet however one looks at it, the Gulf crisis did form the testing ground for the crystallization of the New World Order, which catapulted the United States into the role of the only superpower in the world and in the Middle East in particular.[6] This new role was evidenced in the geostrategic, military, political, and ideological domains.

The American military presence in the Middle East was boosted significantly, both quantitatively and qualitatively, after the Gulf crisis. The causes for this development were obvious, yet they would have been quite unthinkable a decade or two earlier. The war itself brought some 532,000 American troops (out of 760,000 of different nations), 2,070 tanks, 1,376 combat aircraft, about 1,900 helicopters, and 180 ships into the region.[7] While on paper 28 nations participated in the anti-Iraq alliance, in practice the lion's share of the burden was Washington's, hence also the spoils of the war. These spoils were not physical domination of territory and nations, as was the case with Britain and France after World War I, but rather the deployment of forces and military hardware in strategic areas. The indecisive ending to the war with Iraq necessitated—or, as America's critics would say, formed the pretext for—such a move. Although Iraq was ousted from Kuwait, Iraq's President Saddam Hussein remained entrenched in power, and was a potential danger both to his neighbors and to his own Kurdish and Shi'a populations. The basic rationale behind the American presence was, therefore, to protect its client states and the defenseless groups in Iraq. But behind this apparent idealism, strong realism was at play: the need to protect America's traditional strategic interest in the Gulf—the flow of oil. The show of force was also to serve another goal: to convince the waverers in the older confrontation—the Arab–Israeli conflict—to opt for peace.

Several developments facilitated the United States establishing a high military profile in the region. First, the demise of the Soviet Union, which could no longer project power into the region and endanger American soldiers. Second, the fact that Saudi Arabia and Kuwait were the main financiers of the Gulf War and troop deployment and of ongoing American military activities.[8] Equally important was the revolution in military technology, which made it possible for Washington to wage war by remote control. The combination of all three factors allowed the United States the luxury of taking intermittent military action in the Middle East over more than a decade, while avoiding the syndrome of the Vietnam War (1955–75), with its severe human, economic, military, and political costs.

If the Middle East was a main theater for the Cold War that had raged between the United States and the Soviet Union for 40 years since the 1950s, then the Gulf War helped to draw the final curtain on that drama. The end of the Cold War and the ensuing collapse of the Soviet Union had far-reaching implications for the region. For individual countries, the greatest impact was on three neighboring states—Turkey, Syria, and Iraq. For Turkey, it meant the disappearance of a potential enemy, the Soviet Union, but also some temporary loss of importance as a buffer state against Soviet encroachment in the Middle East. For the other two it signified the loss of a patron, which, although its role had gradually diminished, had nevertheless served to the end as a balancing factor in the region. The USSR's withdrawal not only affected the balance of power within the region, as, for example, in the triangle of Turkish–Syrian–Iraqi relations, it also changed the stance of almost each country toward the Soviet Union's rival—the United States. Curiously enough, while the disappearance of the USSR moved Syria to seek to improve its relations with the United States, it triggered Iraq into challenging Washington. Accordingly, while the fault line between the countries of the region during the Cold War was between pro-Americans and pro-Soviets, it was now between pro-Americans and anti-Americans, with an additional category of waverers.

Although the end of the Cold War and the demise of Soviet influence became apparent only in the late 1980s and early 1990s, the process of diffusing the intense rivalry between the two superpowers started, in fact, a decade earlier. The clearest evidence was their position on the Iraq–Iran War (1980–88) and their relations during it. Despite the important strategic assets that both held in the two warring countries and in the Gulf region as a whole, and despite the proximity of their bases to the battle arena, at no time during the eight-year war was there a danger that the Soviets and Americans would be drawn in as rivals. Moreover, one can say that a kind of détente—even entente—developed between them with regard to the war, which led to the virtual containment of the warring parties, as well as to the prolongation of the war itself. For the Soviet Union, the Iraq–Iran War ushered in the dismantling of its assets in the region in the early 1990s. In spite of its formal treaty of friendship with Iraq since 1972, the USSR at first tilted toward Iran. It began to support Baghdad militarily only in 1982, and then attempted to balance relations with both countries.[9] Thus, during the 1990–91 Gulf crisis and war, the USSR played the part of neutral mediator to Iraq, rather than the ally that Baghdad must have expected. Taken together, these developments finally led to the marginalization of the Soviet Union and its heir, Russia, in the region. For the first time in almost two centuries (one could even say four), the region had to contend with one major world power rather than two or three. It was against this background that President Bush developed his vision of the New World Order, with its pretensions of shaping the world, starting with the Middle East.

The "New American Order" in the Middle East was inaugurated by the Gulf War in January–February 1991. For the United States, this was a real turning point: never before had it been involved in a war against any country of this region. Indeed, the war marked the climax of the incremental involvement of the United States in the Middle East. This had started with the period between the two World Wars, when its main interest was economic—the quest for oil—and continued in the period from the end of World War II to the end of the Cold War, when it diversified its interests to include political and ideological fields. It now culminated in the Gulf War, which added yet another dimension—military strategic interests.[10] This process involved the gradual dismantling of the two important powers in the Middle East—first Britain, which had lost its final assets by the early 1970s, and then the USSR, which lost them by the 1990s—leaving the United States to fill, or attempt to fill, the vacuum left by both.

Much has been written about the 1991 Gulf War and its reverberations.[11] Some points should be highlighted, however, in order to understand the American role in shaping the region's destiny in the 1990s. In spite of the United States being the dominant force behind the anti-Iraq coalition and the major military power in the war, its strategy was, on the whole, reactive, in the sense that it reacted to Saddam Hussein's actions or provocations and did not, for example, initiate a preemptive move before his invasion of Kuwait. Indeed, this was to be the characteristic U.S. posture on Iraq until the September 11, 2001 bombings of the World Trade Center in New York caused a sea change in U.S. strategic thinking. Although the United States became engaged in a ten-year war of attrition against Iraq during the 1990s—in itself an innovation in American policy in the region—its military strikes or bombing of Iraqi sites were still mostly in reaction to Hussein's moves and not preplanned initiatives. Also, while the United States had a clear sense of direction with regard to the war itself, it became less and less focused in its aftermath. The end of the war ushered in an era of American bewilderment, indecision, ambiguity, and double messages on Iraq, which found expression in reactive policies.

Similar ambiguities were reflected in the American stance on the Iraqi Kurds, which set another precedent for U.S. policy in the region—involvement in the domestic affairs of a foreign country. Initially, President Bush sought to disengage himself altogether from Iraq's Kurdish and Shi'a issues. Even though he had encouraged the Iraqi population during the war to rise up against Saddam Hussein,[12] and in spite of his lofty ideals of bringing freedom and security to the people of the world, he remained aloof to the Kurdish (and Shi'a) plight after Saddam had crushed their uprising in April 1991. Moreover, he declared himself unwilling to commit even "a single [American] soldier" to "a civil war in Iraq that's been going on for ages."[13] As time went on, however, he himself, and especially his successor, President Bill Clinton, became more and more involved in the Kurdish issue. In the past, the few contacts that the United States had had with Iraqi Kurds were in total secrecy, but now they were made openly. The United States had ignored intra-Kurdish fighting altogether, but from 1996 it increasingly played the role of mediator between the two rival Kurdish groups—the Kurdistan Democratic Party (KDP) headed by Mas'ud Barzani, and the Patriotic Union of Kurdistan (PUK) headed by Jalal Talabani—even inviting their representatives to Washington (e.g., the initiation of the

"Washington process" of 1998). Similarly, in the past the United States had secretly encouraged the Kurds to destabilize the Iraqi regime, but it now did so quite openly. Taken together, America's policy shift on the Iraqi Kurds reflected and amplified its dilemmas on the Iraqi issue as a whole. The United States sought to destabilize Saddam Hussein's regime, but feared that in the process Iraq would break up into two or three parts. It considered the Kurds an important tool for precipitating the fall of the Iraqi dictator, but was reluctant to grant them the necessary support, lest they would "succeed too much" and end up separating from the state. It did not wish to be directly involved in the Kurdish issue, but feared that aloofness or indifference might encourage Saddam Hussein to initiate a military action in order to regain control of the Kurdish areas. This, in turn, might trigger an exodus of the Kurds and hence strengthen the central government. As far as the Kurds were concerned, then, the United States looked like a person who had kindled a fire and did not want it to be smothered, but was unable to control it all the time. The ambiguities and the limitations of the Kurdish–U.S. relationship would be superseded only in spring 2003, with the American war to overthrow the Ba'thi regime and remake Iraq, in strategic partnership with the Iraqi Kurds.

## America's Three Policy Pillars in the Middle East

While it was President Bush who came up with the notion of the New World Order, it was left to his successor, President Clinton, during his eight years in office, to plan and execute these policies in the Middle East. The most important ingredient of the new order was an extensive American presence in the region, reflected in military might, political clout, economic influence, and diplomatic activity. Within a few months of his election, Clinton developed a two-pronged policy for the Middle East—"the two policy pillars"—later to be supplemented by a third, undeclared one. The most articulate presentation of this policy was made by Martin Indyk, Senior Director for the Near East and South Asia on the National Security Council, in a speech on May 18, 1993.[14] Analyzing the changes in the Middle East since the demise of the Soviet Union and the Gulf War, and their implications for U.S. policy, Indyk stressed the following points:

1. The United States no longer needed to view the region through "a competitive global prism," but could judge developments there in terms of their impact on American regional, rather than global, interests.

2. For the first time since the 1950s, the United States emerged as the "unchallenged dominant power" in the region, and all sides were looking to Washington "to exert its influence." The paradox was that, while the United States was "tasked with greater regional responsibilities," it was less able to fulfill them, since the absence of superpower competition also brought in its wake "less influence" over the policies of regional powers.

3. The region could no longer be dealt with "in compartments," since the proliferation of ballistic missiles on the one hand, and the spread of religious extremism on the other, meant that what happened in the east of the region had immediate impact on the west of the region, and vice versa.

4. The end of the Cold War necessitated a redefining of the region, and the inclusion of the newly emerging Muslim states of Central Asia as a factor in U.S. strategy, something that endowed Turkey with an "increasingly important role" in American regional calculations.

Along with these reformulated strategies, Indyk outlined four abiding American interests in the region: the free flow of oil at reasonable prices; reciprocating the friendship of Arab countries that sought good relations with the United States; the survival, well-being, and security of Israel; and settlement of the Arab–Israeli conflict. This led to the forging of a regional strategy that combined all the above considerations, and was based on the three policy pillars of "dual containment" of Iraq and Iran in the east, encouraging an Arab–Israeli peace process in the west, and promoting "a vision" of a more democratic and prosperous region for all the peoples of the Middle East.

Identifying Iraq and Iran as the major source of threat to the region and, for that matter, to the United States, the new policy sought to neutralize them, not by balancing one against the other, as in the past, but rather by containing both. The best way to do this was through tight economic and political sanctions. In this way, the United States hoped to strengthen its hold on a strategically vital region of the Gulf and to defend its clients there more effectively. Indeed, no other region in the Middle East better represented the fault line between pro-American and anti-American countries than did the Gulf. Roughly speaking, the northern part belonged to the anti-American camp, the southern to the pro-American camp; Iran and Iraq were in the former, other Gulf states in the latter.

The second policy pillar was promotion of the peace process between the (more moderate) Arabs and Israel, now made possible by the changing strategic circumstances in the region and the realization by both sides that, after four decades of attempting to settle their conflict by force, the time had come to try direct negotiations. The Clinton administration was thus following in the footsteps of its predecessor. However, it decided to step up its role in the negotiations by offering to become a "full partner" to all the parties. According to this conceptualization of the Middle East, there was to be an interdependence between the two pillars, so that containing the threats posed by Iraq and Iran was to have a positive impact on promoting the peace process between the Arabs and Israel, and promoting the peace process was to facilitate containment of the Iraqi and Iranian threats.

On the third pillar, the promotion of democracy in the Middle East, Indyk did not elaborate, saying that the articulation of this policy would be deferred to a later date and to other people. Indeed, this is what eventually happened, not during the eight years of the Clinton administration in which Indyk served, but the subsequent Republican administration of George W. Bush. No coherent policy was ever articulated during the Clinton years, as policy-makers seemed to recognize that democratization was, after all, a long process and could not be imposed from outside. They also seemed to recognize that forceful advocacy of democratization would bring the United States into conflict with friend (e.g., Saudi Arabia) and foe (e.g., Iraq) alike, in which the risks outweighed the rewards. Indeed, the discrepancy between the American preaching of high ideals, and what was regarded as total inaction in implementing them, came under strong attack from the administration's critics at home and abroad.

The ideal of promoting democracy seemed to undergo a metamorphosis in the mid-1990s. Instead of trying to introduce democracy to countries ruled by authoritarian and totalitarian regimes, the United States shifted its policy toward promoting alignment between two self-styled democracies in the region, Turkey and Israel. Indeed, the Turkish–Israeli alignment would emerge as the third, undeclared, American policy pillar in the region during the latter part of the 1990s, and it is the focus of this book. From the vantage point of 2003, one may conclude that it alone of the three pillars was truly durable and commensurate with American interests in a volatile region: dual containment had eroded even more quickly than expected during the late 1990s, helping to prepare the ground for the strategic shift in U.S. policy after September 11, 2001.

The other pillar of U.S. Middle East policy, the peace process, was characterized by ups and downs throughout the decade. The progress made was not, however, due to the United States being a full partner.

In fact, in the September 1993 Oslo Agreement between Israel and the PLO, the United States was not a partner at all. Nor were the successes or failures in this area linked to the viability of dual containment. The linkage between "east" and "west" hardly existed in reality. The signing of the Oslo Agreement had no connection with dual containment, and the same was true of the peace agreement between Jordan and Israel in 1994, and the negotiations with Syria. Insofar as Damascus joined the peace process, it was for quite different domestic, regional, and international reasons. Furthermore, Syria's alliance with Iran neither stopped it from joining the peace talks, nor was it the cause of their failure. Overall, the peace process seemed to have no direct impact on the success or failure of dual containment, and the collapse of the containment policy had no bearing on the peace process. Indeed, it can safely be said that dual containment and the peace process progressed largely on parallel lines. It will be intriguing, however, to find out if there were fine linkages between the peace process and the alignment between Turkey and Israel. This is discussed in chapter 5, which deals with the triangle of Turkish–Arab–Israeli relations.

Iraqi officials and the media often spoke of American "neo-imperialism." Whether one agrees with this or not, a comparison with "old" imperialism may provide some clues about the U.S. role in the region and the new order it set out to establish.[15] If the term applies at all, it may be in the sense that the United States has emerged as the only "empire" in the world that can, and does, actively seek to establish its order in the Middle East. The old imperialism represented by Britain and France, occupied key areas for various strategic, economic, and political reasons, while also purporting to bring civilization to the people (the famous French *mission civilisatrice*). Washington's main goal during the 1990s was to bring stability to the region and to integrate it into the American world system. Instead of imperialism by occupation, one could speak of imperialism by integration, and instead of drawing new maps, of jealously preserving the old ones. However, following the September 11 attacks, the United States added a new twist to its policy: direct military intervention to topple regimes deemed threatening to U.S. interests, and pro-active, intimate involvement on the ground to refashion Middle East realities. Those opposed to America's grand strategic plan viewed its actions as a combination of old and new imperialisms; all observers could agree that it was certainly a different, and unabashedly imperial strategy.

To return to the 1990s: another important difference between the pre- and post-1991 eras was that in the old system, the region was torn by rivalries and influences between different powers, while in the after-math of the 1991 war and the end of the Cold War the United States stood unrivalled, with no major power to counterbalance it, the efforts of Russia, France, and China notwithstanding. In the early age of Western imperialism, the different British spheres of influence—Iraq, Palestine, and Egypt, for example—earned more or less similar treat-ment from London, while in the *Pax Americana* era, the only hegemonic power, divided the Middle East into two zones, reminiscent of the "zone of war" (*dar al-harb*) and the "zone of peace" (*dar al-salam*) of clas-sical Islamic thought. The *dar al-harb* zone (the Middle East portion of what later became George W. Bush's "axis of evil") consisted of those countries that should be fought against, either militarily or through sanctions, such as the Ba'thi Iraq regime, Iran, Sudan, and Libya. The *dar al-salam* zone, namely America's Arab friends (Egypt, Jordan, Morocco, and the Gulf Arab states) and potential partners (Syria and the Palestinians), were to be encouraged to engage in peacemaking with Israel.

In the eyes of Ba'thi Iraq, the difference between the old imperialism and the new was striking. Under the old, Britain was deeply involved in day-to-day activities, while under the new, America sought to police Baghdad by remote control. In the old imperialism, Britain (in the Mandate period) protected its client governments from the often-dissident Iraqi Kurdish and Shi'a communities, even through the use of air strikes against them,[16] while the United States sought to protect the Kurds and (to a far lesser extent) the Shi'as against the regime in Baghdad by establishing no-fly zones in the Kurdish north and the Shi'a south, in 1991 and 1992 respectively.[17]

To sum up, the United States, after a decade of intensive involvement in the affairs of the region, had not managed to bring its *enfant terrible, Ba'thi* Iraq, to order. Iraq remained the main spoiler of the American order and, in Baghdad's perception, the only rival to the United States in a uni-polar world. It was only in March–April 2003 that the United States brought a final end to what was, in essence a 12-year war against Saddam Hussein's Iraq, opening up a new era of uncertainty.

## Breaking Taboos, Deconstructing Myths

The Iraqi invasion of Kuwait in August 1990 had a kind of domino effect on the Middle East, in that the breaking of one taboo—an attack on an Arab country by a sister Arab country—led to the breaking of other taboos, myths, and conventions. So strong were the shockwaves of that one event that they changed the map of the region, not geo-graphically, where it remained intact except for a few months, but in terms of the relationship between different actors within the region, and between them and others outside it.

The term "taboo" in social science refers to practices that are generally prohibited because of religious or social pressures. On the other hand, one of the meanings of "myth" is a belief or set of beliefs, often unproven or false, that accrue around a person, phenomenon, or institution. The Iraqi president, Saddam Hussein, attempted to juggle with both, in an attempt to deflect attention from reality and to lull his enemies, but ended in breaking a taboo of his own making.

When Saddam Hussein assumed power in 1979, the central myth that informed his worldview was of Pan-Arabism and Arab unity. Although by that time this had become mostly cliché,[18] Saddam seized on the idea and attempted to resurrect it in his famous declaration of February 1980.[19] However, while promoting a Pan-Arab facade, he quite consciously shackled himself with some taboos that were to boomerang on him in later years. One of these was Article No. 2 of the declaration, calling for "the banning of the use of armed force by any Arab state against any Arab state and the solution of any disputes that may arise between the Arab countries by peaceful means and within the context of the principles of joint Arab actions and supreme Arab interests."

Equally interesting was Article No. 1, which called for "the rejection of the presence or the facilitation of the presence of any foreign armies, bases or armed forces in the Arab homeland in any form, under any pretext and guise and for any reason; the isolation of any Arab regime which does not adhere to that principle; the boycott of such an Arab regime politically and economically and opposition to all its policies by all available means."

Another notable article was No. 4, which advocated the solidarity of all Arab countries "against any aggression, violation or state of actual war that any foreign side may undertake against the territorial integrity of any Arab country. These countries will jointly repulse that aggression or violation and will thwart it by all methods and means, including military action, collective political and economic boycott and any other method dictated by necessity and pan-Arab interests." Most instructive of all was Article No. 8, which stated that "Iraq declares its readiness to be committed to this declaration before every Arab country."

Banning the use of force by one Arab state against another was noth-ing new, and this was but a rephrasing of a principle contained in the

1945 Charter of the Arab League.[20] Nor was the breaking of it new. The list of Arab states that had preceded Iraq in their use of force in inter-Arab conflicts is long. They included Egypt in its intervention in the civil war in Yemen in 1962, Syria's brief intervention in the Jordanian–PLO conflict in Jordan in September 1970, and from 1976, Syria's military involvement in Lebanon. The novelty was that Baghdad had resurrected the ban and publicly committed itself to be the first to honor it, yet in practice did not limit itself to military intervention or even to creeping annexation, but sought with a single stroke to erase another Arab state from the map. Iraq's cynical breaking of its own taboo set in motion a chain reaction that led to the breaking of other taboos as well. The irony was that Article Nos. 1 and 4 were implemented almost verbatim by certain Arab countries, chief among them Egypt, Syria, and Saudi Arabia, not in support of Iraq, as the declaration had envisaged, but against it.

In breaking this taboo, which finds expression in the famous saying, "I and my cousin against the foreigner," these three and other Arab countries allied themselves with foreigners, non-Arabs, and non-Muslims against an Arab and Muslim country.[21] This alliance of leading Arab states with the United States, Britain, and France also signified an ad hoc historical reconciliation with "imperialist" forces past and present. For certain Arab countries, the road they traveled was long indeed. Syria, for one, joined the "American camp" in spite of being a politically radical regime and the ally of the Soviet Union and Iran. Saudi Arabia, although belonging traditionally to the American camp, went out of its way, for the first time in its history, to sanction an extensive American presence on its soil. Similarly, since the end of the Gulf War, Arab countries of the Gulf—especially Saudi Arabia and Kuwait—have flagrantly violated Saddam's Article No. 1 by allowing the deployment of American forces on their soil, as well as agreeing to sporadic attacks on Iraq launched from their territory. Hence the punishment of isolation prescribed by Iraq for such aggressive actions boomeranged against him.

Another change in the map of Middle East relations after the 1991 Gulf War was the initiation of the peace process between Arabs and Israel. It was true that the taboo on such a process had been dramatically broken by Egypt more than a decade earlier. The difference now was that the process was much more encompassing, and was more than one isolated track. Also, the inclusion of both Jordan and Syria proved that the fault line between moderates and radicals in the Arab world was becoming blurred. Although the Syrian track would remain relatively blocked, the country's very participation in the process proved that this particular taboo or psychological barrier was no longer the main stumbling block.

A third change of great magnitude, and the focus of this study, is the alignment between Turkey and Israel. While one cannot speak here of breaking taboos in the strict sense, because relations between Turkey and Israel had existed since the establishment of the state of Israel in 1948, the intensity and deepening of these relations was nevertheless closely connected with the breaking of taboos and psychological barriers elsewhere in the Arab world.

That such sweeping changes could have occurred in such a short period was also connected with the erosion of some pervasive underlying myths in the region. The de-mythification of Pan-Arabism highlighted the diminishing of Arab solidarity—if it ever existed. Nevertheless, most Arab states had subscribed to it before the Gulf War. The most blatant case of breaching the solidarity myth was Syria's support of Iran during its eight-year war against Iraq. This created a precedent for other Arab countries to redefine their "Arab solidarity" during the Gulf War. Since the war was initially between two Arab states, Iraq and Kuwait, it was easy for those who backed Kuwait to depict their support as part of Arab solidarity and to blur its other aspect—support of the United States and its Western allies against an Arab country.

Another set of myths that was severely shaken was the perception of the United States and its relations with the Arab world.[22] The dominant myth was that the American position in the Middle East was fragile and depended on Arab goodwill. In fact, the alignment of leading Arab countries, including radical Syria, with the American-led alliance proved just the opposite. Arab countries needed American support to repel a military threat from a sister Arab country. A related myth was that America's regional standing was vulnerable because all Arabs or Muslims might unite against it. This, too, was disproved during the Gulf War and its aftermath. A third myth was that the Arab obsession with the Palestinian issue meant that nothing else counted when determining their stance toward the United States. Reality, however, was more complicated, with state interests relegating ideological tenets to secondary importance.

Simultaneously with these changes, a different perception of Israel and the Arab–Israeli conflict began to emerge. The myth that Israel was the most dangerous enemy for each Arab country individually, and for the Arabs as a whole, was invalidated on two levels. First, it dawned on many regimes in the Middle East, both Arab and non-Arab, that their greatest danger emanated from domestic forces and conflicts instead. According to the Egyptian scholar, Sa'd al-Din Ibrahim, civil wars and conflicts between minorities and the state in Arab countries had taken a much higher toll than the Arab–Israeli conflict. He estimated the number of Arab casualties in all the Arab–Israeli wars to be 200,000, while that of Arab civil wars was 1,690,000. The casualties in Sudan alone, in a relatively short period, were 900,000 and in Iraq, 400,000.[23] These figures are partly corroborated by the Institute for Strategic Studies in London, which put the number of fatalities from Sudan's civil war during 1963–72 at 500,000, and those of Iraq from 1961 to 1970 at 105,000.[24] Even if these numbers are exaggerated, there is no doubt that civil wars in certain Arab countries, in particular Iraq, Sudan, and Lebanon, were much longer than all the Arab–Israeli wars put together, and that the threat to the state from radical Islamist groups or ethnic and religious minorities, was much stronger and more violent than the wars against Israel.[25]

If anything, the Iraqi invasion of Kuwait proved that when contemplating a danger from the outside, an Arab sister state could be as dangerous as Israel, if not more so. This shocking realization went a long way to explain the sustained military, economic, and political efforts made by Kuwait and Saudi Arabia to weaken, isolate, and ostracize Iraq, such as they had never done to Israel. Indeed, the Iraq–Iran War and the Gulf War diversified the conflicts in the region, so that it was no longer monopolized by the Arab–Israeli conflict. The long war between two Muslim regimes, and the short war between two Arab countries that developed into a bloody conflict among many Arab countries, had the effect of relegating the Arab–Israeli conflict to a secondary place at times, as well as causing certain Arab countries to consider the possibility of coming to terms with Israel.

Like many countries in the region, Israel, too, underwent a process of de-mythification as a result of the Gulf War and related developments. This is discussed in more detail below, but suffice to say that in Israel's case as well, the erosion of prevailing myths and concepts played an important role in changing its thinking on the peace process, especially in regard to the Palestinian track, and also in its push for closer strategic relations with Turkey.

In one sense, then, by the beginning of the 1990s, the region was significantly different from a decade or two earlier. In another, it remained quite static. Arab coalitions had formed and reformed, but overall the state system had proved to be the strongest. Countries such as Kuwait,

Lebanon, Iraq, Sudan, or the two Yemens, which were in the throes of dismantlement, disintegration, or civil war, proved resistant enough to survive these severe crises. Linked to this was the triumph of state interests over ideologies. Not only did Pan-Arabism and Arab unity become mere slogans, but the old–new ideology of Islamism had failed to change the systems in Arab countries—except for Sudan. The myth that the Islamic Revolution of Iran would sweep over the region evaporated. Even Iran opted for state interests when these clashed with Islamic ideology.[26]

But the vacuum was soon filled by new myths and concepts. "Democratization," "globalization," and the "clash of civilizations" became the new catchwords. Although totally different from each other, they had one characteristic in common: they emanated from the West or reflected Western conceptualization. Hence, the prospect that they might influence the rhythm of social, economic, and political life was not particularly attractive to most countries of the Middle East. Democratization was threatening to those leaders and regimes that had hitherto ruled through totalitarian or authoritarian political systems. Globalization was considered to be a threat on all social, economic, political, and cultural levels. The concept of the clash of civilizations had been put forward by only one person[27] and was highly controversial even in the West. But the very idea that, instead of peaceable interaction, the world might expect a clash between the West and Islam was considered by Arabs and Muslims to be widespread enough in the West, and sufficiently frightening, not to be dismissed so easily.

If these three new concepts formed a dividing line between West and East, could it be possible that, conversely, they acted as a glue between two countries in the Middle East—Turkey and Israel? I shall try to answer this question in later chapters.

## Turkey's Return to the Region

Turkey's perception of the outside world, and its role in it, underwent dramatic changes within the short space of two years. So did the outside world's perceptions of Turkey. The causes of these changes are well known: the end of the Cold War, the outbreak of the Gulf War, and the collapse of the Soviet Union. The fall of the curtain on the last act of the Cold War in 1989 threatened to marginalize Turkey's role in the West. Just one year later, however, the Gulf crisis and ensuing war promised a quick restoration of Turkey's strategic role—even its enhancement—while the final collapse of the Soviet Union in 1991 opened new vistas for Ankara and freed its hand to steer foreign policy in new directions, one of which was the Middle East. Indeed, the combined effect of these three events was to facilitate Turkey's return to the Middle East.

Turkey's policy toward the Middle East during the 45 years of the Cold War was marked by a certain degree of aloofness, non-intervention in intra-regional affairs, and strict neutrality in regional conflicts. The causes of this were twofold. Ankara's main economic, political, and strategic interests lay in the West, evidenced in its position as the only Middle Eastern country to belong to NATO and to have applied for membership of the European Union (EU). On the other hand, Turkey's traditional threat emanated from the north—the Soviet Union. Both orientations relegated the Middle East to secondary importance in Turkish eyes. It was true that in the mid-1950s and 1960s Turkey engaged in a more active policy toward the region, signified by its participation in the Baghdad Pact in 1955 and by its secret "peripheral alliance" with Israel in 1958. But even this short-lived activity reflected Ankara's interests and concerns in other areas rather than in the Middle East per se. Joining the Baghdad Pact was much more the result of prodding by the West (Britain and the United States) than the appeal of Baghdad.[28] Similarly, Ankara's fears of being caught in a vise between the Soviet Union in the north and a Soviet client or Communist regime to the south, or between Communism in the north and Pan-Arabism in the south, went a long way to explain its involvement in both pacts. This policy sucked Turkey unavoidably into intra-Arab regional conflicts, such as the struggle between Egypt's Gamal 'Abd al-Nasser and the Hashemite rulers of Iraq and Jordan, when Turkey sided with the latter. (Traditionally, Turkey had good relations with Jordan and especially with Iraq, which reflected also its long-standing rivalries with other countries, such as Syria or Egypt.) Another conflict was that between Syria and Egypt, following the dissolution of their United Arab Republic (UAR) in 1961 and Turkey's rapprochement with Syria, which led Egypt to sever its relations with Ankara.

By the mid-1960s, when Soviet activity in the Middle East began to wane, Turkey adopted a multidimensional foreign policy, part of which was termed "Turkish Ostpolitik" and was aimed at mending fences with the Arab world.[29] Accordingly, Turkey tilted more and more to the Arab side, especially by its growing sympathy with the Palestinian cause, while remaining neutral in other intra-regional affairs. This neutrality became a kind of trademark of Turkish foreign policy, and was best illustrated during the eight-year Iraq–Iran War, where it notably paid off.

Not only was Ankara saved from military hostilities, but it was also the main beneficiary of the war, since both Iraq and Iran maintained and even expanded trade and other economic relations with Turkey.[30]

The end of the Cold War, coming as it did in the wake of the Iraq–Iran War, was a two-edged sword for Turkey. On the one hand, it seemed to have removed a potential danger that had overshadowed the country for more than four decades. On the other hand, as one observer pointed out: "the end of the Cold War threatened to undermine Turkey's geostrategic role and its principal institutional link with the West," because "the West might no longer need strategic outposts such as Turkey" following the disintegration of the Eastern Bloc.[31] Turkey's fears of marginalization found expression in the analysis of the Deputy Chief of General Staff Çevik Bir, who charged that by adopting "a Central Europe–oriented" approach, the Europeans had marginalized Turkey and invited what he termed the revival of the Cold War, by raising a "Western curtain" in the place of "the iron curtain."[32] Indeed, by 1990 Ankara had suffered certain setbacks in western Europe and the United States that either coincided with, or were the result of, this sudden loss of importance.

Turkey's application in 1987 for full membership of the EU was turned down in 1989. Although this did not come as a complete surprise, it intensified Ankara's sense of exclusion from European institutions. At the same time, Turkey's chief ally, the United States, also seemed to be giving it second-class treatment. Ankara's relations with Washington were soured in the first half of 1990 by the resurfacing of the Armenian and Cyprus questions, two traditionally thorny matters.[33] In early 1990, Senator Dole proposed a resolution in the U.S. Senate that sought to designate April 24 as "a national day of remembrance of the Armenian genocide of 1915–23." Turkey, which has long denied that there was such a genocide, promptly reacted by placing restrictions on American training flights and naval visits to Turkey. However, the defeat of the resolution in the Senate at the end of February brought a quick lifting of these restrictions.[34]

On April 24 1990, President George Bush issued a message of "sympathy for the Armenians," which, it can be assumed, greatly irritated the Turks. Then, in July, the United States signed a Defense Cooperation Agreement with Greece. It stated, among other things, that Washington would come to the help of Athens if there was an outside threat. The agreement did not specify a source of threat, but it took little imagination to assume that Turkey was a possibility. Similarly, in reciprocating Greece's attitude of rapprochement, the Bush administration again showed sympathy to Greece on the Cyprus issue. It declared, for example, that the status quo on the island was unacceptable to Washington. The United States had never recognized the independence of that part of the island occupied by Turkey in 1974 (see below). However, restating this during a crucial period of flux in the region was not reassuring for Ankara. Added to its concerns was a similarly negative attitude displayed by the European Community (EC), which stated that Turkey's membership in the EU would be considered in the light of concessions it would make on Cyprus. (Turkey's human rights record and treatment of its Kurds were also of concern to the EC.)

Concurrently, Turkey had a series of problems with most of its other neighbors. Beside Cyprus, which was the main bone of contention between Turkey and Greece, the two governments had disputes over territorial rights in the Aegean, with no solution in sight. Relations with Bulgaria also started to deteriorate, following Sofia's expulsion of some 300,000 ethnic Turks across the border in summer 1989. Turkey's call for support from the Arab world went unheeded and it had to absorb a large number of these refugees. The affair left psychological and political scars on Turkey's relationship with Bulgaria. Nor were relations with Iran free of concern. Ankara feared that the end of the Iraq–Iran War might free Tehran's hands to pursue more vigorously the export of its Islamic revolution into Turkey. Indeed, Iran began to be involved in the assassination of Turkish intellectuals, as well as of Iranian opposition figures who had found refuge in Turkey.

Meanwhile, new threats appeared in the southern sector. Already in the early 1980s, Turkey had begun to feel that the balance of power with its two southern neighbors, Iraq and Syria, was shifting in their favor. Turkish officials watched with anxiety the build-up of conventional forces and strategic weapons systems in both countries, and of chemical and nuclear weapons in Iraq.[35] If Ankara learned one lesson from the Iraq–Iran War, it was that Iraq, and to a lesser extent Iran, were able and willing to use chemical weapons and missiles, and that in different circumstances these might be directed against Turkey. Reports on Iraqi and Syrian efforts to acquire chemical and nuclear weapons were no more reassuring, as Ankara had no defense against these. In January 1990, Turkish papers published a report by France's Institute for International Relations, predicting that a new war in the Middle East would involve the use of chemical and even nuclear weapons. The report added that both Turkey and Israel would be within striking distance of Iraq and Syria's warplanes and long-range missiles.[36] Turkey's concerns were heightened by reports in March 1990 about the seizure in Jordan of devices from a nuclear weapon triggering system that were being smuggled to Iraq.[37] Equally worrying was an April report in *Time* magazine, publicized in the Turkish press, claiming that Iraq would be able to manufacture nuclear weapons within a short period.[38] An illustration of Iraq's continuing build-up of its war machine was revealed the same month, when Turkish customs officials uncovered Iraq-bound shipments of pipes that were believed to be parts of the planned Iraqi "supergun." All these revelations alarmed the Turkish military, which was already concerned about the changing balance of power in the region.

The Iraqi invasion of Kuwait in August 1990 greatly increased Turkish anxieties, but also changed overnight Turkey's perception of itself and the West's of Turkey. Ankara's sense of marginalization gave way to a newfound confidence in its strategic value, both regionally and internationally. The West, for its part, began to realize Turkey's vital importance in the management of the developing crisis. The anti-Iraq operations did not qualify as a NATO activity, but for the first time, NATO's concept of "out of area intervention" was operationalized. Turkey's status in NATO was thus boosted significantly. It also dawned on European governments that they were incapable of defending their own interests, or those of their allies in the Middle East, without substantial support from both the United States and Turkey. Moreover, Turkey's strategic position was enhanced in their eyes, in that it was perceived as the most stable and reliable partner in the region. These perceptions were soon translated into action. A Conference on Security and Cooperation in Europe, held in Paris in November 1990, reached a decision on European disarmament—but exempted Turkey. In recognition of Turkey's strategic value, the conference decided to exclude a wide belt of territory along the Turkish border with Syria and Iraq from the zone in which conventional forces were to be reduced under the disarmament process. Moreover, because much of the equipment decommissioned by the Europeans was more modern than that of Turkey, it was handed over to Ankara in what was termed "the cascade effect."[39] In this way the Turkish army began to modernize itself. But its readiness to participate in the war was a different story.

Like the Cold War, the Gulf War had a paradoxical effect on Turkey. Although the crisis catapulted the country into a key strategic position regionally and internationally, its aftermath heightened security concerns about northern Iraq, and had the political consequence of further intertwining domestic security and foreign affairs. Another notable effect was that the war prepared the way for Ankara's return to the

Middle East, in that the Turkish state became far more active and involved in the region's affairs than in previous decades. As Şükrü Elekdağ, former ambassador to the United States who was close to foreign and security policy circles, argued that Turkey should take its place among the architects of the period, lest others use Ankara as "construction material."[40] In fact, Ankara abandoned its former strict neutrality and unequivocally sided with the allies. Although it refrained from sending troops to the battlefield, its contribution to the allied war effort was crucial.

First, shortly after the invasion Turkey closed the Iraqi–Turkish oil pipeline that was Baghdad's main economic artery, and to some extent Turkey's as well—on the eve of war, Iraq exported 50 percent of its oil via Turkey, while Turkey imported 65 percent of its oil from Iraq.[41] Turkey thus helped to institutionalize the sanctions regime against Iraq that was to endure in one form or another for more than a decade. Second, at the end of 1990 Turkey began a substantial build-up of troops along its border with Iraq. Although they did not take an active part in the fighting, their deployment on the border pinned down some 100,000 Iraqi soldiers in northern Iraq and helped to neutralize them from fighting in the south. Third, and equally important, was Ankara's permission to the allies to use the Incirlik air base near Adana for launching sorties over northern Iraq. Although this agreement had to be renewed every six months, it endured for more than a decade. All three moves amounted to Turkey forsaking its long-standing tradition of friendly, at times even close, relations with Baghdad, as had been reflected in the Baghdad Pact. Curiously, in spite of Ankara's *volte face* and Saddam Hussein's habit of issuing threats to his neighbors whenever they failed to support him, he maintained a low profile toward Turkey.

Turkey's alignment with the West earned it a new importance in American eyes, complementing its long-standing role as a bulwark against Soviet expansionism. Although the perceived threat from Iraq to Western interests could in no way be compared to that from the Soviet Union, Turkey still appeared to have a key role in warding off both dangers. Moreover, for Turkey, the 1991 Gulf war came at a perfect moment, giving it the opportunity to "prove" its value to the West precisely at a time when the Soviet Union's break-up might have caused Turkey's status to become diminished in the minds of Western strategists.

In addition, Ankara's siding with the West was yet another indication that, when it had to choose between its interests in the West and those in the Muslim East, it consistently opted for the former. Ankara's enhanced status in American eyes was given symbolic expression by President Bush's visit to Turkey in July 1991, the first presidential visit since that of Eisenhower in 1959. This was a far cry from the American coolness toward Turkey in the period between the end of the Cold War and the beginning of the Gulf crisis.

However, Turkey had to face negative effects of the war as well. Although it did not fire a single shot against Iraq, and no missiles were launched against it by Baghdad—as happened to the more neutral Israel—Ankara paid a high price on the political, economic, and strategic levels. Domestically, the decision on whether it should participate in the war was neither easy nor smooth. Turkey's dilemmas reflected the tension between its friendly relationship with Iraq and its equally historic endeavors to belong to the West, to which it also had commitments. In addition, there was the long-standing tension between the country's politico-military generals and its civilian politicians, and between the Western-oriented elites and the more traditional and Islamist groups of Turkish society. The traditional groups took the lead in opposing the war, but the antiwar mood was relatively widespread throughout the country. It was reflected both in the press and in the parliamentary opposition, which came out vociferously against Turkey's involvement.[42]

More serious was that the issue of participation set politicians and the military at loggerheads. Paradoxically, while the President Turgut Özal, pushed for active participation of the Turkish armed forces, the military vehemently opposed it. Özal might have been motivated by the desire to curry favor with the United States, and perhaps even to fulfill his latent aspirations of bringing back the oil-rich border area of Mosul Vilayet under Turkish influence. The military, however, appeared to have purely professional concerns—fear of the Iraqi military machine and doubt that the Turkish army was sufficiently well prepared for such a campaign.[43] In the final analysis, the military had the upper hand, since the Turkish army did not take an active part in the war, but the dispute triggered the resignation of the Chief of Staff Necip Torumtay, Defense Minister Safa Giray, and Foreign Minister Ali Bozer. However, Turkey retained its strategic importance by permitting the anti-Iraq coalition to use the Incirlik air base for attacks on Baghdad. The whole episode signaled the encroachment of the military on the political sphere, and foreshadowed a deepening of this trend in the future.

The economic price that Turkey paid, both in the short and long term, was one of the highest among the participants because it touched

everyday life. First, the oil that Turkey bought from Iraq before the closure of the pipeline comprised 65 percent of its total consumption and
had been purchased on preferential terms. Second, Ankara earned royal-
ties amounting to $250–300 m. annually from the transportation of
Iraqi oil through its territories, in addition to revenues from services
related to operating the pipelines. Further, Turkish exports to Iraq
amounted to more than $1 bn. a year, while Turkish participation in
various Iraqi development projects earned contractors, technicians, and
suppliers a total of about $3.5 bn. Accordingly, by mid-1991 Turkish
economic losses were estimated at between $4 and $10 bn.[44] Although
the West compensated for some of the losses, Turkey would continue to
carry much of the burden for several years to come.[45] Its willingness to
endure such huge economic losses proved that political and strategic
factors were held to be more pertinent than economic considerations.

Another set of concerns resulting from the Gulf War arose from the
vacuum created in northern Iraq, which again had a paradoxical impact
on Turkey. On the one hand, the vacuum offered a pretext for acquiring
a foothold in the region. On the other, it opened a Pandora's box of all
kinds of problems, caused by the flight of approximately 800,000 Iraqi
Kurds immediately after the war toward the Turkish–Iraqi border.[46] It
also led to the enlargement of the military bases of the dissident Turkish
Kurdistan Workers' Party (Parti Kerkeren Kurdistan; PKK) in northern
Iraq, and the deepening involvement of neighboring countries—Syria,
Iraq, and Iran—in Turkey's Kurdish affairs.[47] This transformed the
Turkish–Kurdish conflict from a domestic into an inter-regional one,
and shifted the perceptions of a security threat from the traditional
northeastern area to the southern border.

These developments coincided with the collapse of the Soviet Union
in the latter part of 1991, which again had far-reaching consequences
for Turkey. Not only did it put to rest the Soviet threat, it also opened
new horizons in the Black Sea and the Caspian rim, as well as in the
Caucasus and Central Asia. What qualified as the enlargement of the
Middle East, or the "Greater Middle East," presented Ankara with new
economic, political, and "ideological" opportunities. Just how far these
opportunities would benefit Turkey was, however, a matter of debate
both in the Foreign Ministry and among the public at large. The
maximalists favored "Pan-Turanism" or "Neo-Ottomanism" and envisaged a Turkish world stretching "from the Adriatic to the Great Wall."
The minimalists, who were the majority, took a more sober view, limit-
ing themselves to a more dynamic and diversified foreign policy. The
Turkish military also had to adapt itself to changing circumstances and

develop a new approach to the Middle East, reassessing it as Turkey's backyard, in which events might even necessitate a projection of power into the region.

This series of changes brought about what might be called the new "Turkish order," of which rapprochement between Turkey and Israel was only a part.

## Israel in Search of Peace and Strategic Depth

As with Turkey, the profound changes in the international arena and in the region brought mixed consequences for Israel. The end of the Cold War and the collapse of the Soviet Union were extremely positive for Jerusalem. The three major benefits were the influx of Soviet Jews to Israel, the resumption of relations with countries that had belonged to the Eastern camp and the opening of new vistas in the Caucasus and Central Asia.

The explanation for these changes should be sought in the Soviet Union, which had severed its relations with Israel after the June 1967 war, in the belief that its interests were best served by putting its weight behind the Arab states. However, the lapse of some 20 years had begun to change this perspective. For various economic, political, and strategic reasons the Soviet Union wished to improve its relations with Washington, but to achieve this it had to meet certain conditions, one of which was resumption of relations with Israel. A related factor was Moscow's concern about Israel's missile capabilities, particularly since the launch of the Jericho missile in 1989. The Soviets claimed that it could carry nuclear warheads and reach not only neighboring Arab countries, but parts of the Soviet Union. It was possible that the Soviet Union raised this issue with American officials in the hope of neutralizing such Israeli capabilities. On another level, Moscow began to realize that if it wished to play a role in the Arab–Israeli peace process, it should have access to both parties in order to influence them. Underlying these changing views was Moscow's gradual relinquishment of ideological dogmas. Among other things, this paved the way for the opening of the gates to Soviet Jewry to leave the USSR.[48] The Kremlin's fear that Zionist activity within its borders and a substantial emigration of Jews would undermine the Soviet political system was no longer valid.

The impressive wave of immigrants to Israel is reflected in the following figures: in 1987, 8,000; in 1988, 20,000; in 1989, 70,000, and in 1990, 200,000. This trend continued, and by the end of the decade almost one million people had left the Soviet Union (and later Russia) for Israel.[49] This immigration of Soviet Jewry, together with the Ethiopian immigration that had already begun, had profound social, economic, and political significance for Israel that does not concern us here. What should be stressed, however, is that it alarmed the Arabs, especially the Palestinians, because of its security and demographic implications. If the Palestinians had hoped that time was on their side in transforming the demographic balance in their favor, then large-scale immigration was a serious drawback. They believed, accurately, that such a demographic change enhanced Israel's security, but their appeals to the USSR to reverse the policy fell on deaf ears. Indeed, the immigration must have played some role (although not a central one) in bringing the Palestinians to the negotiating table.

The other positive aspect of the Soviet-Communist upheaval was the resumption of relations with Israel. The trend of rapprochement began even before the end of the Cold War, in the East European countries that belonged to the Soviet bloc. It reached its peak in the late 1980s and early 1990s, with relations re-established with all these countries and also with the Soviet Union. It was indeed symbolic that the Soviet Ambassador to Israel, Alexander Bubin, presented his credentials to Israel's president just days before the formal dismantling of the USSR at the end of 1991. The formation of the newly independent states in the Caucasus and Central Asia out of the debris of the Soviet Union opened new areas of potential activity for Israel. Jerusalem was quick to recognize these countries and establish diplomatic relations with them, and this was to add another flavor to the Turkish–Israeli rapprochement.

All these developments signified a number of critical changes for Israel: it had ceased to be an outcast in half of the world; it had gained greater legitimacy and flexibility in the international arena; the "Eastern Camp" was no longer available on demand to back Arab countries against Israel—this was especially true for the former Soviet clients, Syria and Iraq; and thus, with Israel having become more "kosher" in the international arena, Turkey was now free to make a qualitative leap forward in its relationship with Israel. Against these generally positive developments, Israel had to face much less benign aspects of the Gulf War, but here a differentiation should be made between immediate and long-term outcomes.

Iraq repeatedly depicted its missile attacks on Israel during the Gulf War as the most important achievement in Arab history. It maintained that by hitting Israeli towns for the first time since 1948, Iraq had eliminated the entire concept of Israeli security, destroyed "the legend of the invincible Israel," and proved that the Iraqi mind and its "legendary steadfastness" had put Israel at the mercy of "the Arab mind."[50] These pronouncements could be discarded as mere propaganda aimed at raising the morale of the Iraqi population after years of sanctions. However, there was no denying that for Israel, the 39 missiles fired into its heartland in the six weeks of the war constituted both a strategic surprise and a traumatic experience. The attack all but demolished certain myths and concepts and brought about far-reaching changes in policy. Among beliefs that were profoundly shaken were those of self-reliance in wartime; the imperative of preemptive Israeli attacks; the ability to repel any aggression single-handedly; and the invulnerability of the civilian population. Indeed, as far as Israel was concerned, the Gulf War was unique on many counts. It was the first time since 1948 that its civilian population came under attack. It was also the first time in Israel's history that it was an absentee participant in a war, unable either to initiate a military action (as its security doctrine dictated), or to react to attacks. In fact, Israel was absent from an impressive list of no fewer than 39 world countries that contributed to the Gulf War (some of them largely symbolically, such as sending medical teams).[51]

The reason for Israel's inaction or restraint were well known, namely, American pressure not to participate. The American motive was also clear: to prevent the collapse of the anti-Iraq coalition and the drifting away of its Arab partners to the Iraqi camp should the war spill over into an Iraq–Israel conflict. Although this was generally known, Israel's stance was interpreted in entirely different ways, with significant implications. The Jewish state's absence from the battlefield implied a certain loss of strategic importance in American eyes, since it "proved" that the United States could form a wide coalition, wage a war and protect its interests much better without Israel's participation than with it. To a certain extent, it could be argued that Israel had ceased to be an asset and even became a liability, at least in this specific case, since the United States had to protect it from missile attacks, although not with great success.[52] The other side of the coin was that Israel, for the first time in its history, had to entrust its security and the protection of its citizens to an outside power, which implied relinquishing the principle of self-reliance. For their part, Iraq and other Arab countries sharing its hostility to Israel interpreted the missile attacks and the lack of response to them in two ways. First, the removal of the "psychological barrier of fear of Israel" and an undermining of Israel's defense doctrine, and second, closely related, the serious assault on Israel's deterrent capability.

In fact, there were two schools of thought regarding Israel's deterrence. One, which included even some Arab commentators, contended that Israel's deterrence was not harmed, and on the contrary, Israel had won "without firing a shot." The other school maintained that Israel's deterrence was eroded and, as a consequence, if an Arab ruler wished to "achieve a specific vital aim," Israel's deterrent capability would not "necessarily function."[53] It is likely that both schools are partially correct, but what was more certain was that the debate in Israel on the implications and consequences of the Gulf War brought about two fundamental changes in its Middle East strategy: the resumption of the peace process with those Arab partners willing to tread the road, and the revival of "the peripheral alliance" with Turkey.

No sooner had the Gulf War ended, than the consensus in Israel started to fall apart and public debate resumed about the country's need for strategic depth and peace with the Arabs, especially the Palestinians, who had been in a state of uprising, or intifada, since the end of 1987. Accordingly, the Gulf War was given two opposite interpretations and solutions. The Likud, the right-wing party that was in power, argued that Iraq's invasion of Kuwait and firing of missiles on Israel were proof of Israel's need of strategic depth, and hence the danger of a pro–Iraq Palestinian state contiguous with Israel. The more dovish group, within the Labor Party and further left, asserted that the Gulf War had provided further evidence "that the notion of strategic depth was nothing more than a myth," and in an era of advanced military technology that included missiles, no strategic advantage could be gained by holding on to occupied lands. Accordingly, the best form of strategic depth, they maintained, would be achieved by "entering into a stable peace agreement and granting the Palestinians the right to political self-determination."[54] As it turned out, the more dovish view carried the day and led Israel into the Oslo agreement.

In retrospect, the Gulf War highlighted three paradoxes for Israel. First, even though the most right-wing government the country had ever known was in power (1990–92), and was expected to be the most militant, it did not react to the Iraqi provocation. Second, during the Gulf crisis Israel (and the United States) rejected out of hand Saddam Hussein's linkage between Kuwait and the Palestinian question, but after the war a hidden linkage seemed to have been formed—that the war to free Kuwait now constituted the most important incentive for Israel to negotiate with the Palestinians. This leads to the third paradox, that even though the Palestinians were Saddam Hussein's staunchest supporters against Israel, it was with them that the peace process was resumed; only later was it joined by Jordan and Syria. If in the perception of some Arabs the Gulf War destroyed the psychological barrier of fear of Israel's might, then, by the same token, the 1993 Oslo Agreement between Israel and the Palestinians destroyed the related fear of "doing business" with Israel and developing open relations.

The Turkish–Israeli relationship should also be seen in this context, as it was one of the most important beneficiaries of this psychological breakthrough, and an example of the post-Oslo avalanche of new relations that began to flourish between Israel and other countries. Relations between Turkey and Israel also reflected the changes in the geostrategic map of the Middle East, and Israel's revised threat perceptions.

The 1990s witnessed an important change in these perceptions, in that the two states of the periphery—Iraq and Iran—emerged as a major source of threat to Israel both in relative and absolute terms. While the core Arab countries, Egypt, Jordan, and Syria, were in different phases of peace or peacemaking with Israel, Iraq, and Iran were escalating their threat: Iraq, by launching missiles against Israel during the Gulf War, followed by a relentless war of words after it, and Iran, by joining Syria in supporting the war of attrition by the Lebanese-based Hizbullah against the Jewish state, and by developing long-range missiles that could reach Israel. Thus, not only were Iraq and Iran the key countries presenting a major viable threat to Israel, they also posed (separately) as the only ones that could defend the Palestinian, Arab, and Islamic causes. This double threat from the periphery required a countermove: an alignment with another country of the periphery, in this case Turkey, which could balance or contain Baghdad and Tehran. In fact, the Turkish–Israeli alignment of the 1990s recalls the "peripheral alliance" of the 1950s, which can be taken as a yardstick for evaluating the changes in the Middle East over the intervening 40 years, and for placing the alignment of the 1990s in its historical context.

# Chapter 2

# Days of Future Past—The Peripheral Alliance

## The Background of the Alliance

In 1958, Israel and Turkey forged a top secret alliance known as "the peripheral alliance" or "Phantom Pact." Although a third party—Iran—was also involved, this chapter concentrates mainly on the first two countries, for the following reasons: the alliance, especially its strategic aspect, had a bilateral rather than trilateral character; the Israeli–Iranian linkage has been treated by some scholars and journalists; and finally, the Israeli–Turkish alliance is more relevant to the present, as it may be considered the precursor of the strategic alignment concluded between the two countries some 40 years later, in 1996. In shedding new light on an important period in the modern history of the Middle East, this study of the peripheral alliance, through archival material, interviews, and other new material, may give a better understanding of the development of regional relations in our times and of the lines of continuity and change between the two periods.

The concept of the peripheral alliance was first launched by a man who would later be a member of the Liberal Party in the Israeli Knesset, Baruch 'Uziel, in a series of lectures delivered before the establishment of the state of Israel. He continued to press for the idea in a memorandum to the Foreign Ministry, and in an essay published in November 1948 in *Beterem*, a journal affiliated to the Mapai party. In it, 'Uziel analyzed the fragile geopolitical situation of the embryonic state and suggested ways to consolidate it. He opined that the greatest danger to the Jewish state was the imperialistic idea behind the Arab League, aimed at forming a large "Arab confederation" or empire, that would "not tolerate in its midst a small and alien country standing as a stumbling block on its way to complete unity and which, moreover, [blocks] the outlet to the sea for its vast lands." To counter this danger, he said,

Israel must develop a "political orientation" that would last for many years to come, and would seek allies among ethnic groups that lived under the same political conditions and faced the same dangers as Israel.

The idea was to forge "a peripheral and minorities' alliance" that would include "the Jews in the land of Israel, the Maronites in Lebanon, the Alawis in northern Syria, Turks, Greeks, Armenians, the people of al-Jazira [probably the ethnic minorities in northern Iraq], Kurds, Assyrians and Persians." All these peoples, who equaled the Arabs in number, and some of whom were even "superior to them in their culture and military power," could, he maintained, "form an alliance that would be much stronger than the Arabs." In 'Uziel's opinion, the alliance would help to achieve a new balance in the region and would ultimately bring peace. The Arabs would be compelled to live in amity and mutual understanding with their non-Arab neighbors, and to desist from using force to establish their "empire." While aware of the great difficulties of forging such an alliance, such as "the political conflicts" between Turks and Kurds, and Persians and Kurds, as well as the Islamic bonds that tied these peoples to the Arabs, he still thought that geopolitical and national considerations would tip the balance. He concluded, "no new and bold idea has ever forged its way in a direct line and without curves."[1]

A full decade would pass before these proposals, or some of them, would be put into practice. Interestingly, 'Uziel himself was to return to the subject ten years later, when he published a booklet promoting these same ideas, although with different nuances. In the new version he added Sudan and Ethiopia to the list of the countries of the periphery, and provided statistics (unsourced, but probably from 1958), according to which the number of Arabs in the Middle East had reached 36 million, while the combined peoples of the periphery amounted to 50 million. He also called for the formation of a political or military alliance and advised Israel to take the initiative, as it was "a dynamic factor" in the region and needed this alliance more than any other nation in the Middle East.[2] It is not known whether 'Uziel was aware of the alliance with Turkey that had been formed two months earlier, or whether it was mere coincidence that he published his views at about the same time. As we shall see, the alliance was kept top secret and was only hinted at in the Knesset Foreign Affairs and Defense Committee, whose debates are, as a rule, highly classified.[3]

The fact that 'Uziel felt the urge to repeat the same ideas ten years after Israel's independence was ample proof that the Jewish state's main concerns had not been adequately addressed, nor its major expectations fulfilled. What were these concerns and expectations, and how did Israel attempt to deal with them? Among them were lack of legitimacy, chiefly among its Arab neighbors; isolation in its geographical neighborhood and an acute sense of lack of security. These three interrelated concerns became, as it were, an Israeli trademark. To address these issues and others, Israel's foreign policy makers identified several core diplomatic aims:

1. Achieving legitimacy, peace, and security.
2. Developing commerce.
3. Winning foreign endorsement for its positions.
4. Forging constructive engagement in international projects.
5. Strengthening links with world Jewry.[4]

Since it became clear early on that most of these were quite elusive, Israel's policy-makers developed two parallel tracks in foreign relations—an open and a secret track, an approach that was so crucial to the survival of the state.[5] For an outcast country such as Israel became, the secret track was an important tool for enhancing security, for breaking the wall of isolation in the region and in the international arena as a whole, and for finding new allies. But this form of international relations has also had several drawbacks. Being secret, it does not confer the legitimacy so longed for by Israel; it can be broken much more easily by one side or the other and it may clash or compete with the open track. The peripheral alliance of the late 1950s illustrates all these expectations, dilemmas, and difficulties.

Notwithstanding the first stirrings of Israeli–Turkish intimacy in the years immediately after 1948, the idea of an alliance remained mostly a pious wish until 1957. It was Reuven Shiloah, an indefatigable individual who was behind much of Israel's secret diplomacy and played a crucial role in the establishment of Israel's intelligence network in the early years of the state who revived the notion.[6] In a meeting he held at the Foreign Ministry on September 11, 1957, shortly after his appointment as special advisor to the foreign minister, he discussed the possibility of improving relations with Turkey.[7] True, he did not mention in so many words the concept of a peripheral alliance, yet it was clear that this was what he had in mind. Shiloah believed that the common danger emanating from the pro–Soviet Syrian regime might facilitate a rapprochement between Turkey and Israel. Still, according to his own assessment and that of the other participants, Turkey would not dare to make any *open move* [my emphasis] for fear of antagonizing its Baghdad Pact partners—especially Iraq—or of prompting the Soviet Union to set

Arab countries against Ankara. The participants also doubted that Britain and the United States would encourage an open move by Turkey. Accordingly, Shiloah recommended strengthening relations with the Turkish military, "something which can be done with less publicity." It was also recommended that Eliyahu Sasson, Israel's ambassador to Italy, who as previous ambassador to Turkey had developed strong ties with the Turkish ruling elite, should approach Prime Minister Adnan Menderes directly on this matter.[8]

A year would pass before the alliance came into effect, yet this document highlighted the major characteristics of the relationship:

1. Israel's role as initiator.
2. The extreme sensitivity of the Turks.
3. The complexity of the Turkish–Arab–Israeli triangle.
4. The personal role of Menderes.
5. The centrality of the Turkish military.
6. The difficulty in bringing Turkey into the alliance.

This last difficulty was highlighted time and again by various Israeli officials who had come into contact with the Turks. Only a short time afterward, Israel's military attaché to Turkey opined that not only was Turkey unwilling to improve relations with Israel, but that in order to keep the Baghdad Pact intact—Ankara's major concern—it was ready to pay any price, "certainly at the expense of Israel."[9] In an earlier memorandum on Turkish–Israeli relations, the Israeli chargé d'affaires in Ankara, Moshe Alon, pointed to Menderes's ascent to power in 1954 and the establishment of the Baghdad Pact in February 1955 as the beginning of the deterioration in relations between Turkey and Israel. Menderes, he said, was fully committed to the Baghdad Pact and was doing his utmost to develop and strengthen it as a means of enhancing his stature as "the leader of the region." In pursuing this policy, Menderes interpreted Israel's moves to improve its relations with Turkey and to "forge cooperation in the military field" as attempts to undermine his policy in the Middle East. Furthermore, while maintaining that the Baghdad Pact might ultimately serve Israel's interests in the region, Menderes advised patience and asked Israel to refrain from publicizing existing relations, such as trade.

In view of this, Alon put forward several proposals to address the situation. First, as Menderes was the "sole leader" in Turkey, Israel should approach him personally and directly. Second, the United States could play an important role in this rapprochement, since Menderes was "very sensitive to public opinion in the United States." In fact, Israel had suspected all along that American indifference was a major reason why relations with Turkey remained cool, after they had been downgraded in 1956 because of Israel's participation in the Suez War. Third, cooperation on the economic and military industry levels should be enhanced, and fourth, Israel should initiate campaigns within Turkey to explain its position, as public opinion there was, on the whole, friendly to Israel.[10]

Against this background, it was quite difficult to see how a rapprochement, let alone an alliance, could be achieved between the two countries. Indeed, for this to happen, several "conditions" would first have to be fulfilled: rapprochement between Israel and Iran, significant changes in the Arab world, and the involvement of the United States. Israel's ability to exploit the opportunities and take initiatives on several levels was a key factor in this endeavor. The rapprochement between Iran and Israel preceded that between Turkey and Israel, and its most important aspects remained secret, as the alliance itself would be.[11] The background was Israel's military accomplishments in the 1956 Suez War and the realization in Tehran—and for that matter in Ankara—that Israel was a strategic asset in the region and could contain the ambitions of Egypt's Gamal 'Abd al-Nasser.[12] It is not my intention to discuss in detail the relationship between Iran and Israel, but suffice to say that at the time it was much deeper and more comprehensive than the ties between Turkey and Israel, and extended into various economic, military, and intelligence spheres. Relations with Iran were important for the rapprochement with Turkey, because both Tehran and Ankara were allies in the Baghdad Pact (signed in 1955 and including Iraq and Pakistan), both were pro-Western and both were concerned about Soviet and Egyptian ambitions in the region. Moreover, Iran was said to have been instrumental in convincing Turkey to join the peripheral alliance.[13]

Much more crucial, however, were developments in the Arab world. During this time, Turkey's change of heart toward Israel went through three phases: the first was Iraq's vote against Turkey over Cyprus at the United Nations in December 1957; the second, the establishment of the United Arab Republic (UAR) between Egypt and Syria in February 1958; and the third, the fall of the monarchy in Iraq in July 1958. Turkey was surprised and greatly frustrated by Iraq's vote with Greece and against Turkey at the UN committee considering the Cyprus issue, which took place (probably) on December 12, 1957 and was to decide the future of the island. Although in the final analysis Greece's demand for the Cypriots's right to self-determination did not secure a two-thirds majority, the voting left a negative impression. As one Turkish commentator pointed out: "we have received with wonder and pain the stand taken up by some of the Arab states, including friendly and allied Iraq ... It is very difficult (to explain this away?)."[14] Indeed, Baghdad had promised to vote with Turkey and even to convince other Arab countries to do likewise. Now, Turkey came to realize that if Iraq had to choose between loyalty to the Arabs and to the Baghdad Pact, it would opt for the former. Also, the Iraqi stance hurt the Menderes government internationally and especially domestically, as the opposition became increasingly critical of Menderes's policy of "flattering" the Arabs.

Turkey's frustration with Baghdad's vote came on top of other grievances: Baghdad's reluctance to pay "the oil debt" to Turkey (TL100 m. owed in return for Atatürk's ceding of the oil-rich Mosul Vilayet area in 1926); its objection to building an oil pipeline between Iraq and Turkey, and to turning Mersin or Iskenderun on the Turkish Mediterranean coast into the central port for the Baghdad Pact countries and NATO; and its opposition to building common dams. Meanwhile, second thoughts began to emerge regarding the viability, "stability," and effectiveness of the Baghdad Pact, at least in regard to the Iraqi partner, which acted at times at cross-purposes to the Pact's objectives. Thus, while Baghdad needed the Pact against Israel and *vis-à-vis* its Arab rivals, Turkey and the other partners sought to use it against "Soviet designs."[15] However, with the growing penetration of the Soviets into Syria, the Baghdad Pact lost some of its importance in the eyes of the Turkish military, since it became clear that it could not prevent such activity. Nor did the Pact enhance Turkey's other political goal—to increase, via Baghdad, Ankara's influence over the Arab states.[16] Yet for all these disappointments, Turkey was not considering a change in its stance toward Iraq at that point. Indeed, it continued to invest much effort into keeping Iraq in the Pact, and many of its decisions—regarding Israel, for example—were related to this policy.

An alarming development, which brought Turkey to change its approach, was the establishment of the UAR in 1958, the union between Egypt and Syria that significantly boosted Egypt's stature in the region. A long-standing rival of Ankara, Egypt now came, in a sense, to border Turkey on the south. Moreover, the fact that the newly established republic was strongly pro-Soviet, or at least perceived as such by Ankara, threatened to catch Turkey in a vise between the Soviets in the north and the pro-Soviet UAR in the south. There was also fear that the expansionism of Egypt's President Nasser would not stop at Syria's border, but would try to engulf other Arab countries as well. The Turkish newspaper *Ulus* maintained that the real danger to the Middle East emanated from Nasser, "who followed in Hitler's footsteps."[17] Nevertheless, as late as May 1958 the former Israeli ambassador to Turkey, Morris Fischer, suspected that Ankara might further downgrade relations with Israel, since "Turkey has been under constant pressure from Iraq, and one can assume that it [Turkey] will pay any price in order to prevent its dissent from the Baghdad Pact."[18]

In the end, it was the fall of the monarchy in Iraq in July 1958 that triggered an immediate change in Turkey's outlook on the region in general and on the role of Israel in particular. Developments in Baghdad were alarming for Ankara on several counts. Notwithstanding Turkey's disappointments and frustrations, relations with Iraq had been stronger than with any other Arab country. Turkey's Menderes and Iraq's Nuri al-Sa'id were also close personal allies. Menderes visited Baghdad at least eight times, while al-Sa'id had returned from one of his many visits to Ankara just one day before the coup. Indeed, this friendship was seen as pivotal to relations between the two countries.[19] Now there was a fear that the new regime would not adhere to the Baghdad Pact (as indeed happened) and that events in Syria and Iraq might engulf the whole region and threaten an encirclement of Turkey from both the north and the south. This upheaval in Baghdad removed the last barrier to a rapprochement with Israel.

Another "silent" player who seemed to have contributed, first to the cooling of relations, then to rapprochement between Turkey and Israel, and ultimately to the formation of a peripheral alliance, was the United States. Before analyzing the American role, a word must be said about the relationship between Turkey and Israel up to July 1958.[20] After Turkey's de jure recognition of Israel on March 28, 1949,[21] the two parties established diplomatic legations in Ankara and Tel Aviv and relations developed quite smoothly until the formation of the Baghdad Pact, when Turkey started to tilt more and more toward Iraq. Even more critical was the Suez War in October 1956, which caused Turkey to recall its ambassador to Israel the following month—a move reciprocated by Israel.[22] After that date, Israel's efforts were aimed at trying to restore the situation and upgrading diplomatic relations. In Israel's perception, the United States could and should have played an important role in promoting these efforts. From the start, Israel assumed that Menderes would not have dared recall the Turkish minister without consulting the Americans, especially as he believed "in the strong influence of the Jews" in the United States. This assumption was reinforced by the Turkish representative to the United Nations, Selim Serper, who maintained that it was Britain, with the support of the United States, that had asked Turkey to make this move in order to save Nuri al-Sa'id from falling.[23] Whether this was true or not, Israel believed that the best way to break the stalemate and change the situation was to pressure Britain, and especially the United States, to take back their "sincere advice."[24] At one point, the Israeli President Yitzhak Ben-Zvi, approached the American ambassador to Israel for such a commitment, to no avail.[25]

As time went by, Israel became more and more convinced that the United States held the key to its rapprochement with Turkey, but was equally convinced that Washington was unwilling to make a move for fear of antagonizing Arab and Muslim states and the Afro-Asian bloc. Moreover, Washington was suspected of having opposed the upgrading of relations in case these countries suspected it of being behind this. Subsequently, Turkish officials intimated that a "foreign power" had obstructed the upgrading of relations.[26] Certain Israeli officials and representatives counseled roundabout tactics for bringing pressure to bear on Turkey, such as "inviting" lobbying by American senators or congressmen on Turkish representatives in Washington or at the United Nations.[27] If this tactic was indeed acted on, it was also ineffective. However, while the United States would not contribute to the improvement of open diplomatic relations, it was to be instrumental in promoting secret ties. For this to happen, the Israeli Prime Minister David Ben-Gurion, had to plunge into the matter and pull all the elements together.

## Ben-Gurion's Initiative

Ben-Gurion had three main motives for initiating the peripheral alliance or doctrine:

1. Breaking the ring of isolation that the Arab countries had imposed on Israel by forming an alliance with the non-Arab countries of the periphery.
2. Stabilizing the region and forming a new balance of power.
3. Strengthening relations with the West, especially the United States.[28]

In seeking to enhance Israel's relations with the Americans, which were not strong at the time, and to raise Israel's status in President Eisenhower's eyes, Ben-Gurion endeavored to portray his initiative as a strategy that would significantly advance American interests in the region. On the other hand, he sought to use American involvement or support for the agreement as an incentive to the countries in question to join in. In other words, Israel sought to use the United States to galvanize the pact, and use the pact to consolidate U.S. support for itself. Thus, in a letter to Eisenhower on July 24, 1958, Ben-Gurion disclosed that Israel had lately been strengthening its relations in the Middle East with four countries of the outer ring, Sudan, Ethiopia, Iran, and Turkey, with a view to stemming the "strong Nasserist-Soviet torrent." He also revealed that relations with Turkey were developing in secret channels in addition to the open negotiations. Ben-Gurion explained that Israel could help these countries in the military, economic, and scientific fields, and it is probable that he also suggested forming an alliance with them (an assumption, since part of the document is still classified). For this to happen, he said, two conditions must be met: that America would provide "political, financial and moral support," and that it would send a message to the countries in question that the United States supported Israel in its efforts [to bring about the alliance].[29]

Analysts are divided on the American reaction and its role in the emerging alliance. Avi Shlaim has maintained that the United States did not need Israeli help, since it had good relations with Turkey and Iran; that it did not provide moral and political backing to Israel's activities in the periphery; and that it "could not be drawn to make any commitment, even a purely verbal one, to the alliance of periphery."[30] In contrast, Haggai Eshed has asserted that during the crisis of July–August 1958 and afterward, "the Americans began to regard Israel as a strategic element of the highest importance in the Middle East, capable of helping to strengthen the parties in the region that the US was interested in supporting." He quoted Ben-Gurion as saying that he had received two letters that [probably] promised support, one from Eisenhower (July 25, 1958) and the other from Secretary of State Dulles (August 4, 1958). He further mentioned that Dulles had spoken twice to the Turks and that other American officials had talked to the Iranians and Ethiopians on the matter. In short, Eshed suggested that the alliance was forged "with the American blessing."[31]

Although neither Shlaim nor Eshed quoted his sources, it seems that Eshed was closer to the truth. In view of the close relations that existed between Turkey and the United States at the time (there were some 65 American military bases in Turkey), and the fact that the alliance was to have a strong strategic aspect, it was unthinkable that Ankara would make any move without consulting or getting the blessing of Washington.[32] The same was true for Iran and probably for Ethiopia. Moreover, a year later Turkey presented to Eisenhower a memorandum that resembled in many points the thinking behind the peripheral alliance. It stated that the Middle East was composed in the main of non-Arab countries, which were pro-Western and freedom- and peace-loving. It maintained that (these countries) Turkey, Iran, Pakistan, and Israel, outnumbered the Arabs in their populations and were stronger than them, that Arabs represented only one-third of the Middle East, and that the United States should strengthen this non-Arab bloc by all possible means.[33]

Ben-Gurion's dramatic and top secret meeting with Menderes in Ankara, on August 29, 1958, laid the foundation for the Turkish–Israeli alliance. The fact that it took place less than two months after the upheaval in Iraq proved how threatening the situation looked to Ankara, and demonstrated its willingness to draw a line between its relations with the Arab world—especially Iraq—and its relationship with Israel, with the latter gaining a greater share, albeit through secret channels. Initially, Ben-Gurion had considered Turkey as the "weak link" in the alliance, since, as he wrote in his diaries, Ankara was a NATO member and hence less dependent on the Baghdad Pact than was Iran; also, it enjoyed stronger American support than Tehran and was less anti-Arab.[34] The new constellation in the region, together with the groundwork laid earlier by Israeli officials who had worked to bring about rapprochement on the bilateral level, helped to remove Turkish reservations.

The Ben-Gurion–Menderes meeting was preceded by almost a year of intensive secret meetings and contacts between Israeli and Turkish officials in Turkey, Europe, and Washington. The leading Israeli negotiators were Foreign Minister Golda Meir, the political advisor to the Foreign Ministry, Reuven Shiloah, and the Israeli ambassador to Rome Eliyahu Sasson. Although now based in Rome, Sasson had retained close ties with high-ranking Turkish officials from his time in Ankara and was instrumental in bringing about the rapprochement. He met Menderes in Paris at the end of 1957 and later sent him a letter that emphasized the importance of cooperation with Israel, as well as the need for Turkey to stand against anti-Israel decisions in the Baghdad Pact, whose members were scheduled to meet in Ankara at the end of January 1958. Interestingly, in early January 1958, Sasson met the Turkish Chief of Staff Ibrahim Feyzi Mengüç in Rome, who encouraged him to pursue his efforts and promised his "full support" for rapprochement.[35] Subsequently, Foreign Minister Meir visited Turkey secretly in the spring and met with the Turkish Foreign Minister Fatin Rüştü Zorlu, on board a boat in the Sea of Marmara. On August 2 she again met him secretly, this time in Zurich.[36] On the whole, Israel was the initiator of these meetings, but in times of emergency, such as the period following the July 14 coup in Baghdad, the Turkish foreign minister approached Israel for consultation and asked for further information on the event, since he considered Israel to have good sources in the Arab world.[37] In any case, the atmosphere of growing threats and considerable uncertainties helped push the two countries into alliance.

## The Unfolding of the Alliance

What kind of alliance was it? What was its content, and what impact did it have on the region? If we compare it to the Baghdad Pact,[38] which was formed in 1955 and included Turkey, Iraq, Iran, and Pakistan, four major differences are evident:

1. The peripheral alliance was secret, and has remained so in most of its aspects.
2. Because of this secrecy it did not generate a counter-alliance in the region as the Baghdad Pact had done.
3. While Ben-Gurion had envisioned a trilateral or multilateral alliance, it boiled down to a bilateral agreement between Israel and each of the three countries, Ethiopia, Iran, and Turkey. However, as we shall see, there were certain areas where trilateral cooperation did exist.
4. Perhaps because it was bilateral, as well as secret, it lasted longer than the Baghdad Pact.

There is a great divergence, hence an asymmetry, between the Turkish and Israeli versions of the Ben-Gurion–Menderes "agreement." To this day, and in spite of the passage of more than 40 years, the Turkish side has largely remained silent on the matter. Since there is no access to Turkish archives, and Turkish newspapers rarely mention it, it is difficult to verify the Israeli version by resorting to documented Turkish sources. The "minimalist" Turkish version maintained that there were no written documents on the meeting; that Turkey did not commit itself to anything; that no regular high-level talks were held between the two parties following the August 29 meeting; and that there was merely an "understanding" between them. It was conceded, however, that the meeting formed an important turning point for the exchange of intelligence between the two countries. In contrast, Sezai Orkunt, the head of military intelligence between 1964 and 1966, maintained that there was an agreement of which only ten military and civilian officials knew about.[39] The tight secrecy that Turkey maintains to this day on the alliance is, if anything, an indication of its extreme sensitivity toward the Arab states and its fear of antagonizing them.

The picture becomes much clearer when we approach the matter from the Israeli side. Israel's archives on that period are public; scholars and journalists have already investigated the issue and one can also benefit from interviews with Israeli officials who served in Turkey in that period. It is true that an important part of archival material relating to the peripheral alliance is still classified (it falls within the higher 50-year classification). None the less, this can be partly compensated for by interviews and private archives. In any case, this higher classification is itself evidence of the importance of the relationship.

In his book on Reuven Shiloah, who participated in the Ben-Gurion–Menderes meeting (together with Golda Meir and Eliyahu Sasson), Haggai Eshed states that Shiloah had prepared in advance a list of topics for proposed cooperation. The list was read and approved point by point by the representatives of both sides. Eshed, who does not mention his sources (he probably used Shiloah's classified archives), maintains that the *agreement*[40] [my emphasis], included cooperation on diplomatic, military, and economic levels. According to Eshed, in the diplomatic sphere it included joint public relations campaigns aimed both at governments and public opinion. On the economic level, the two parties agreed on cooperation, particularly in regard to industrial development in Turkey and increased trade between the two countries. On the military level, agreements were reached for the exchange of intelligence, information, and joint planning for mutual aid in emergencies. Turkey also promised to support, both in the Pentagon and NATO, Israel's demand to strengthen its armed forces.[41] Another Israeli historian, who likewise does not mention his sources, asserts that the comprehensive agreement included scientific cooperation in "highly sensitive" areas, as well as the export of Israeli military equipment to Turkey.[42] This general outline was confirmed to me by Israeli officials who served in Turkey at the time.[43] It is clear, then, that the agreement was bilateral, and that at least from the Israeli side it was viewed and referred to in top secret documents as the "alliance" (*brit*) and not as the "agreement" (*heskem*). Thus the Israeli military attaché referred to his discussions with his counterparts as "the talks of the alliance."[44] In his dispatches from Ankara, Moshe Sasson did occasionally use the term "periphery." However, he mentioned this in connection with Israel's "policy of the periphery" with various countries, such as Iran and Ethiopia, and not as a multilateral alliance.[45]

There was most probably trilateral cooperation between Israel, Turkey, and Iran in the exchange of intelligence. According to a CIA report captured by Iran in 1979 from the American Embassy in Tehran, and later distributed in the West, at the end of 1958 Israel, Turkey, and Iran signed an agreement to form an organization called Trident. This organization aimed to exchange intelligence information between the Israeli intelligence service (the Mossad), the Turkish National Security Services (then *Milli Amele Hizmet*—MAH, later *Milli İstihbarat Teşkilati*— MIT), and the national organization for intelligence in Iran (Savak). The heads of the three services met twice a year.[46] In one of his dispatches, Moshe Sasson, the Israeli chargé d'affaires to Ankara from 1960 to 1966, mentioned such a tripartite meeting in Tehran. He later confirmed the existence of these meetings in an interview.[47] A high-ranking Turkish military officer, who was in charge of coordinating the meetings between the military intelligence organizations of Israel and Turkey and was in contact with the Mossad as well, said he did not remember ever having organized or heard about such tripartite meetings of the Mossad, the MAH, and Savak.[48] Similarly, the Israeli military attaché from 1964 to 1967, Baruch Gilboa, denied knowledge of such meetings. Gilboa did, however, refer to a tripartite understanding, whereby Turkey tacitly agreed to Israeli flights over its airspace on their way to Iran[49] (probably to bring aid to the Iraqi Kurds, who were in rebellion against the Iraqi government). The divergence between Sasson and the military attachés possibly had to do with the high degree of compartmentalization between the different parties in contact with the Turks.[50]

The Turkish–Israeli axis of the peripheral alliance lasted formally for eight years and experienced many ups and downs, mostly because of fluctuations on the Turkish side. There were, indeed, basic asymmetries and disagreements between Israel and Turkey, which went a long way to explain the course the relationship took. Israel's motives for strong relations with Turkey were strategic, coming as they did in response to inherent problems of isolation, lack of legitimacy, and ongoing conflict with its Arab neighbors. Turkey's needs, on the other hand, were more tactical in nature. Although many of its leaders would admit that Turkey needed a strong Israel to check Pan-Arabism and Pan-Islamism in the region, the immediate motive was more transient. And while Israel did not have to be overly concerned about the impact of the alliance on third parties,[51] Turkey felt it had to give great consideration to certain Arab countries and to other sensitive issues, such as Cyprus (see below). This fundamental difference left its mark on the relationship. Thus, while Israel strove to make relations as open and as public as possible, Turkey sought to keep them secret and unpublicized. This reflected another asymmetry. While in Israel there was quite a strong consensus for relations with Ankara, no such consensus existed in Turkey, where the government had to take into account anti-Israel sentiments, especially among the more traditional Islamic sectors of society in the rural areas and small towns of Anatolia. In the very early years of the state of Israel, the leftist parties—Mapam and the Communist Party—had objected to relations with Turkey.[52] However, by 1958 such opposition had all but disappeared. In the debate on July 16, 1958 of the Knesset Foreign Affairs and Defense Committee, which dealt with relations with the peripheral countries, the Mapam representative did not object in principle to the need to find friends in the periphery, or "the belt," as he termed it. However, he cautioned against the illusion that these countries would come to Israel's aid in its hour of need.[53] The opposite was true for Turkey. As time went on, Turkish governments had to show growing deference to Islam and to Turkey's Islamic elements opposition to ties with Israel—an additional reason for keeping them secret. Israel, therefore, as the more vulnerable and dependent party of the two, had to constantly take into account Turkish sensitivities on various domestic and foreign issues, in particular the Kurds, the Armenians, and the Arabs. Finally, while Turkey was a member of two pacts, NATO and the Baghdad Pact (later to become CENTO), Israel belonged to none and even its relations with the United States were at that time quite precarious.

In spite of this, the basic common denominators and the convergence of interests between the two states in 1958 moved them to forge an alliance. These shared interests can be summed up as follows: keeping Soviet expansionism at bay, containing Pan-Arabism and Pan-Islamism, and fighting terrorism. In addition, Turkey (and Iran as well) hoped to use the alliance and Israel's good offices to improve its image in the West, both in popular and government opinion.

The Ben-Gurion–Menderes meeting laid the foundations for the "special relations," which then took their course at various political, economic, and military levels. Interestingly, the fluctuations toward Israel in that period did not so much reflect domestic developments in Turkey as events in the regional and international arenas. The new regime of General Cemal Gürsel, which came to power following the coup of May 27, 1960, did not renege on the agreement, but even strengthened relations with Israel in various ways.[54] (This could not have been taken for granted, since those behind the coup were highly critical of Menderes's policy on the Middle East and maintained, for example, that had he not deployed forces on the Syrian border in 1957 the formation of the UAR might have been forestalled.)[55] The reason for the continuity of the accord may, in fact, be that Turkey's powerful military elite appreciated the military-strategic importance of relations with Israel and put its weight behind it even in that critical period. In a meeting with Fischer on August 15, 1960, Gürsel himself described relations with Israel as an "important bastion" of stability, peace, development, and progress in the region.[56] Israel's eagerness to maintain relations with Turkey was highlighted by its prompt recognition of the new regime—the third country in the world to do so.

In examining the peripheral alliance with Turkey, a distinction should be made between the open and secret levels as well as between the political–diplomatic, economic, and military links. The least gratifying, from the Israeli point of view, was the public political–diplomatic level. For all Israel's endeavors and all Turkey's promises, Ankara did not upgrade diplomatic relations with Israel, even in the period of relative honeymoon—compared, of course, with what would follow. Needless to say, Turkey's failure to keep its commitment was a major source of frustration for Israel, which had pinned great hopes on this. Israel probably did not fully appreciate the inherent contradiction between one of its own most important policy aims—gaining legitimacy by establishing high-level/open relations with as many countries as possible—and Turkey's basic instinct to keep as low a profile as possible on its relationship with Israel, so as not to hamper its relations with the Arab world. Since it was Turkey that held the key, the contradiction was resolved in Ankara's favor. Indeed, it seems that the secret agreement made Turkey even more reluctant to upgrade the public rapprochement, in case this aroused Arab suspicions.[57]

This need to take Arab reactions into account was the main argument that Turkey put to Israel when explaining its failure to upgrade relations. Indeed, the Arab states have consistently put pressure on Turkey to break off relations altogether. Ankara's most important partner in the Arab world was Iraq, and the need to buy Baghdad's goodwill was obvious to successive governments both in Iraq and Turkey. Menderes, who had forged the agreement with Ben-Gurion, promised in that "fateful meeting" to upgrade relations with Israel to the ambassadorial level.[58] He later undertook to do this in October 1959. Yet he did not keep his promise, and one of the key reasons was Baghdad. Although the new regime of 'Abd al-Karim Qasim repudiated the Baghdad Pact in March 1959, Menderes still wished to support Qasim and maintain relations with him, either as a counterweight to the UAR, or to prevent his veering into the Soviet orbit, or to prevent anarchy in Iraq, or for all these reasons combined.[59] Israel felt victimized by these moves. Its arguments to the effect that it had supported Qasim in different ways, even alerting him to a planned coup by his rival, 'Abd al-Salam 'Arif, and its request that Turkey inform Qasim of Israel's endeavors, were to no avail. In fact, when Menderes was again approached on the matter in November 1959, he stated that Turkey should "take into consideration Qasim's possible reaction" to the country with whom he "finally" achieved close relationship.[60] But even at that point he once more promised that relations would be upgraded "very soon."[61]

Unaware of the changes that were taking place in Turkey, Israel attempted to interest Menderes in a (probably secret) visit to Israel, as he had promised Ben-Gurion. But Menderes rejected the idea. Nor did a proposed meeting for consultations in Ankara between Ben-Gurion and Menderes take place.[62] To judge from impressions gained by Israeli officials who were in touch with Turkish politicians at the time, it was Foreign Minister Fatin Rüştü Zorlu who prevailed upon Menderes to prevent the upgrading of relations. The Israeli chargé d'affaires in Ankara, Moshe Sasson, maintained that although Menderes had promised the upgrading, Zorlu was the person in charge of relations with Israel and at times obstructed face-to-face meetings, such as one planned between Sasson's father, Eliyahu Sasson—then ambassador to Rome—and Menderes. Moshe Sasson maintained that Zorlu preferred relations "with no marriage" and sought the best of both worlds.[63] On the whole, the Turkish Foreign Ministry was considered to be much more pro-Arab than other ministries and also than the military, and was at pains to act with great caution on relations with Israel, to avoid antagonizing the Arabs.[64] In the end, Menderes and Zorlu were both ousted (and executed in September 1961) without having normalized relations with Israel.

The same trend was evident under the new regime of General Gürsel, the strongman in 1960–65. Although he declared himself willing to strengthen relations with Israel, Gürsel was nevertheless reluctant to do so openly on the political–diplomatic level. His reasons were straightforward: he did not want to fall into the same trap as the Shah of Iran, whose announcement of his recognition of Israel caused Egypt's 'Abd al-Nasser to sever relations with him, and he wished to "befriend" the Arabs. This, he argued, would help Israel too, as it would facilitate Turkey's role of explaining the Israeli case to the Arabs.[65] As it turned out, Gürsel did actually strengthen relations on many levels, on condition that this would be kept secret. Under Gürsel too, the Iraqi factor was important.[66]

The new government under Ismet Inönü in 1961 was no more forthcoming. Although it was Inönü who had established relations with

Israel back in 1949, and had renewed his promises to upgrade these,[67] he too left office (in 1965) without having carried this out. His primary concern, once again, was the reaction of the Arab states in general and of Iraq in particular. Not that Inönü's Arab concerns helped endear him to the Iraqis. Indeed, his gesture of proposing condolences on the death of Israeli President Yitzhak Ben-Zvi in May 1963 won him the following commendation from an Iraqi newspaper: "An old man who had stabbed the Arabs in the back, went to weep on the tomb of a dog."[68]

As time went on, the Arab factor gained greater significance in the Turkish–Israeli agenda, and added new dimensions beyond the strictly bilateral. The strategic threats that persuaded Turkey to form the alliance with Israel in the first place began to lose their urgency. By the end of 1963, Turkey had improved relations with four potential sources of threat: the Soviet Union, Iraq, Syria, and Egypt. The dissolution of the UAR in 1961 was an important turning point. Interestingly, Turkey was quick to recognize Syria, even before Arab countries such as Iraq did. This so frustrated Egypt that it broke off relations with Turkey for two years. Ankara had to swallow its pride and ask for their resumption, which took place in May 1963. Expectations were raised in Israel that Turkey would balance this move by normalizing relations with Jerusalem. In fact, the Israeli chargé d'affaires considered the time very opportune for such a Turkish gesture and increased his pressure on Ankara. He even opined that not "merely" the normalization of relations was at stake, but "bringing Turkey to such a political orientation that [would put] Israel in the first place in the Middle East."[69]

Israel's expectations for upgraded diplomatic ties ran high in the first part of 1964, when the relationship reached its peak. In early 1964 two Turkish officials on a secret visit to Israel declared, in the name of Prime Minister Inönü, that the upgrading would take place within four to five weeks. Later, in July, Inönü secretly met Eshkol in Paris and again promised that this would happen.[70] Soon, however, these expectations would prove mere wishful thinking, and Israel would instead have to fight against downgrading relations rather than for their improvement. It seems probable that Turkey had never intended to upgrade relations, but Israel chose to close its eyes to reality.

Israel's frustration with the way that relations on the political–diplomatic level developed was mitigated by economic cooperation. This was also part of the peripheral alliance, but was generally more immune to Arab pressure. The reasons for this were threefold: diplomatic–political relations were by their very nature in the public eye, while certain aspects of economic cooperation could be kept discreet; Turkey was in need of

Israeli technological know-how in certain areas; and the economic sector was from the start an important incentive for bilateral relations, because the two economies were complementary.[71]

Even before the peripheral alliance, Israel had hoped that strong economic ties would be a stimulus for Turkey to normalize relations. According to the Israeli chargé d'affaires in Ankara, the "great importance" that Turkey attached to economic ties with Israel "contributed significantly" to its decision not to downgrade relations too far in 1956. He therefore suggested that Israel should continue to cultivate economic links by deepening trade relations or setting up joint projects, so as "to establish political facts with the help of economic tools."[72]

Turkey did show an interest in maintaining and deepening economic ties. Süleyman Demirel, who in 1959 was the head of Turkey's water authority, visited Israel that year. He was so impressed by Israel's achievements that, in a public lecture to some 300 people in Ankara, he advised the Turks "to take the Israeli people—the perfect people in every respect...as a model and to make the Israeli achievement as a goal [for Turkey]." Demirel was especially interested in Israel's manufacture of irrigation pipes.[73] It was true that his enthusiasm did not survive his rise to power in 1965, when relations continued to decline. Nevertheless, this firsthand acquaintance with Israel was the background to Demirel's revival of the political alignment in the 1990s, this time openly.

One of the most promising areas for developing ties was agriculture. Israel sought to export its know-how in this field, to reach out to Turkish villages and peripheral regions, and thus introduce itself to the more traditional Muslim section of the population, often disposed to be less friendly to Israel than city dwellers. In one of his dispatches, the Israeli chargé in Ankara recommended putting great emphasis on the villages. He considered this "the most important activity" in such a Muslim country, aimed at correcting "the wrong impression" that the villagers, who comprised most of the voters, were "pro-Muslim, pro-Arab and anti-Israeli." He asserted that the fact that the villager was "pro-Muslim" did not prevent him from being pro-Israeli.[74] There is no doubt that the Israelis who came to live in the villages and train local people made a great difference.

Furthermore, the results of Israel's agricultural methods were reportedly spectacular. According to Moshe Sasson, in the area of Adana, where the Israeli methods were introduced, the cotton crop quadrupled within six years.[75] By 1968, the cotton crop approximated that of Israel. Indeed, the Turkish Ministry of Villages considered the Adana Project to be Israel's most important achievement in Turkey.[76] Sasson maintained that Israeli know-how in agriculture was widespread all over Turkey, that there were Israeli experts in nearly every province, and that some Turks from the agricultural sector visited Israel. He, too, considered agriculture to be an important area for economic cooperation. Little wonder, then, that the minister of villages pressed for an increase in ties that would include sending hundreds of Turkish officials to study in Israel, and was one of Israel's best advocates in Ankara.[77]

By early 1965 the annual volume of bilateral trade between the two countries had reached $30,000,000, although Israel was concerned that the trend might change for the worse.[78] Other areas of economic cooperation included joint research projects, joint industrial projects, and tourism. Israeli experts were also engaged in the planning of the Keban dam, on which both Israel and Turkey tried to keep a low profile because of its domestic and external ramifications (the resettlement of Kurds and the downstream impact on Syria and Iraq).[79]

Turkey remained keen on economic ties as long as Israel kept quiet about them, and as long as they did not clash with Ankara's economic interests in the Arab world. Indeed, this would be the case from the mid-1960s onward, when Turkey's interests led it to try to penetrate the markets of Arab countries, while also taking heed of their oil weapon. Turkey, then, did not live up to Israel's expectations: it was unwilling to pay for economic ties in political coin.

## Strategic Relations: The Heart of the Matter

The strategic relationship was the most important aspect of the alliance, since it was common strategic threats that had brought the two countries together. In fact, relations on all other levels flowed from and were subordinate to the strategic partnership. However, on this subject we are on very shaky ground, since that part of the agreement has remained classified even in the Israeli archives, and of course on the Turkish side with its great sensitivities.

Although the alliance was signed between two civilian leaders, the military area gained overwhelming importance in time. The Turkish military was eager to develop these relations, and on the whole its attitude toward Israel was far more positive than other sectors of the Turkish elite. There was also great frustration in the army with the way Turkey was treated in the West, especially in the United States, and with the level of military support given it. Not only was Turkey looked down on by other NATO members, but it was felt that the United States exploited its military bases in Turkey, without paying the requisite fees or supplying Turkey with sufficient weaponry. It was not, of course, that Israel could supplant the United States, but that it was easier to share or ask for certain information or technology from a small country, which as such did not threaten Turkey. (The notion of a small country had two aspects: admiration and willingness to cooperate, mixed with uneasiness or contempt, and reservations.) Nor did the Turkish army lose sight of the concept that a strong Israel was important for the balance of power in the region, even at the times when Turkey was trying to court the Arabs. One Israeli dispatch from Ankara mentioned that Turkey's Deputy Chief of Staff Refik Tulga, had expressed to Israel's chargé d'affaires his conviction that the Turkish general staff "sympathized very strongly with Israel," and that he did not know any "high Turkish officer who did not support Israel unconditionally." He further expressed his regret that Turkish policy did not reflect the army's point of view.[80] In short, the army became a kind of guardian of the relationship.

Military cooperation with Turkey, which in Israel was given the code name Merkava, was unique, being the only case of a military agreement between Israel and another country.[81] Regular meetings were held every six months, alternately in each country, between the heads of military intelligence[82] and possibly at times the chiefs of staff.[83] The military relationship with Turkey was termed by the then Chief of Staff, Yitzhak Rabin, as a "special relationship" and by the head of military intelligence as "very close."[84] It included exchange of intelligence, views, and information; coordination and cooperation on various military issues; exchange of know-how in the field of military industry,[85] and probably a lot more that is still classified. The common threats about which the two states shared intelligence were the Soviet Union, certain Arab countries—especially Syria—and terrorism. It was true that Turkey could get most of its intelligence on the Soviet Union from the United States, but there were certain aspects to which Israel could contribute.[86] With regard to Arab countries, Turkey had become "Israel's eyes" into the Arab world, as one anonymous officer termed it. To be sure, this was an additional, albeit important source as Israel's intelligence on the Arab countries was much better than Turkey's, and it was here, especially in regard to Syria, Iraq, and probably Egypt, that Jerusalem made most of its contributions to Ankara.

In writing this book, I did not have access to military documents about the strategic coordination between the two countries. However, according to a high-ranking Israeli officer who was involved at the inception of the alliance, in 1959 the two armies had prepared a joint strategic plan for a war against Syria (and possibly against another Arab country), to meet any contingency. According to this informant, it was the first time in either country's history that there was such a joint plan. Undoubtedly, the military staff of the two countries developed close ties. The Israeli Chief of Staff Haim Laskov, came on a top secret visit to Turkey in that year, together with other senior officers, and his visit was reciprocated by all the Turkish chiefs of staff, including the Chief of General Staff Mustafa Rüştü Erdelhun; Deputy Chief of General Staff Cevdet Sunay; Commander of the Air Force Tekin Arıburun; Commander of the Navy Fahri Korutürk, and Commander of Land Forces Cemal Gürsel. Yitzhak Rabin, then head of operations, played a leading role in developing the plan, which included all three forces—land, naval, and air. It was also the first time that there was a plan for a joint naval force, able to undertake strategic action against a third party. The existence of such a plan was corroborated by the Turkish chief of military intelligence.[87]

The 1960 coup in Turkey, and the change of guard in the military staff, were said to have caused some coolness in relations between the two armies. Yet, in one of the early Israeli dispatches from Turkey, it was mentioned that Turkey "would interfere if we were attacked" and that relations and "cooperation" would continue in all spheres. Later, in August 1966, an Iraqi Mig-21 that was flown to Israel was allowed to make a refueling stop in one of the joint Turkish–American bases.[88] Another example of strategic coordination (or exchange of information), which took place even after military relations were formally frozen, was that Israel notified Turkey about the massing of its forces on the Syrian border in September 1970.[89]

Other forms of cooperation and coordination included a joint enterprise to manufacture mortars for Germany; Israel's sale of parachutes to the Turkish Air Force; its training of Turkish armed forces in various domains; and permission to the Israeli Air Force to train on Turkish territory,[90] as well as the use of Turkish airspace for lifting military supplies to Iran and on to the Kurds of Iraq. In all likelihood, Israel's support of the Kurds was known to only a handful in the Turkish military high command, who kept it strictly secret, especially from the Turkish Foreign Ministry.[91] Generally speaking, the two air forces seemed to have quite close relations, as the Turkish Air Force was keenly interested in developing itself by using Israeli expertise. It should also be mentioned that at one point Turkey showed interest in Israel's development of atomic energy, but Israel was reserved about sharing information on this subject.[92]

On the whole, it can be said that in the alliance's heyday, relations between the two military establishments were quite intimate. One indication was the treatment accorded to Israel's military attaché to Ankara. Two former incumbents of this post said, when interviewed, that they had enjoyed preferential status, on the same terms as representatives of the three powers, the United States, Germany, and Britain. They would meet the director of Military Intelligence every two weeks, and hold regular meetings with the Chief of Staff and other high-ranking officers. One of them was also permitted to visit military bases without the usual lengthy bureaucratic formalities.[93] The exchange of visits, mostly in complete secrecy, was also common. For example, General Cemal Tural, later Chief of Staff, visited Israel in 1964,[94] while the Head of Israel's Military Intelligence Meir Amit, and other senior Israeli officers visited a closed American base in Erzurum, causing some embarrassment to the Americans there.[95] On one occasion in 1964, however, there was an open visit to Turkey by the Israeli military academy, which was headed at the time by Uzi Narkis.[96] The Commander of the Air Force Ezer Weizman (later president of Israel), was also scheduled to come on an open visit at the end of 1964.[97] By that time, however, the Cyprus crisis had begun to take its toll and the visit had to be cancelled.

## The End of the Affair: Cyprus and Its Aftermath

The Cyprus crisis, which erupted in December 1963 after three years of independent statehood for the island, had far-reaching implications for Turkey's worldview, priorities, and relations with the outside world, including Israel. It is beyond the scope of this book to analyze in detail the development of the crisis. However, an outline is needed to understand its impact on the present subject. In 1960, the London Conference brought about the formation of the Republic of Cyprus, an island populated for hundreds of years by a Greek majority and a Turkish minority. The British, Greek, and Turkish participants at the conference reached a compromise that rejected Enosis—the Greek movement to unite Cyprus with Greece—as well as Taksim, which represented the claims of Turkish Cypriots, who sought to divide the island into Greek and Turkish sections. Instead, they created an independent Cyprus. However, the Turks suspected that the Greek Cypriots, headed by Cyprus's president, Archbishop Mihail Christodoulou Mouskos Makarios III, had never relinquished the goals of Enosis. Makarios had declared, for example: "Either the whole of Cyprus is to be united with Greece or become a holocaust..." Turkey and the Turkish Cypriots were accused by the Greeks of plotting to achieve partition of the island.[98]

By December 1963, tension had increased between the two parties, leading to severe clashes at the end of that month between Greeks and Turks, for which each blamed the other. However, according to a Turkish analyst who had access to new documents, it was the Greeks who deliberately provoked the Turks, in order to have an excuse to crack down on them. Indeed, it was Makarios who had undermined the governmental formula decided upon in London. Thus the year 1963 ended with many Turkish Cypriot casualties and a few Greek Cypriot ones. Some 30,000 Turkish Cypriots were relocated from 103 mixed villages, and their houses were demolished and burned after their departure. A complete blockade was imposed on the Turkish enclaves by the Greeks.[99] At that point, Turkey warned Makarios that if he did not accept a cease-fire, it would take action on behalf of the Turkish Cypriots. On March 4, 1964 the matter was discussed at the United Nations, which passed Resolution No. 186 (calling for the cessation of violence and the establishment of a UN peacekeeping force), considered a major diplomatic success for Makarios and a setback for Turkey. As a result, Makarios managed to neutralize Anglo-American efforts to send a NATO peacekeeping force to Cyprus, as well as have his own administration, composed completely of Greek Cypriots, recognized as the government of Cyprus. Meanwhile, notwithstanding the arrival of the UN peacekeeping force on the island, the situation continued to deteriorate, and Turkey prepared to intervene. However, Ankara backed down at the last moment, following a threatening letter dated June 5, 1964 from U.S. President Lyndon Johnson to Prime Minister Ismet Inönü, warning that NATO might not be able to come to Ankara's support if it were to be attacked by the Soviet Union for invading Cyprus.[100] The letter, which was written "in a crude and brutal tone," generated considerable anti-American feeling in Turkey, and while it prevented a Turkish invasion, it did not stop a Turkish Air Force bombardment on August 8 and 9 of Greek Cypriot positions, in support of Turkish Cypriots.[101] A Turkish invasion, however, would be postponed for ten years, until July 1974.

The Cyprus crisis was traumatic for Turkey. It felt helpless to aid those whom it considered its own nationals; it was left isolated and with almost no support at the United Nations and it felt betrayed by its allies in the West, chiefly Britain and the United States. As a guarantor power, Britain "did little to protect the Turkish Cypriots," while both the Americans and the British began to favor Enosis.[102] These developments focused all

Turkey's concerns on Cyprus, turning it into a major yardstick for reevaluating and developing its relations with the outside world.

Against this background, Prime Minister Ismet Inönü initiated a new foreign policy, which eventually had an impact on Israel as well. The most important lesson that he drew from the crisis was the need to break the ring of isolation at the United Nations, by attempting to diversify as much as possible Turkey's relations with other countries. Turkey's frustration with the United States led it to make new overtures to the USSR,[103] implying that the Soviet danger that had once united Turkey and Israel was now reduced significantly. Even more worrying from the Israeli point of view was Turkey's attempt to court the Arab states (as well as Third World countries), whose sheer numbers might determine the voting at the United Nations. At the end of the day, the significance of the crisis was that it shattered Israel's hopes of upgrading relations and brought about Turkey's strong tilt toward the Arab states, at least on the open political level. This tilt was exacerbated by the eruption of the Palestinian problem at the same time. Together, these two issues proved that the level and quality of Turkey's relations with Israel were not a function of bilateral content or considerations alone, but increasingly a reflection of Ankara's relations with third parties, mainly the Arabs.

Aware of Turkey's vulnerability, the Arab countries began pressuring Ankara on the issue of its relations with Israel, making their support on the Cyprus issue conditional upon Turkey's severing ties with Israel. Certain Arab states, conscious of the strong economic links that had developed between Turkey and Israel, had begun, even before the Cyprus crisis, to compete positively with the Israeli influence and infiltration in the economic field. Ironically, it was this cooperation with Israel that prompted the Arabs to court Turkey and try to diminish Israel's role.[104] Simultaneously, representatives of the Arab countries in Ankara had started to coordinate their activities by early 1964, when relations between Turkey and Israel reached their peak. While warning Turkey of the negative impact that rapprochement with Israel might have on the Arab vote on Cyprus at the United Nations, they launched a political, diplomatic, and popular campaign to explain their own point of view. In addition, they sent warning letters to journalists who wrote articles in favor of Israel, and attempted to "buy" journalists for their cause. Later that year, they raised the stakes higher by demanding that Turkey freeze relations with Israel altogether and announce this publicly. Then, in 1965, they offered to mobilize all 13 Arab countries to vote for Turkey at the United Nations if Ankara would break off relations with Israel.[105]

Turkey was not prepared to go to such extremes, probably because it doubted the seriousness of such an offer.[106] The Arab states were not a monolith. Egypt, for example, supported Makarios militarily.[107] More important, Turkey explained, the Arab demand to sever relations with Israel infringed on its sovereign right to determine its own foreign policy. There were even those in the Turkish Foreign Ministry who believed that the downgrading of relations with Israel back in 1956 had been "a very serious mistake," since it put a "terrible mortgage" on Turkey's foreign policy in the Middle East.[108] Nonetheless, by mid-1965 Turkey did adopt new guidelines in its Middle East policy, which were not favorable to Israel, to say the least. Their aims were:

1. To maximize efforts for achieving rapprochement with the Arabs.
2. To limit relations with Israel to the minimum possible.
3. Not to give in to Arab pressures beyond this minimum.
4. Not to permit relations with Israel to obstruct rapprochement with the Arabs.[109]

How did Israel react to these developments? What role did it play in the crisis? And how did relations develop until the informal freeze of the alliance in 1966?

## Israel's Reaction

Israeli officials and scholars agree that the Cyprus problem was a turning point in Turkish–Israeli relations. The question is: to what extent was the change in Turkey's stance brought about by the Arab side of the triangle, and to what extent did Israel too play a part? Most Israeli observers believe that once the crisis erupted, Turkey's tilt to the Arab side was a foregone conclusion, since its interests lay with the Arabs at that point in time.[110] In other words, whatever Israel did or did not do would have made little difference. I will attempt to examine this hypothesis by reconstructing the developments of bilateral relations in that critical period.

Shortly after the Cyprus crisis blew up, Turkish Prime Minister Inönü sent a message to Israeli Prime Minister Levi Eshkol, in which he described developments on the island from the Turkish standpoint. Inönü explained that Turkey had decided "to use the right of unilateral intervention" on the basis of Article 4 of the Treaty of Guarantees [of 1960], but that it had confined its intervention to a single warning flight over Nicosia on December 25, 1963. In his reply, Eshkol expressed distress "for the human loss and suffering" and a hope that "harmonious relations" would be established between "all sections of the population of Cyprus."[111] It was clear, then, that initially Turkey had not asked for, nor had Israel committed itself to, anything specific. Nevertheless, Turkish expectations were that Israel would support it on this issue. Indeed, from the start, the Israeli chargé d'affaires in Ankara, Moshe Sasson, cautioned against Israeli neutrality or abstention at the United Nations, on grounds that such a stance was likely not only to hurt prospects for upgrading relations, but more importantly, to harm the "mutual sympathy existing between the two countries." He was already skeptical about the promise of normalization, because, as he said: "The Turks are known for their talent to issue promises and not to stand behind them in due time."[112] Indeed, normalization was never achieved, but relations in other spheres continued to flourish, as evidenced by the visit to Istanbul on May 9 and 10, 1964 of the College for National Defence, which was even reported on Radio Ankara, although not in the Turkish press.[113] This was followed by the July meeting between Inönü and Eshkol in Paris, which dealt with the Cyprus issue, among other things.

This cordiality, however, began to wane, at least on the public level, following the Turkish bombardment of Greek Cypriot positions in August 1964. After that attack, Archbishop Makarios sent a circular to heads of state, including Israel's President Zalman Shazar, in which he referred to the "barbaric" Turkish action and "the unprovoked and indiscriminate attacks" in which hundreds were killed, and appealed to the international community to put an end to this crime against humanity.[114] After consultation with Israel's prime minister and foreign minister, President Shazar sent Makarios a message in which he expressed sorrow on a "humanitarian basis," and explored the possibilities of sending aid.[115]

The circular and the reply, which were published in the Israeli media, triggered a wave of frustration and criticism from Turkish officials, the Turkish media, and the public at large. Prime Minister Inönü sent a message to Eshkol saying that: "we were disappointed to see that this message was interpreted as a sign of support for the Archbishop" and expressing the hope that relations between Turkey and Israel would be further strengthened by "a close cooperation on the problem of Cyprus as well."[116] What infuriated the Turks, especially the rank and file, was that they interpreted Shazar's statement as "Israeli neutrality," or worse, support for Makarios and the Greek position.

The Israeli military attaché, Paul Kedar, who was shortly to leave his post, was told by military officer friends that he was leaving in good time, meaning that from then on relations were going to cool.[117] An Israeli official who used to visit Turkey frequently and happened to be there after the event, described the sudden change of mood toward Israel. One of his contacts expressed his frustration and astonishment at Israel's behavior, saying that Turkey was the only Muslim country that had recognized Israel and had quarreled with the Arabs because of Israel, whereas Greece did not recognize Israel de jure, while Makarios, for his part, was improving relations with Israel's enemy, Egypt.[118] The Israeli chargé likewise lamented the change, saying that: "before the miserable message, Israel's political standing in Turkey was similar to that of [Ankara's close allies] Persia and Pakistan."[119]

The Cyprus crisis put Israel on the horns of a dilemma. On the one hand, it did not wish to take sides in the conflict and tried to remain neutral. On the other, it knew full well, and made clear to Turkey, that its interests lay with the Turks for various historical, ideological, and political reasons, and, most important, because of their close association in the peripheral alliance. To make things even more difficult, Israel was cognizant of Cyprus's recognition of the state of Israel. Furthermore, it owed the people of Cyprus "a moral debt" for aiding the immigration of Jews to Palestine during the British Mandate.[120] The solution that Israel found to this dilemma was to increase its secret support to Turkey. As soon as this Turkish–Israeli mini-crisis occurred, Israel sent the head of the Mossad, Meir Amit, for talks with Turkey's deputy prime minister and foreign minister. Amit was said to have taken with him a "very important dowry" and "very important and far-reaching commitments."[121] The source of this information did not disclose the contents of this "dowry," but one can assume that it had to do with important military support of some kind. Thus, Sasson and other officials kept repeating that if the secret could be revealed, public opinion in Turkey would not have thought that Israel was neutral,[122] but instead rather pro-Turkey, and there would not have been such a divergence between the senior officials and officers who shared the secret and all those who did not. Although Inönü dropped certain hints to his ministers, these could not be released to the public. From other dispatches it became clear that Israel supported Turkish "efforts" on Cyprus on the basis of "anything they asked us for," and in various other ways that remained secret, such as lobbying for Turkey in African and Latin American capitals; providing legal support; gaining access to the American media; or preventing Egypt, Makarios's arms supplier, from spreading its influence in the island. Israel itself rejected the Archbishop's request to sell him arms.[123]

No doubt both parties insisted on this secrecy because it served their ends. Israel did not want to mar its relations with Greece and the government of Cyprus, nor its façade of neutrality, while Turkey did not want to harm its relations with the Arab countries now that it was courting them so eagerly. But this secrecy had a price. First, Israel lost some ground in Turkish public opinion. Second, because the support was secret, it gave the Turkish government an excuse to avoid the upgrading of relations, using Israel's so-called neutrality as a pretext. Third, if Israel had hoped to use the secret track as a lever for improving open political relations, it failed completely. The secret track continued to operate without interruption,[124] but it had no influence whatsoever on the public level. Nor was Turkey satisfied with the secret support, insisting on open backing as well in case the issue came to a vote at the United Nations. Indeed, Israel's special emissary, Meir Amit, who held talks in Turkey following Shazar's message to Makarios, warned on his return that if Israel did not vote with Turkey at the United Nations, relations would "collapse."[125] The chargé d'affaires, Sasson, kept repeating the same warning, saying that taking a neutral stand would make Israel lose both worlds. Whether in response to these warnings or not, both Prime Minister Levi Eshkol and Foreign Minister Golda Meir prepared messages to their counterparts in January 1965, in which they said that Israel was thinking of standing behind Turkey at the Security Council at the appropriate time.[126] However, as far as can be established, these messages were never sent.

By that time, however, relations had slowly begun to deteriorate. True, in early November 1964, Yosef Almogi, the minister of Housing and Development, made an official visit to Turkey, the first by an Israeli minister. Although the Turkish government did its best to keep the visit from the public eye—for example, by not inviting Almogi to visit Atatürk's mausoleum and not flying the Israeli flag—Israel considered it an important gesture of goodwill.[127] Furthermore, the Commander of the Israeli Air Force Ezer Weizman, was scheduled to come on an official, open visit on December 8 that year. This invitation, sent by General Irfan Tansel, Commander of the Turkish Air Force, was to include meetings with the minister of defense and the Chief of Staff as well as visits to air force and missile bases and other installations. However, some ten days beforehand, the visit was postponed indefinitely and never took place.[128] There are two Israeli versions of this. The then Israeli military attaché, Baruch Gilboa, maintained that the forthcoming visit was somehow "leaked" to the Turkish Foreign Ministry, which then took steps to prevent it.[129] For his part, Moshe Sasson reported in a dispatch to Jerusalem about his meeting with a Turkish Foreign Ministry secretary whom he wished to prepare for the visit, so as to prevent the last-minute embarrassment of a cancellation. However, Sasson asserted that the message of cancellation had been sent shortly before he returned to his office, and that even if the Foreign Ministry had tried to stop the visit it would not have succeeded, as Tansel's standing was very strong in Turkey, much more so than the Foreign Ministry's. In the final analysis, Sasson suspected, it was Prime Minister Inönü himself who had intervened at the last minute to postpone the visit, after the UN debate on the Cyprus issue.[130]

Whatever the truth, one thing was certain—that the Turkish Foreign Ministry had spearheaded the policy of lowering the profile of Turkish–Israeli relations. An official in the Turkish Foreign Ministry, Ilter Türkmen, explained that two "fronts" had formed in the cabinet: on one side, all the ministries that had cooperation agreements with Israel, and on the other, the Foreign Ministry. "People from the ministries of housing, agriculture, villages, work, tourism and others keep pressuring us to enlarge cooperation with Israel," he said, while the Foreign Ministry, "including myself, keep advising caution in the few coming months." It was also clear that both the Turkish army and the intelligentsia were either pro-Israel or else against the pro-Arab line that was gaining ground in Turkey.[131]

By the turn of 1964–65, the Foreign Ministry and all the political parties, including that of Inönü himself, had tipped the political balance to the Arab side. The main reason, as has been mentioned, was the "bitter lesson" of the Cyprus issue and the need to devise a new foreign policy that would be much more flexible and proactive, so as to appeal to countries or groups of countries with which Turkey had not always been on good terms—while the government of Cyprus was. These were the Soviet Union, the Arab states, and the Third World or non-aligned groups. This, together with the need of Turkish politicians and parties to cater to the more traditional and Islamist part of the population at home,[132] and Israel's "neutrality" on the Cyprus issue, turned the Jewish state into more of a liability than an asset, and put an end to Jerusalem's hopes of upgrading relations, as it now had to fight against a reduction or freezing them altogether.

On the Israeli side, archival documents have shown that there was a certain difference of opinion between the legation in Ankara and the Foreign Ministry on how best to cope with the situation. Sasson, for six years chargé d'affaires in Ankara (until mid-1966), emerged as the strongest advocate for Turkey. He argued that Israel should show understanding for

Turkey's sensitivities and the difficult times it was undergoing;[133] that between Cyprus and Turkey, Israel should choose Turkey, since it was the only Muslim country with which Jerusalem had open relations, and that in spite of Arab pressure, Ankara had not severed its relations with Israel, so that there was a need for Israel to reciprocate. This is not to say, of course, that Sasson did not criticize Turkish policy on many occasions, or that he did not express deep frustration with the fact that for all Israel's endeavors, the friendship that had developed over the years was not translated into that most important symbol, ambassadorial and open relations.

The Israeli Foreign Ministry, on the other hand, held a different opinion, which reflected in a kind of mirror image the more critical line of the Turkish Foreign Ministry. Looking from a broader perspective, the Foreign Ministry had to take into consideration Israel's interests not only in Turkey, but in the region and the world at large. In their dispatches back to Sasson, ministry officials argued that Cyprus had an ambassadorial relationship with Israel, which, in spite of Arab pressure, it had not downgraded; that Israel's role as a "good guy" was not always rewarded (it was Egypt that had supported Cyprus militarily, and was being courted by Ankara, and not Israel); that Turkey wanted "everything" and gave nothing in return; and finally, that Turkey should not feel that Israel was in "its pocket," and that for all of Israel's support, Ankara's "gratitude" was "nil." In one of the dispatches, the official suggested that Israel should change its tactics and policy *vis-à-vis* Turkey. But it was too late: Turkey was already in the process of changing its own policy toward Israel.[134] The downward trend signs of Turkish uneasiness over its relations with Israel began to appear when the relationship was at its zenith, in mid-1964. In a meeting with the Israeli chargé d'affairs in early June, a Turkish Foreign Ministry official, while conceding that Israel could publish as much as it wished about the two countries' relations in the media, still suggested that Israel's Arabic language radio limit its reports on Turkish–Israeli relations to "the most important events," such as ministerial visits or important delegations, and ignored the less important ones. The reasons, he said, were twofold—not to provoke the Arabs against Turkey, and not to provide them with all the details of Turkish–Israeli cooperation, "since the Arabs hear and absorb everything."[135] As time went by, this modest, polite request turned into a sweeping demand that Israel Radio in general, and the station's Arabic Service in particular, stop broadcasting anything on Turkish–Israeli relations.[136] Later, this request came to include other media as well.

Israel, despite its instinctive need to publicize relations as much as possible, so as to acquire the longed-for legitimacy, committed itself to almost total secrecy, heeding the Turkish warning that any leakage might bring about a total rupture of relations. Its deference to Turkish sensitivities could be inferred from the stern directives issued to Israel Radio's Arabic service not only not to broadcast reports on Turkish–Israeli relations, but to refrain from broadcasting reports from the Turkish press that were hostile to Egypt and Syria. Furthermore, at the end of December, Israel Radio was directed "to refrain from broadcasting any report on Turkish–Israeli relations on the political and economic level in the coming weeks."[137] It should also be mentioned that the Arabic service received directives to refrain from using the term "the Kurdish people" in its broadcasts, or to quote Israeli newspapers that mentioned the Kurdish problem.[138] Even so, from time to time the Turkish Foreign Ministry blamed Israel for publishing reports on Turkish–Israeli relations and harming Ankara's relations with the Arabs.[139]

Concurrently, leaks began to appear from the Turkish Foreign Ministry to the press that Turkey had decided to "limit" its relations with Israel.[140] Designed initially to appease the Arabs, these leaks would prove true as time went on. By the end of 1964, Sasson summarized the areas in which there were "limitations" or a downgrading of relations:

1. The policy of exaggerated and even petty secrecy on any contact with Israel.
2. The postponement of some of the official government-to-government agreements.
3. A "temporary" veto on any action that required open contacts between the two states.
4. Stagnation in trade with Israel, as opposed to a host of Arab trade delegations invited to Turkey.
5. The cultivation of a pro-Arab atmosphere at the expense of relations with Israel, in all the ministries as well as in public opinion.[141] It later transpired that the Turkish foreign minister had demanded that the chargé d'affaires refrain from inviting members of parliament to Israel, even for private visits.[142]

What worried Israel most was Turkey's intensive courting of the Arabs at its expense. This found expression, among other things, in sending "delegations of goodwill" to each of them (but not to Israel) to explain the Cyprus issue; pro-Arab coverage in the media; upgrading of economic and trade relations; and the establishment of an Arab Information Center in Turkey.[143] The most serious development, from the Israeli point of view, was a series of Turkish declarations in favor of the Palestinians, for example, the use of the term "Palestinian refugees," or mentioning the

1947 Partition Plan. This about-turn on Turkey's part elicited the dispatch of messages from the Israeli prime minister and foreign minister to their counterparts, as well as meetings of the Mossad representative with the head of the Turkish secret services, but to no avail.[144]

The erosion of the relationship, which continued under three different governments—those of Ismet Inönü, Suat Hayri Ürgüplü, and Süleyman Demirel—would gain even greater impetus after 1967. Turkey had reached the conclusion that, in regard to Cyprus, there was much to be gained from Arab friendship, while on the other hand, Israel was unable to help much on this issue, but neither could it harm Turkish interests in this or other fields. Turkey was to be deeply frustrated at the end of 1965 when its intensive efforts produced very poor results: in the UN vote on Cyprus only five states—the United States, Libya, Iran, Pakistan, and Albania—voted with Ankara, while 51, including Israel, abstained and 47, mainly the developing countries, voted against it.[145] Although the Arab countries did not fulfill Ankara's hopes, Turkey's courtship of them would intensify in the next two decades. Israel would pay the price of this Turkish–Arab rapprochement, but perhaps also of its abstention, or its failure to adopt a clear-cut pro-Turkish stance.[146] The final blow to the military "special relationship" would take place in April 1966.

This relationship began to show signs of wear from the end of 1964, but the final break came on April 27, 1966, when the Turkish Director of Military Intelligence, Sezai Orkunt, conveyed to the Israeli military attaché Turkey's decision to freeze relations—or, as the Chief of Staff later put it, to "dissolve the intelligence connection."[147] This move was significant, because it put a formal end to the military aspect of the peripheral alliance. The official reason given was an anti-Turkish announcement published on April 10, 1966 in the *New York Times* which expressed "growing anxiety for the safety and future of the Ecumenical Patriarchate of Constantinople and the Greek Orthodox Church in its historic setting in what is now Istanbul." What infuriated the Turks was that Reform Rabbi Maurice N. Eisendrath (as well as the national chairman of the Anti-Defamation League of B'nai B'rith, Dore Schary, of whom the Turks were not aware) was among the signatories, most of whom were bishops and church leaders, including those from the Armenian and the Greek Orthodox churches. Both Orkunt, and Ilter Türkmen from the Foreign Ministry (who summoned the Israeli chargé d'affaires two days later) expressed their frustration, saying that nothing in the Turkish treatment of the Jews or Turkish–Israeli relations could justify such an anti-Turkish act.[148]

Israel was thus accused of not dissuading the rabbi from signing. The military attaché, Gilboa, and the chargé d'affaires, Sasson, tried in vain to convince their accusers that Israel's influence did not reach that far and that it could not stop American rabbis from signing such an announcement. The truth was that the Israeli Foreign Ministry had received prior information about the Greek Archbishop's attempts to enlist the signatures of the American rabbis, and did try to prevent it. The ministry explained that such a move was bound to harm Turkish Jewry as well as Turkish–Israeli relations, since Turkey identified American Jewry both with Turkish Jewry and Israel. But the two Jewish leaders signed against the ministry's advice.[149]

Israel reacted promptly, attempting to dissuade Turkey from putting its decision into effect, or at least to cut Jerusalem's losses. Prime Minister Levi Eshkol summoned the Israeli military attaché for consultations and suggested that Israel be instrumental in publishing an opposing announcement, so as "to put an end to the incident" and help improve relations. However, Gilboa rejected the idea, saying that since the announcement was a mere pretext, such a move would be useless. Privately, he revealed that Orkunt himself had admitted to him that the real issue was Turkey's pro-Arab policy.[150] Next, came a top secret meeting in Brussels on May 17, 1966 between Israeli Foreign Minister Abba Eban and Turkish Foreign Minister Sabri Çağlayangil. Eban maintained that international experience did not justify an "exaggerated concern" over the Arab reaction and that Turkey should therefore follow a more balanced foreign policy. Çağlayangil, for his part, insisted that "direct contacts" between senior officials, including military ones, should stop "for the time being" and that Israel should refrain from publicizing its relations with Ankara, as was the case with Iran, with which Israel was doing "big things without noise." He explained that the Arabs had a "womanish character: they get excited, shout and disturb."[151]

Nor was Israel's Chief of Staff Yitzhak Rabin, more successful in his letter to Turkey's Chief of Staff Cemal Tural. In his meeting on June 9, 1966 with Gilboa, who had delivered this letter, Tural explained that in light of the political and military circumstances prevailing in the Middle East in 1958, "there was a need for an agreement between the governments for the exchange of military information directly between the armies." However, things had since changed. Turkey now wished to "clean the tables" of "secret agreements," since they interfered with its desire to develop friendly relations with its Arab neighbors. Maintaining contacts with Israel, he emphasized, meant "giving away information on friends; it is not necessary, it is not good and it disturbs."[152]

Failing to change things directly, the Israeli Foreign Ministry toyed for a while with the idea of using the Jewish lobby in the United States to influence matters indirectly to reduce the damage to Israel. This proposal was inspired by a mixture of myth and reality. The myth was that Turkey, like other states and people in the world, believed that American Jews had an overwhelming influence on American policy. It was suggested that one of the underlying reasons for the Turkish rapprochement with Israel was the special relationship that Turkey believed existed in the triangle of Israel, Jews, and the United States, and Ankara's hope of using this to bolster its relations with the United States and gain its support on various issues, such as Cyprus.[153] Indeed, this belief goes a long way to explain Turkey's anger at the signature of the rabbis on the announcement. The Turkish foreign minister even went as far as to state that "Turkish public opinion was shocked" by the appearance of Jewish leaders among the signatories.[154] The reality was that the Jewish lobby did exert its influence at times in support of the Turkish case and attempted to offset the strong Greek lobby in Washington, but this role should not be exaggerated.

Probably at the request of Israel's Foreign Ministry, the chargé d'affaires, Sasson, prepared a detailed proposal "for using the Jewish influence as a political lever in the Turkish–Israeli relations." The long, tentative list of proposals, in which the Turkish Foreign Ministry could have been engaged, included, among other things, a secret meeting between Turkey's ambassador to Washington and the influential Jewish senator, Jacob Javits, together with the presidents of major Jewish organizations, as well as helping the Turkish Embassy in Washington to choose a leading journalist to visit Turkey and write a "positive" article on Ankara. In addition to helping Turkey, such actions could be useful in the following areas: Turkish–Israeli relations in general; the Jewish community in Turkey; curbing the growing influence of anti-Semitic and anti-Zionist elements in Turkey; and consolidating the emigration of the Jews of Syria.[155] Later, in a meeting between the Israeli and Turkish foreign ministers (probably in New York), the former described Israel's endeavors to impress upon the U.S. Jewish leadership the importance that Jerusalem attached to its relations with Turkey, and to try to influence this leadership to support the Turkish cause in the United States.[156] In December 1966, Senator Javits met the Turkish ambassador to the United States and expressed to him the Jewish concern over the cooling of Turkish–Israeli relations, and proposed helping to promote the Turkish cause in the United States.[157]

Reality, however, was stronger than myth, and Israel's endeavors to salvage the peripheral alliance with Turkey were unsuccessful. Indeed, from 1966 onward, relations began to enter a deep freeze, with no signs of thaw appearing until some two decades later. Nevertheless, it must be stressed that even in this low period, Turkey never considered cutting relations with Israel altogether, and low-level ties continued in various areas.[158] Contacts between the secret services went on uninterruptedly in all times. Turkey also allowed Israeli Air Force flights to cross its airspace on their way to and from Iran.[159] On a minor level, Israel was even quicker than the Turkish government in sending immediate support (300 doses of plasma) to help the victims of the earthquake at Adapazarı, in summer 1967. The Turkish Foreign Ministry Director General thanked the Israeli chargé d'affaires, saying: "Only Israelis can do things so quickly."[160]

In assessing the demise of the peripheral alliance with Turkey, the following questions should be asked: What was the relative role of the Turkish Foreign Ministry and the army in bringing it to an end? What was the weight of side issues and third parties in Turkish decision-making? Could Israel have prevented the rupture? From dispatches sent at the time by various Israeli diplomats in Turkey and from interviews with some of them today, it became clear that the Turkish Foreign Ministry was the prime mover behind the freezing or downgrading of relations. It was true that if the prime minister had stood out against it, the picture might have been different, but it seems quite clear that the various prime ministers, from Menderes to Demirel, shared the Foreign Ministry's view that, for all the importance of relations with Israel, those with the Arab countries far outweighed them. The same could be said of the military. It was true that relations between the countries were much stronger on the military than on the political–diplomatic level. In fact, the military used to conceal things from the Foreign Ministry, for example, the planned visit of the Israel's Air Force commander, which was, however, frustrated once the Foreign Ministry got wind of it. It was also true that, as we have seen, relations began to cool on the civilian–political level earlier than on the military one. Yet it would be a mistake to think that the Foreign Ministry had to impose its view on the military. Nor is it likely that the Chief of Staff took the decision personally and single-handedly, without informing the Foreign Ministry, which once it learned about it, tried to soften the decision. The Foreign Ministry's Secretary General Ümit Bayülken, who had conveyed this piece of information to the Israeli chargé d'affaires, explained the decision as the "impulsiveness" of the Chief of Staff and his "rigid," "sensitive," and "rough" character—"the way soldiers are."[161] Yet, such assertions should be taken with a grain of salt. First, Bayülken himself was considered the architect of the new pro-Arab policy[162] (the main motive behind the decision). Second, in a meeting with the Israeli military attaché, the director of Turkish General Security admitted that there was "a connection between the decision to cut the special military relationship and Turkey's pro-Arab policy."[163] Third, the Turkish military had accepted the line followed by the Foreign Ministry, because it considered the matter to be of vital importance to Turkey, and the decision was not haphazard, but was taken after a balanced debate.[164] In fact, it was possible that the decision was taken at the highest level, namely, at the National Security Council (NSC), which included, among others, the president, the Chief of Staff, the prime minister, and the foreign minister.[165]

The eruption of the Cypriot problem concurrently with the Palestinian issue was the most damaging to the Turkish–Israeli relations. Theoretically, the inherent isolation of the state of Israel and the increasing isolation of Turkey on the Cyprus issue might have further consolidated relations between the two. In practice, however, the unenviable status of both nations had the opposite effect, and Turkey sought to break the ring of isolation by distancing itself from Israel, while moving closer and closer to the Arab states in the hope of winning them over on the Cyprus issue. Thus, the emergency situation that propelled Turkey into the alliance in 1958 was replaced by another emergency that moved it to disengage from that alliance a few years later.

Faced with such strong Turkish national interests and a decisive shift in foreign policy priorities, could Israel have done anything more to change the course of events? In hindsight, it can be said that Israel was probably unable to stop the erosion, but might have been able to minimize the damage. Both in the Makarios–Shazar incident of August 1964 and the rabbis' signature of April 1966, it became clear that the Turks felt a sense of betrayal, in spite of the substantial support Israel granted them behind the scenes. Thus, as Sasson explained in one of his dispatches, in order to understand Turkey's reactions on the Cyprus issue one should not use logic, but rather "the finer tools which deal with phenomena in the realm of emotions," and that "what is going on in this issue is by no means in the realm of pure political logic but rather in that of national feelings," which were full of contradictions, lack of logic, and inconsistency.[166]

I suggest, therefore, that had Israel done nothing to offend Turkish feelings, and had it gone all the way in supporting Turkey *openly* at the United Nations and other forums, the atmosphere between the two states, or rather their peoples, might have been better and the strong tilt to the Arab side might have been scaled down somewhat, although not prevented altogether. It was indeed ironic that at the end of this specific period, a certain symmetry formed between the two parties, in the sense that each needed the other's open support as much as secret cooperation, but both were unable to deliver the goods. This would take another three decades.

What is the relevance of the peripheral alliance to the Turkish–Israeli alignment of the 1990s? As a historical precedent, the pact proved that when there was a common danger, the two countries could unite to contain it. In 1958 it was the triple threat of the Soviet Union, the UAR, and the upheavals in Iraq; in the 1990s it was Iran, Iraq, and Syria. The peripheral doctrine, although not stated in so many words, has been a constant in Israel's foreign policy, coming as it did in response to other ongoing preoccupations: Israel's isolation, and the political upheavals and changing strategic circumstances in the region. Accordingly, the development of relations with the countries of the periphery was not limited to non-Arab states, but included, at different times, Arab states as well[167]—among them the secret relations with Morocco[168] and Oman.

The alignment of the 1990s with Turkey, which was another metamorphosis of the peripheral alliance, served several Israeli ends. While addressing imminent threats from other countries of the periphery, it was also designed to complement the peace process with core Arab states. The alignment with Turkey was intended to compensate Israel for loss of strategic depth, in the event that it had to give up territory to Syria and the Palestinians in return for peace. On another level, the alignment diversified Israel's strategic reliance and broadened the base of its support by adding a regional state—Turkey—to the almost exclusive bulwark of the United States. Lastly, it was to bolster Israel's position in the region, in that the Jewish state had allied itself openly and publicly with another strong country in the area. Thus, Israel's endeavors to reach out to the periphery, and Turkey's endeavors to turn back to the Middle East, met in middle ground in the 1996 alignment.

# Chapter 3

# The 1990s Alignment: Motives and Players

I f the peripheral alliance of the late 1950s was initiated, activated, and cultivated mainly by one side—Israel—the strategic alignment of the 1990s can be considered more as a joint project, in which the two partners contributed equally to its formation and success.[1] And whereas the peripheral alliance came into being to address threats of Communism and Pan-Arabism, the new agreement addressed threats emanating from radical Islam and individual states. Similarly, where Iran had been a leading partner in the Israeli–Turkish–Iranian triangle, it was now considered to be a potential threat to both Turkey and Israel, thus adding another motive for the new alignment. Moreover, Turkey now felt confident enough to proceed on its own with a *rapprochement* with Israel, without needing an additional Muslim partner (as in the 1950s, Iran), to provide legitimization to an "unholy" alliance with the Jewish state. In fact, it was Israel that initiated the additional, involvement in the alignment of its long-time tacit ally in the Arab world—Jordan.[2] Most important, unlike the peripheral alliance, which was and still is considered highly secret by both Turkey and Israel, the new agreement has been public from the start. The explanation for this transformation needs to be sought in Turkey, and not Israel, which has always been very keen to develop strong and open relations with Ankara. Events in the regional and international arena played an important role in the new Turkish approach. But equally, or even more significant, were developments on the Turkish domestic scene, which are discussed below.

These changes notwithstanding, a certain continuity in the relationship should not be lost sight of. It was true that almost 40 years, some of them very difficult as far as Israel was concerned, separated the first and second alignments. Yet the foundation laid in the peripheral alliance four decades earlier was strong enough to provide a springboard for the special relationship of the 1990s. Needless to say, in both cases military-strategic cooperation dominated all other aspects.

## Turkey's Change of Heart

In his important study on Turkish–Israeli relations between 1948 and 1960, George Gruen suggested that the most salient feature of the Turkish stance toward Israel was ambivalence.[3] While it could be argued that a certain ambivalence governs relations between any two countries, in Turkey's case it was reinforced by various historical, cultural, political, economic, and strategic factors. It must be stressed, however, that this ambivalence was largely on one side—Turkey's—and was far less apparent in Israel.

The legacy of the Ottoman Empire went a long way to explain this ambivalence, and in many ways the unique relations between a Muslim and a Jewish state. From the start, the Ottomans opened their gates to Jews who were fleeing persecution in different countries in Christian Europe, and in turn the Jews contributed to the flourishing of the empire, at least in its early years, and remained loyal to it throughout.[4] This laid the basis for future Turkish acceptance of the state of Israel, as well as for the development of bonds of friendship between the two peoples. On the other hand, a dichotomy had existed during the reign of Abdül Hamid II (1876–1909), who welcomed the Jews and allowed them to prosper, but at the same time totally rejected the idea of a state for the Jews in Palestine, as proposed to him by Theodore Herzl.[5] This was to reinforce an opposite or more negative attitude toward Israel. The reasons for Abdül Hamid's objection to Zionism were manifold, but two of them would be pervasive up to the end of the twentieth century. These were Islamic sensitivities and sentiments on the one hand, and on the other, opposition from the Arab inhabitants of Palestine to Jewish settlements. However, even Abdül Hamid himself, who had formally prohibited the settlement of Jews in Palestine (but not elsewhere in the empire), turned a blind eye to their immigration to the holy land, thus allowing the Jewish Yishuv (the pre-state Jewish community) to develop.[6]

This ambivalence was reflected in a book written by Falih Rıfkı Atay, one of the aides to Cemal Paşa, who was the commander of the fourth army in Palestine during World War I. While Atay could not hide his admiration for the prosperous and modern life of the Jews in Palestine, even during the war, he warned of the inherent political problems between "the handful of Jews" in Kudüs—Jerusalem—"as against

600,000 Arabs." Describing local life, he said: "The new towns and villages of Palestine are the achievements of the Jews. This is . . . a brand new Palestine . . . The grapes are squeezed by the Arab day-laborer and the wine is drunk by the pretty well-fed Jew."[7]

This ambivalence carried over into the era of the Turkish Republic, affecting its relations both with the Jewish minority in Turkey and the Jewish Yishuv in Palestine. While Turkish Jewry, which became a kind of glue in Turkey's relations with the future Jewish state, continued, on the whole, to enjoy a high degree of tolerance, it still suffered anti-Semitic attacks from time to time. The causes of this hostility were various, but two of them would be relevant in later years. The first was conspiracy theories accusing the Jews of plotting to bring about the disintegration of the Ottoman Empire, in order to facilitate the founding of the "infidel" Jewish state. The second was the overwhelming share by ethnic minorities, especially the Jews, in trade and manufacturing in Turkey, which fueled animosities and anti-Semitism. These sentiments were in the background of what may be called the pogrom against the Jews in Thrace in July 1934, which caused the flight of most of them to Istanbul.[8]

Against this, the state of Turkey itself largely upheld a policy of tolerance toward the Jews. President Kemal Atatürk, who was himself accused of being a *dönme* (a Jew who had ostensibly converted to Islam, but secretly practised Judaism), was quoted as saying, as early as 1923, that because the loyalty of the Jews to the Turkish state and nation had been proved, "they would continue to live in comfort and happiness."[9] Although Atatürk's statements concerning the Jews were very rare, they regarded him as their protector and called him "El Gadol" ("The Great" in Ladino).[10] Atatürk's tolerance of the Jews can be inferred from the election of the first Jewish MP, Abravaya Marmaralı, to the Turkish Parliament in 1935.[11] More significant, during the 1930s Atatürk welcomed to Turkish universities and institutes some 200 Jewish academics, scientists, and physicians from Nazi Germany. These immigrants played a crucial role in the development of Turkey's academic, scientific, and artistic life throughout the 1940s.[12] Little is known about Atatürk's views on the Jewish Yishuv in Palestine. However, Turkey's positive attitude may be inferred from its permission to a large group of Turkish Jewish sportsmen to participate in the Maccabi games in Israel in 1935,[13] and its close relations with the Jewish Agency, the paramount Zionist organization in Palestine in those days. Turkey also took part in the Zionist-sponsored Levant Fair in Tel Aviv in 1936. The Yishuv, for its part, participated in the 1938 Izmir International Fair.[14]

As is well known, Turkey's attitude to the creation of Israel was ambiguous. While Ankara was opposed to the 1947 Palestine Partition Plan, it recognized the new state of Israel in 1949 and was at the time the only Muslim country to engage in diplomatic relations with Israel. But what should be noted was that, although the Jewish state was established on previously Ottoman- and Muslim-dominated lands, Turkey, unlike the Arab states, has not taken the view that Israel was born in sin. Turkey's official attitude toward Israel has been governed by one word—balance, namely, balance between Jerusalem and the Arab world. However, this term disguised a multitude of Turkish vacillations and ups-and-downs *vis-à-vis* Israel.

Turkey's ambivalence, was best illustrated in the three major wars in the region after the 1948–49 Israeli War of Independence: the 1956 Suez War, the June 1967 War, and the October 1973 War. Militarily speaking, Turkey remained neutral and did not send troops to support either side. Nor did it sever its relations with Israel after the wars, in spite of Arab pressure. Yet Turkey did lean toward the Arabs in various declaratory and practical ways. In the aftermath of the 1956 Suez War, Turkey downgraded relations with Israel to chargé d'affaires level, justifying the move by Israel's occupation of the Sinai Peninsula. However, Israel's withdrawal shortly afterward did not result in the return of the relations to the previous level. In the 1967 crisis, which led to the war between Israel, Egypt, Syria, and Jordan, Turkey refused to contribute to the efforts to reopen the Gulf of Akaba to Israeli shipping and declared Incirlik air base off limits to U.S. forces. After the war it supported UN Resolution 242, which demanded Israel's withdrawal from the territories it had occupied during the fighting, in return for secure borders. In the 1973 War, Turkey again adopted a pro-Arab stance by not allowing the United States to use the Incirlik base to assist Israel. Furthermore, there were reports that Turkey permitted Soviet cargo planes carrying military equipment to Egypt to use Turkish airspace.[15]

Turkey's tilt toward the Arabs became even more evident after the 1973 War and the ensuing world oil crisis, when in 1974 it recognized the Palestine Liberation Organization (PLO) as the sole representative of the Palestinian people, and in 1975 voted for the UN resolution that equated Zionism with racism. The most drastic measure against Israel was Ankara's decision on November 26, 1980 to further downgrade diplomatic relations to second secretary level, which came into force in February 1981. The official reason given was Israel's enactment, on July 30, 1980, of the "Jerusalem Act," which affirmed that a united Jerusalem was the capital of Israel. However, the lapse of four months between the enactment of the law and the Turkish decision begs other explanations. First, the military coup of September 1980 made a significant difference, since its leaders brought with them a new agenda and set of priorities. Second, although the Turkish military elite was on the whole sympathetic to Israel, this did not help Israel this time, since Turkey was on the brink of bankruptcy and its new Foreign Minister Ilter Türkmen, and Economic Minister Turgut Özal, both thought that the best way to overcome the crisis was to strengthen relations with the Arab countries, at the expense of Israel if necessary.

According to an Israeli representative in Ankara, it could not be mere coincidence that the decision to downgrade relations was made on the same day that Türkmen returned from Saudi Arabia with a check for $250 m. in his hand.[16] Türkmen himself was known for his anti-Israel views and, priding himself on the change of policy, he declared: "We brought more clarity to our Middle East policy by downgrading relations with Israel to the minimum meaningless level." He further added that Israel had proved that "she is being unconstructive about the Middle East peace."[17] In an interview with the author in October 2001, Türkmen spoke of himself as the "bad guy," confirming that he had initiated the move. He justified it on grounds of the Jerusalem law; Turkey's dire need of Arab oil, especially from Saudi Arabia; the fear that Turkey would be expelled from the Islamic Conference, as Egypt had been from the Arab League, because of its peace agreement with Israel; and a belief that such a policy change would not "practically harm Israel too much." He denied, however, the reports of the $250 m. Saudi assistance to Turkey, and even emphasized that Turkey's expectations of Saudi and Arab support were never fulfilled.[18] Thus, official relations remained all but frozen until the mid-1980s, when a thaw started to take place. In fact, as we shall see, intelligence and military relations developed secretly during the 1980s, until the public upgrading of relations at the end of 1991.

## Domestic Politics and Israel

What was the position of Turkish political parties in regard to relations with Israel? Generally speaking, the mainstream parties accepted the Foreign Ministry's official line. However, opposition came from marginal groups, both on the Left and Right of the political spectrum. In the late 1960s and early 1970s, the radical-leftist groups were strongly pro-PLO, regarding the Palestinian movement as a model to emulate. A sizeable number of them went to Lebanon and Jordan and joined the ranks of the PLO. Several factors, including guerrilla romanticism, the struggle for national independence, revolutionary solidarity, and escaping arrest by the Turkish police, pushed many outstanding student leaders into the arms of the PLO; some Turkish radicals ended up in Israeli prisons.[19]

On the other side of the spectrum were the Islamists, with all their conspiracy theories about Jews, Zionists, and the state of Israel. From its inception in 1970, the Islamist National Order Party (*Milli Nizam Partisi*, MNP), headed by Necmettin Erbakan, continually propagated the idea that "International Zionism" aimed at "cutting off the head of the Islamic world," with Turkey as its prime target. The creation of the state of Israel, the MNP maintained, threatened Turkey, since Jerusalem's aim was to "swallow" Ankara either by partition or integration. Erbakan himself later argued that Herzl's Zionist project aimed at seizing large parts of *Turkey* [my emphasis] and annexing them to Israel. His conspiracy theory further led him to argue that any Western project was the result of a Zionist plot. For example, he claimed that the European Common Market, formed in the early 1970s, was the product of Zionist conspiracies and its aim was to achieve world hegemony, hence Turkey should never join it.[20] The Islamists would continue to propagate these ideas throughout the 1990s, because Israel served as the perfect tool for mass mobilization of public opinion in Turkey, against either the Turkish government or "American imperialism," or both.

Unlike the radical Left and Islamic parties, the position of the nationalist Right was quite ambiguous. On the one hand, most of the parties or groupings had in their background anti-Semitic tendencies. This was especially true of the Republican Peasants' and National Party (*Cumhuriyetçi Köylü Millet Partisi*, CKMP), which later became the Nationalist Action Party (*Milli Hareket Partisi*, MHP), headed by Alpaslan Türkeş. In the 1930s the Turkish ultranationalists were strongly influenced by Nazi propaganda, and anti-Semitism became one of their trademarks. Although for most of the 1930s they were kept at bay, they still managed to disseminate their anti-Semitic ideas, especially against Turkish Jews. Hitler's *Mein Kampf* was published and extensively distributed by Turkish nationalists.[21] However, after the establishment of Israel in 1948, the Jewish state became a source of admiration and emulation for many in ultranationalist circles. They admired the nation-building efforts of the Zionists, their struggle for independence, and their revival of the Hebrew language, especially turning it into the official language of the state. The fact that Israel had friendly relations with the United States and was on poor terms with the Soviet Union only added a point in its favor. Similarly, the 1967 and 1973 Wars were another cause for admiration. Unlike the Islamists, the ultranationalists had always kept their distance from the Arabs because of "the stabbing in the back" syndrome, a memory they kept alive. Also unlike the Islamists, the ultranationalists did not view with concern Israel's occupation of Gaza and the West Bank in 1967, but rather admired the Jewish state's victory and sought to imitate it in Cyprus, Kirkuk, and Mosul.

An example of someone who traveled all the way from extreme anti-Semitism to admiration of the Jewish state was Hüseyin Nihal Atsız, one of the ideological fathers of the nationalists and very influential among the rank and file of nationalist organizations. In 1934 he stated that "the Turkish nation's internal enemies are three; the Communist, the Jew and the flatterer" and that the God of the Jews was money.[22] However, in 1947 he wrote that the Jews, whose "cowardliness became proverbial," had set an example of how to fight for an ideal and realize it against all odds.[23] They managed, he said, "to get back the land they had lost 2000 years ago, and to revive Hebrew which has remained only in the books and turn it into a spoken language." In the same vein of anti-Semitism mixed with genuine admiration, he wrote after the 1967 War that the Jews of Israel were no longer the Jews of Balat (a neighborhood in Istanbul), but that Israel was like Prussia, and was justified in not returning the occupied territories so long as the Arabs did not recognize the state of Israel. He declared that Turkey should learn from Israel's example and fight for northern Iraq.[24] The MHP leader, Türkeş, also lauded Israel's consecutive victories in the wars against the Arabs, while criticizing the Arab states for lack of unity and lack of progress in scientific, technological, and economic fields. The conclusion that Türkeş drew was that Israel had become a reality in the region, and that the Arabs should come to terms with this and make their peace with the Jewish state.[25]

On the popular level, too, ambiguities and fluctuations were discernible in Turkish attitudes toward Israel: while the more sophisticated circles admired Israel's nation-building achievement,[26] the ordinary people envied its consecutive victories and despised the Arabs for their inadequate fighting ability. However, this perception changed radically after the outbreak of the Palestinian intifada at the end of 1987, when most Turks began to admire Palestinian youths for their courage in the face of heavily armed Israeli soldiers. At times, strong anti-Israel sentiments were evident, for instance, after the 1982 massacre of Palestinians in Sabra and Shatila camps in Lebanon carried out by Israel's Maronite Christian allies.

In spite of these varying attitudes, both official and popular, there were certain common denominators that made the coming together of the two parties, when the time was right, far more natural and enduring than initially seemed possible. These ranged from issues of identity to those of orientation, economy, and strategy. Both countries saw themselves as democracies surrounded by totalitarian or authoritarian regimes. Their ruling elites were Western-oriented, identified themselves with Western values, and belonged to the Western orbit in both ideological and strategic terms. Each country felt distinct from its neighbors by virtue of non-Arabness, which was at times accompanied by feelings of superiority—even contempt—that, paradoxically, was stronger among Turks than Israelis. In addition, the two countries had complementary economies, and their armies were considered to be the strongest in the Middle East. It was true that Turkey also had certain common denominators with the Arabs, especially through Islam, cultural bonds and shared economic interests, which stood as stumbling blocks in its relations with Israel (see below). However, by the early 1990s, Ankara's common interests with Israel significantly outweighed those with the Arab world, paving the way for a dramatic change in relations to take place.

On December 19, 1991, Turkey announced its decision "to raise the Ankara representation of both Palestine and Israel to embassy status."[27] According to the Israeli scholar Efraim Inbar, Israel was unaware of the debates that had taken place in the Turkish Foreign Ministry long before this decision, hence the considerable surprise with which the announcement was received in Jerusalem.[28]

For all the importance of the revised policy in the Turkish Foreign Ministry, it seems that such a metamorphosis could not have occurred without the political and strategic changes that had come about in the region in the short space of a year (see chapter 1) and which had prompted various Turkish institutions, especially the army, to adapt to the new circumstances. On the psychological–conceptual level, the breaking of some powerful political and cultural taboos in the Arab world, described in chapter 1, freed Turkey's hands in its relations with Israel. It was now able to break a taboo of its own making and establish full diplomatic relations with Israel, regardless of what the Arab reaction might be. In fact, Ankara must have come to the conclusion that the deep political fissure in the Arab world after the Gulf War, the weakening of the oil weapon, and the fact that the Arab countries had become more inward-looking, meant that their ability to bring pressure to bear on Turkey, either as individual countries or collectively, had decreased significantly. No less important was the change in international attitudes toward Israel, which gathered momentum after the Gulf War. For example, Turkey's main rivals in the region, the Soviet Union and Greece, had established full diplomatic relations with Jerusalem in March and May 1991 respectively, setting both an example and a precedent for Turkey. In this case, the domino effect was in Israel's favor. The most important development as far as Turkey was concerned was the peace process that started between the Arab states and Israel at the Madrid Conference in October 1991. Although the conference itself achieved only modest results, the fact that a Palestinian delegation took part in it, along with several Arab countries, and that its representatives sat together with Israelis, provided Turkey with the legitimacy to make its own overtures toward Israel. A positive correlation was now created between progress in the Israeli–Palestinian peace process and the development of Israeli–Turkish ties. This linkage was no coincidence, revealing as it did Turkey's extreme sensitivity to the Palestinian issue as well as its fundamental need to strike a balance between the two sides. Indeed, Turkey welcomed any improvement in relations between the PLO and Israel, as it was likely to remove the main source of friction between itself and the Arabs in general, and the Palestinians in particular.

The positive correlation between Israeli relations with the Palestinians and those with Turkey was demonstrated after the September 1993 Oslo Agreement between Israel and the PLO. No sooner was the agreement signed than the Turkish Foreign Minister Hikmet Çetin, came on a first visit to Israel in November that year. Later, in July 1994, the Turkish Prime Minister Tansu Çiller, attended the ceremony awarding the Nobel Peace Prize jointly to Israel's Prime Minister Yitzhak Rabin, Foreign Minister Shimon Peres, and Palestinian leader Yasir 'Arafat, and held talks with all three. On that occasion, Çiller stated: "Turkey is a very important country in the region. We believe that it is in a position to contribute to world peace," adding that "both countries have showed us that they want us to fulfill the function of leadership and contribution."[29]

The movement on the Jordanian and Syrian tracks in the peace process also contributed to the growing rapprochement between Turkey and Israel. Thus, just nine days after the signing of the peace agreement between Jordan and Israel (October 26, 1994), Çiller came (on November 3) on the first visit to Israel by a Turkish premier. The fact that Jordan traditionally had good relations with both Turkey and Israel must have greatly helped to legitimize such a visit. In fact, Turkey and Jordan had one thing in common: for years both had engaged in covert strategic cooperation with Israel, but only in the 1990s were they confident enough to establish full diplomatic relations. To balance the visit, nonetheless, Çiller also visited the Palestinian Authority and Egypt.

The Israel–Syria peace track appears to have created another powerful incentive for the strategic agreement reached between Turkey and Israel in February 1996. It would have been noted in Ankara that between December 27, 1995 and January 5, 1996, and January 24–31, 1996, at Wye, Maryland, Israel, and Syria held what Syria's head of delegation, Walid Mu'allim, described as the most fruitful peace talks in four years.[30] Although in the final analysis nothing came of these discussions, the perception at the time that a breakthrough was about to happen must have propelled Turkey into concluding an agreement with Israel soon afterward, in February 1996, and to send President Süleyman Demirel to Israel the following month on an official visit—another first. However, unlike the Palestinian and Jordanian tracks, which directly encouraged the positive Turkish attitude toward Israel, the peace process with Syria was viewed negatively. Ankara feared that an agreement between Syria and Israel might cause it to lose strategic cards *vis-à-vis* Damascus. Ironically, this made Israel even more attractive to Turkey, as Ankara sought to counterbalance a Syrian–Israel agreement with a deal of its own. Turkey's alarm about the Israel–Syria talks was displayed during a visit to Israel in January 1996 by Deputy Foreign Minister Onur Öymen. He was quoted as saying: "How come you talk to these bastards? We beg you officially to stop the talks with Syria."[31]

The Arab–Israeli peace process gave Turkey outward legitimacy for initiating its own moves toward Israel, but the real motives and incentives were to be found in the changes in the region at the beginning of the 1990s, the way in which the Turkish military interpreted them and the role it played in the renewed relations with Israel. Indeed, there is a direct line between the changes of 1990–91 and the Turkish–Israeli agreement of February 23, 1996, which became the cornerstone of bilateral relations in the 1990s and beyond.[32]

## The Turkish Military: Driving Force Behind the Agreement

Like the peripheral alliance of 1958, the 1996 agreement also focused on the strategic partnership. However, the Turkish military now took a much more active part, turning the army into the main driving force behind the agreement. General Çevik Bir, Turkey's deputy chief of general staff in 1996, and considered to be a primary architect of the agreement on the Turkish side, told the author that "it was the achievement of all the Turkish institutions," meaning that all Turkish institutions contributed equally, and that the Turkish Foreign Ministry had prepared the agreement and laid down its guiding principles.[33] However, in spite of Bir's attempts to play down the role of the military, I argue that it did play the major role, driven as it was by its need to address various internal and external threats. This led it, among other things, to encroach on the territory of the Foreign Affairs Ministry.

Indeed, the most striking feature of Turkey's foreign and security policy-making in the 1990s, especially in the latter half of the decade, was the military establishment's enlargement of its de facto and de jure authority *vis-à-vis* the political–civil authorities in these domains[34]. This was made possible by the various mechanisms developed by the military over the years; the relative weakness and instability in the office of the Foreign Ministry; and the twin challenges posed to the state's security and political orientation by Kurdish separatism and Islamic fundamentalism.

One of the areas in which the military increased its influence in the 1990s was foreign policy. A possible explanation was the frequent change of foreign ministers during this period. In the course of the decade, no fewer than 11 ministers held this office. This stood in sharp contrast to the 1980s, when there were only three. The turnover also compared unfavorably with the position of Chief of Staff, which had just four incumbents in the 1990s.[35]

The military sought to bypass politicians by appealing directly to public opinion on important foreign and security issues. One way of doing this was to give briefings to leaders of public opinion explaining its point of view.[36] In addition, high-ranking officers sometimes took part in public debates on foreign policy issues.[37] Such involvement became even greater when the issue in question might involve a military operation, such as northern Iraq, Cyprus, or the Aegean Sea.

Several factors worked in favor of the military's dominance in Turkish politics. Its traditional role as guardian of the Turkish state and its unity; the legal capability it had acquired over the years; and the broad interpretation of security, covering almost all societal and political spheres, all granted the military elite the final word in domestic and foreign policy-making. The changing regional and domestic settings were the catalyst for putting into effect its latent aspirations.

In its position at the forefront of Turkish society in contending with these changes, the military forged a new security and foreign policy.

It assumed this role because it felt that it bore the brunt of the changes, since most of the developments touched on the military-security sphere; civilian leaders were either too weak or too "dangerous" to be trusted with the task of steering policies in such a crucial period; and Turkey's internal and external problems had become so intertwined that only military involvement could find solutions. It should be stressed, however, that the military did not perceive these developments solely as threats, but as opportunities to enlarge its sphere of influence in various areas, above all in foreign policy.

Analyzing the "dramatic developments" of the 1990s, General Bir stressed that most important was the end of the Cold War, which amounted to "a victory for the Western alliance gained without firing a shot."[38] Indeed, the end of the Cold War and the concomitant collapse of the Soviet Union and Yugoslavia urged the military to take action, either because the boundaries between security and foreign policy issues were becoming blurred, or because these events by their very nature impinged on its areas of interest.

Generally speaking, the Turkish military had to reformulate policies toward the three "near abroad" regions: the Caucasus and Central Asia, the Balkans, and the Middle East. On the whole, the opening of vistas toward these regions was perceived by Turkish politicians, especially Turgut Özal, as an opportunity for a more dynamic foreign policy and for extending Turkey's influence. But the military had to contend with its more negative aspect—the need to prepare for any conflict that might flare up, from the Gulf to Chechnya and Bosnia. At the same time, the military had to "prove" to the Europeans that not only had Turkey not lost any of its importance to NATO, but that this had increased significantly. As Çevik Bir put it: "The new risks and challenges that could affect the whole Western World have transformed Turkey from a 'flank' to a 'front state.' " Accordingly, he maintained that Turkey was one of the few Western countries whose importance was enhanced in the post–Cold War period. These assertions, however, were far from convincing to the Europeans, who, as Bir charged, by adopting a "Central Europe-oriented" approach, marginalized Turkey and invited what he termed the revival of the Cold War, but this time by raising a "Western curtain" (against Turkey) instead of an "iron curtain."[39]

These feelings of marginalization had already troubled the Turkish military at the end of the Cold War, and now drove it to shore up an old partnership with the United States and build a new one with Israel. Together or separately, these two alliances were to compensate for strategic losses in Europe, act as a conduit for a new Turkish role in the

region, and help modernization of the Turkish armed forces. All three
issues were embedded in the Gulf War and the operational conclusions
drawn from it by the military elite.

The experience of the Gulf War had other far-reaching implications
for security perceptions. First, the war highlighted the shortcomings of
the Turkish army compared to the sophisticated techniques of the allies.
These inadequacies were most evident in the fields of electronic warfare, mid-air refueling, and night air combat. Second, the war enlarged
the spectrum of threats emanating from the Middle East, most importantly the sudden emergence of nonconventional weapons—in particular the long-range ballistic missiles, against which the Turkish army had
no defense. Although Turkey itself was not targeted by these missiles
during the war, the need to prepare for such a contingency was one
of the war's most important lessons.[40] Third, Turkey's relations with
Europe had been called into question because of the EU's reluctance to
come to Ankara's help with sufficient military equipment and technological know-how both during and after the war.[41] This European
rebuff, which amounted to a near embargo on sales of military equipment to Turkey, would determine the military to look for new suppliers
who were both willing to meet Ankara's urgent military requirements
and capable of doing so.[42] The greater dynamism and fluidity that the
1990s brought to Turkey's relations with the outside world, in contrast
to the Cold War era, was reflected in the military's switch from reactive
to proactive policies; in a change in the structure of the armed forces,
with the objective of achieving more efficient and flexible power
projection capabilities; and in the reformulation of threat perceptions
and options.

Developments in the 1990s also greatly complicated the military–
civilian political scene. Domestically, there was a significant change of
stance toward Israel by Turkey's political parties. This occurred almost
simultaneously with the setting up of covert ties between the military
and Israel, and at the right time made it possible for these relations to
come into the open. By the early 1990s, Turkish political parties had
slowly shifted toward a more even handed attitude to Israel and the
Palestinians.[43] The two major social democratic parties gradually shed
their anti-Israel policies, and even Alparslan Türkeş, then leader of the
ultranationalist MHP, declared in 1993 that his party supported the
improvement of relations with Israel.[44] This reflected changes in Turkish
public opinion toward Israel, whose popular image, because of the
Arab–Israeli peace process, had now greatly improved. Indeed, many in
Turkey had become to believe that the two countries were *ipso facto*

natural allies. The major exception to the rule remained the Islamist Welfare Party (Refah Partisi, RP), headed by Necmettin Erbakan, which continued to propagate anti-Semitic, anti-Zionist, and anti-Israeli views until it was banned at the end of the 1990s. Thus, in propaganda pamphlets probably from early 1996, the RP blamed what it called "the order of slavery in Turkey" (*köle düzeni*) on the Zionist American banks and on Israel for "milking" 60 million Turks and using their money to equip Israel with tanks and combat aircraft in order to fight Palestinians and Turkey.[45]

Another major development in the first half of the 1990s was the rise of the Kurdistan Workers' Party (Parti Kerkeren Kurdistan, PKK) as a force in Turkish domestic politics. Moreover, the Turkish military and civilian establishments became increasingly concerned that the Kurdish issue was now involving additional parties beyond its borders. According to the Turkish journalist Ismet G. Imset, whose book on the PKK is based on Turkish security service documents and interviews with Abdullah Öcalan and others, the PKK received support from Syria, Iraq, Iran, Lebanon, Libya, the Soviet Union, and the PLO. The PKK's links with Turkey's neighbors enabled its militants to infiltrate into Turkey and stage hit-and-run attacks on Turkish targets. Syria's support for the PKK, which began in 1980, was far and away the most far-reaching and durable. It included sanctuary for PKK guerrillas and officials, the establishment of political headquarters and branch offices in a number of Syrian cities, and permission for various training and organizational activities, including the recruitment of Syrian Kurdish citizens to the cause. Understandings that were reached between Turkey and Syria in 1987 and 1992 regarding the cessation of support for PKK were not honored. Similarly, the PKK's cooperation in the 1980s with the Iraqi Kurdish Democratic Party (KDP), and then with the KDP's rival, the Patirotic Union of Kurdistan (PUK), enabled it to increase its presence in northern Iraq. (Subsequently, during the 1990s, the PKK clashed with the two Iraqi Kurdish groups, while receiving support from the Iraqi government.) Iran was also said to have allowed the PKK to use its territory during the early 1990s.[46] Before it would be brought to an end, the Turkish authorities' war with the PKK insurgency would result in an estimated 30,000 fatalities.[47]

The regionalization of Turkey's Kurdish question forced the hand of the Turkish military. Regarding the PKK entirely as a security issue, it devised military solutions and corresponding policies to meet the changed threat perception.[48] Thus, in the National Security Policy Document of 1992, the main threat perception shifted from that of an external source—the defunct Soviet Union—to an internal one, "Kurdish separatism." Because the "southeastern question" was considered a security—rather than political—issue by the majority of civilians and politicians as well, a certain consensus built up behind the military's approach, and had the effect of legitimizing its role in domestic political issues.[49] This, in turn, precluded a political solution to the Kurdish question. Because neighboring countries, especially Syria, and to a lesser extent Iran and Iraq, became embroiled in PKK affairs by supporting the movement in one way or another, the military was able to significantly enlarge its sphere of influence over foreign affairs. The impact of the Kurdish question on Turkish–Israeli relations will be discussed in chapter 4, but it should be noted here that, as a security issue, it formed one of the motivations for the rapprochement with Israel.

The most important cause or justification for the military's "soft intervention" in domestic and foreign policy making in the 1990s was the rising power of the RP (coinciding with the emergence of the PKK) and the failure of the center parties to check or counterbalance it. At the same time, this intervention set the military at loggerheads with a prominent party that enjoyed considerable popular support. The RP's success in the elections of December 1995 alarmed the military establishment, because it was the first time in modern Turkish history that an Islamist party received more votes than each of its rivals from the Center and Right, and because it proved that political Islam could appeal to the electorate in spite of the predominantly secular nature of Turkish society. The military, in its assumed role as guardian of the secular state, could not but be challenged by this event. It was, indeed, pressure from the military that frustrated the formation of a coalition government between the RP and the Motherland Party (Anavatan Partisi, ANAP).[50]

Subsequent developments were even more alarming. First, the RP brought down the coalition government of the two Center–Right parties, the True Path Party (Doğru Yol Partisi, DYP) and ANAP, and then, in July 1996, the RP became the leader of a coalition government formed with the DYP. This time, the military did not apply strong pressure to prevent the RP from coming to power, but the party's action amounted to a kind of declaration of war against it, as General Fevzi Türkeri later expressed it unequivocally: "We shall fight with arms if it were necessary."[51] Thus, the struggle for power that ensued between the military and the RP-led government was both the symptom and the outcome of the clash of interests and worldviews between them.

In the 11 months that the RP was in power (July 1996–June 1997), it had numerous confrontations with the military, but it seems that one of the fiercest was over foreign relations. As a result, a unique phenomenon developed—a bifurcation in the steering of Turkish foreign policy. While the Foreign Ministry, backed by the military, pushed in one direction, Prime Minister Necmettin Erbakan and his party pushed in another. Erbakan attempted to challenge the military on the very ground that the military considered to be in the vital interests of the state, and over which it enjoyed substantial autonomy. In declarations and actions, Erbakan and his party sought to give a new direction to Turkey's conventional foreign policy by promoting and intensifying ties with Muslim countries—manifested, for example, in Erbakan's visit to Iran in August 1996.[52] The military responded by increasing its involvement in foreign affairs and bolstering policy trends that had been in the making since the end of the Gulf War.

The main bone of contention between the military and the RP-led government was the rapprochement with Israel. This stood in sharp contrast, for example, to the relatively smooth manner in which the improvement in Ankara's relations with "former enemies," such as Bulgaria and the Russian Federation, had taken place, with no criticism from any of the Turkish parties or from other political and social groups. Evidently, the success of establishing relations with Israel, in the face of continuing opposition, was because the military was the moving force behind the policy, if not its architect.

The military was motivated by three sets of considerations in its approach to Israel: purely military/professional; regional/strategic; and political/ideological domestic concerns. In the 1980s, the military had initiated an ambitious modernization and armament program[53] for the Turkish Armed Forces (TAF). However, this received a boost in the aftermath of the Gulf War because of the weaknesses that were exposed in the TAF.[54] Yet one of the major obstacles to its success was the virtual embargo that West European countries and the United States, for various political reasons, put on the supply of up-to-date arms to Turkey.[55] In these circumstances, Israel appeared to be a natural ally: first, it did not attach any political strings to the supply of arms; second, its military equipment was compatible with that of Turkey; and third, it possessed sophisticated weapons and technological know-how, which turned it into a kind of "back door" through which Western armaments of this kind could reach Ankara.[56] Indeed, it seems that military technological know-how was also the main motivation for the Turkish military establishment's approach to Israel back in the 1980s.[57] It was generally assumed that the fighting with the PKK, which began in 1984,[58] had motivated the military to seek out such technology, which Israel either possessed or had developed in the course of its own warfare, for example, against the Hizbullah in Lebanon.

The Turkish military establishment was also attracted by Israel's defense industry experience, and hoped to draw on this to develop its own defense industry or in various cooperation programs and joint projects.[59] In this sense, it can be said that Israel looked more appealing to the Turkish military than the Arab countries with which Ankara was on friendly terms, such as Egypt or Saudi Arabia, if for no other reason than their lack of the self-sufficient military programs that could benefit the Turkish arms industry. Turkey's changing strategic perceptions and new concerns made the partnership with Israel appear even more attractive. Ankara's rebuff in Europe led it to look for compensation elsewhere, including the Middle East. In fact, the peripheral strategy that the military developed after the Gulf War meant engaging in strategic partnerships with Turkey's second belt of neighbors, including those that had emerged from the dissolution of the Soviet Union and the Yugoslav federation, as well as "old" neighbors like Israel. In the Middle East, while the partnership with Israel came to fulfill Ankara's latent aspirations to reach out to the Mediterranean and spread its influence there, it also enabled the Turkish military to respond to the new strategic threats emanating from the south and east—Syria, Iraq, and Iran. Syria, because it stepped up its support for the PKK in the aftermath of the Gulf War; Iraq, because of the vacuum formed in northern Iraq and the lessons learned from its use of missiles and nonconventional weapons during the Gulf War; and Iran, because of the convergence of the ideological threat—the spread of Islamism into Turkey—with the strategic one, the development of nonconventional weapons, including long-range missiles and nuclear weapons. Israel was therefore a natural partner, because it had to contend with common threats, and because together the two countries could devise responses and share information on various military issues.

Underlying these military and strategic motives were ideological and political affinities. The Turkish military's perception of itself as the guardian of democracy and secularism, and its strong pro-Western leaning, certainly helped in its approach to Israel, a country that upheld the same values.[60] It was true that the military's involvement in politics in Turkey was far from compatible with the sort of Western liberal democracy that Israel believed itself to be. Nor can the role played by Israel's military establishment in Israeli politics be compared to that of Turkey. The Israeli military elite is influential, but by no means decisive. Nevertheless, such discrepancies raised few doubts on the Israeli side about the merits of strengthening relations with Turkey. On the contrary, in Israel, too, political rhetoric emphasized the common value of democracy as the unifying factor between the two countries.

The Western orientation of Turkey and Israel, or rather, their relentless efforts to belong to the West, was another element that helped to cement their partnership. The more Turkey was rebuffed in Europe, the more it sought to enhance its strategic relations with the United States and the more valuable Israel was in achieving this. It was, indeed, ironic that after such a long period of close relations between Turkey and the United States, Ankara should need to use Israel as a conduit to Washington. In fact, Israel was most instrumental in the very domain that was so crucial for the military—helping Turkey to circumvent the American arms embargo (with the tacit approval of Washington itself) by allowing supplies to go through Israel. On the whole, the close relations of both Turkey and Israel with the United States helped to create a strategic triangle. Although it would not admit it outright, the United States was fully supportive of rapprochement between Turkey and Israel, because at the time it complemented the other two pillars of American policy in the Middle East after the Gulf War: the Arab–Israeli peace process and the dual containment of Iran and Iraq.

Secularism also played a role, although to what extent and in what way was a matter of debate. According to one scholar: "In Turkey, the *basic reason* [my emphasis] for rapprochement with Israel was the role of the central military [*sic*] and civil bureaucracy, which defined the cooperation with Israel as a policy *to protect the secular system in the country*"[my emphasis]. Such claims often derived from conspiracy theories accusing Israel and America's Jewish lobby (held to have played an "enormous role") of manipulating Turkey and bringing about the rapprochement.[61] A more accurate and nuanced interpretation would be:

1. The military would have forged the agreement with or without the Islamic challenge.
2. The military would have curtailed the RP's power irrespective of the agreement with Israel and, of course, without "Israeli help."
3. Secularism, the most controversial issue on the Turkish domestic scene in the latter 1990s, merely added another layer to the communality of interests between the Turkish and Israeli military establishments.
4. The agreement of February 1996 with Israel coincided with a rising tide of political Islam in Turkey, led by the strongly anti-Israel RP, and turned the issue into a contest between the military and the RP.[62]

5. This development added further complications both to domestic relations between the Islamists and the military and to the Turkish–Israeli agreement, but at the same time it forced the military to stand even more firmly behind the agreement, and to use all the means at its disposal to make it succeed.

## Israel's "New Middle East": Vision and Reality

Shortly after the Oslo Agreement between Israel and the Palestinians in September 1993, Shimon Peres, then Israel's foreign minister, published a book entitled *The New Middle East*.[63] In it he outlined his vision of a region once torn by wars and conflicts, but now heading toward a new era of peace, prosperity, and cooperation between Israel and the Arab countries, to the benefit of their peoples. He envisaged that it would encompass all walks of life—agriculture, industry, trade, tourism, communications, and transport—and would promote and consolidate peace in the region. Peres's vision was later the butt of severe criticism, even mockery, from various Arab countries. Interestingly, it did not accord Turkey a significant role in the realigned region, but mentioned it only in passing as a possible source of water.[64] As it turned out, less than three years later, when Peres himself was Israel's prime minister, Turkey became a major player in the new configuration of the Middle East. Peres did not give up his original vision, but continued to endorse it against many critics, both in Israel and the Arab world.[65] Like George Bush, Turgut Özal, and Saddam Hussein, Peres was inspired by the concept of a world on the threshold of a new era, hence the urge to shape it according to his own vision. That Turkey and Israel would eventually form a major pillar of the new order in the region, completely escaped the vision of all four.

From Israel's point of view, this was the main difference between the peripheral alliance of 1958 and the new alignment of 1996. Whereas the first was concluded against the background of Israel's isolation and serious threats from the Arab world, the new agreement was achieved in the midst of the ongoing peace process between Israel and the Palestinians, and when discussions were underway with key Arab states and certain other Arab regimes on the periphery. In addition, many countries that had long ostracized Israel, such as Russia and China, began to normalize relations, thus giving Israel certain advantages when negotiating new terms with Turkey. Israel was now more confident, and did not need to appear as the keener partner. Nor was there a need for the strict secrecy that had surrounded the peripheral alliance. Not only Turkey, but Israel too, could now portray the alignment as being part of a series of international agreements.

## Asymmetries, Parallels, Dilemmas

From the very beginning there were some inherent asymmetries between Turkey and Israel. Perhaps the most striking was that in Turkey the alignment was controversial. It was opposed by an important section of society, the RP, which was the largest single party in the 1995 elections and had won 21.4 percent of the vote.[66] In Israel, on the other hand, there was near consensus in public opinion about closer links with Turkey. Thus there were no acrimonious debates in the Knesset— the Israeli Parliament—or the media, or in any other public forum. Similarly, none of the political parties spoke out against the blossoming relationship with Turkey. The reasons for this popular consensus are not hard to find: there was a long tradition of relations between the two countries; there were no real bilateral problems with Turkey— certainly no military conflicts; and there was no residue of traditional animosity, as with the Arab states.

A second striking difference was that whereas Turkey's existence and legitimacy were never called into question, Israel frequently had to defend its very right to exist. It followed that while Turkey was courted to join various strategic alliances, like the Saadabad Pact of 1937, NATO in 1952, the Baghdad Pact in 1955, and CENTO in 1959, Israel was excluded from any such treaties. Third, whereas Turkey had not engaged in a major war since the end of its War of Independence in 1922, Israel, since its own Independence War in 1948–49, had engaged in at least four major wars.[67] Indeed, the military experience and victories that Israel, a small country, had gained in these wars went a long way to explain its attraction to Turkey, a large country with a substantial army. A fourth difference or asymmetry was that the Turkish military, since the founding of the modern state in the 1920s, has been able to dictate the country's domestic politics and foreign policy orientation, either by coups or less violent methods, while in Israel this was not the case. Israel's military elite participated in debates on certain issues, but did not dictate an agenda to the government.

The implications of these asymmetries and differences will be discussed below, but it should be mentioned that some observers, especially in Turkey, believe they will eventually lead to the demise of the alignment.

Israel's enthusiastic welcome of the alignment with Turkey did not mean a lack of debate within the Israeli establishment, either about the depth of the agreement, or the risks that it might entail.[68] Revelations to this effect came long after the actual signing. However, it is important to discuss them here because they touched on some fundamental dilemmas and choices that confronted Jerusalem's decision-makers—on sensitive issues that concerned Israel's identity, orientation, and place in the region.

In early 1998, Israel's Foreign Ministry was reported to have held a series of internal discussions about relations with Turkey. The occasion was the appointment of a new ambassador to Turkey, Uri Bar-Ner, and the discussions brought into the open certain differences of opinion within the ministry. Some warned that close and intensive relations with Turkey might hinder relations with other countries in the region, especially Egypt, Syria, Greece, Cyprus, and even Russia (which had armed the Greek Cypriots with missiles). Others blamed the Defense Ministry, and more specifically David Ivri—the man considered to be the architect of the Turkish relationship—for disregarding Israel's overall interests and concerns in the Middle East.[69]

Some three years later, Leon Hadar, in a highly critical essay on Turkish–Israeli relations, asserted that two schools of thought had developed in Israel: the "Turks" and the "Egyptians." The debate between them, he said, was not on the need to improve ties with Turkey, but rather on their strategic significance and their impact on Israel's policies in the region. The "Turkish" coalition or school of thought consisted of "Israeli officials and business executives with strong ties to the Defense Ministry and the country's industrial complex, as well as politicians and experts who tend to subscribe to a hawkish position on the Arab–Israeli process." These people, Hadar said, argued that a "military alliance" with Turkey might strengthen Israel's hands in the negotiations with the Palestinians and Syria, and pave the way to what he called a Turkish–Israeli hegemony in the Middle East.

By contrast, the "Egyptian" school of thought emphasized the need to direct Israel's strategy toward building a stronger relationship with Egypt. This group, Hadar maintained, was closer to the Foreign Ministry than to the Defense Ministry and tended to advance more dovish positions on the negotiations with the Palestinians and Syria. The Egyptian school argued that while Israel should advance its ties with Turkey, "only a reconciliation with the Palestinians, peace with Syria and Lebanon, [and] the evolution of close ties with Egypt . . . will provide Israel with a permanent sense of security."[70] On the same lines, Uri Saguy, the head of Israel's Military Intelligence under Rabin's premiership in the 1990s, expressed his reservations about the rapprochement with Turkey, fearing that it would harm the peace process with

Syria. These reservations led to strategic discussions behind the scenes, which resulted in Rabin's decision to proceed with the rapprochement with Ankara.[71]

The leading academic exponent of the "Turkish coalition" was, ironically, the director of the Begin-Sadat Center for Peace at Bar-Ilan University, Efraim Inbar. In articles published in the *Jerusalem Post* and *Ha'aretz* he strongly advocated the deepening of ties with Turkey for several reasons: strong relations with Turkey would not hamper relations with the Arab countries, but were likely to reinforce the peace process with them; relations with Turkey were important for the containment of rogue states such as Iraq, Syria, and Iran; they were useful in fighting the international terror encouraged by these rogue states; and they were helpful in providing limited deterrence for Turkey, should Syria and/or Iraq attempt to invade it.[72]

Without being explicit, Inbar, here and on other occasions, revealed his skepticism about the feasibility of a warm peace with Arab countries—even Egypt, with which Israel had full diplomatic relations from 1979, a time when Jerusalem's relations with Ankara were at one of their lowest points. The other leading advocate of the "Turkish" policy was Barry Rubin, at that time also from the BESA Center. Besides these two, little was heard from this school of thought, either in public or in the media. This did not mean that the policy lacked support. On the contrary, the BESA academics seemed to express the views of the silent majority who backed the rapprochement and even began to take it for granted. They also reflected the majority in the Israeli establishment, who pushed unremittingly for closer ties.[73]

In another historical irony, the most vocal exponent of the "Egyptian school," was Alon Liel, who had been Israel's chargé d'affaires in Turkey in the early 1980s when relations were at their nadir, and had worked tirelessly, but unsuccessfully, to upgrade them.[74] A decade later, however, rather than enthusiastically welcoming the improvement in bilateral relations for which he must have striven when a second secretary in Ankara, he now became their most outspoken critic. To do him justice, he was not against the ties as such, but against the manner in which it was being done: their intensity, the parties involved in them, and their impact on Israel's relations with other countries in the region. He argued that:

1. The publicity given to these relations was likely to be damaging, because of the "hostile" and "jealous" environment at the time.
2. The strategic component of the relations was overemphasized, making the relationship more vulnerable to Turkey's domestic upheavals and external pressures.

3. Relations with Turkey endangered the peace process with the Arabs, because this would encourage in Israel what he termed a new concept of "security without peace."
4. Relations with Turkey would be seen as an alternative to good relations with the Arabs.
5. There was no chance that a strategic alliance would develop or survive between Turkey and Israel.

Liel therefore called for a lowering of the public profile of the whole issue, or, as he put it: "We can love each other but we don't have to kiss and hug in public." He further suggested that Israel's Foreign Ministry, and not the Defense Ministry, should handle relations with Turkey, that the United States be kept out of the joint training exercises, and that Israel should shift the overall emphasis to the peace process with the Arabs.[75]

Shortly afterward, another scholar from Bar-Ilan University, Stuart Cohen, also cautioned against close relations with Turkey, because, he said, the "Turkish-Israeli connection rests on a rather narrow base," from the point of view of common interests. He asserted that close ties might hamper the peace process with Syria, which should be the real focus of Israeli attention; that they might entangle Israel in Turkish problems, such as the Kurdish issue; that "full military cooperation" seemed far from practicable; and that "the alignment helps turn the clock back to the bad old days from Israel's point of view, when the most important regional distinctions were between those states which are Arab and those which are not."[76]

Pouring water on the "unencumbered enthusiasm" with which many Israeli decision-makers have embraced the links with Ankara since the early 1990s, another Bar-Ilan scholar, Gerald M. Steinberg, warned about "entangling alliances." He opined that such an alliance had the potential of dragging Israel into a conflict that was "none of its business," such as the Kurdish issue or Turkey's problems with Greece over Cyprus. Steinberg did not, however, think that the alliance was a mistake, but that Israel should be aware of its limitations and potential complications and "avoid," as he put it, "emotional responses and romantic approaches to international and regional relations."[77] Invoking the peripheral alliance, a journalist from Ma'ariv, Chemi Shalev, also warned against Israel's "romance" with Turkey, whose value, even in Ben-Gurion's day, had proved transient.[78]

The debate about the peripheral alliance was taken up by an Israeli analyst living in the United States, Leon Hadar, who called on Israel to learn from the mistakes of forming close ties with "undemocratic governments." He argued that the case of Iran in the peripheral alliance had demonstrated that when a diplomatic and military alliance was not seen as a core national interest by the majority of the political elites and the public, it was vulnerable to changes in the regime (there was a reversal of policy toward Israel after Khomeyni came to power in 1979). While conceding that (unlike Iran) Turkey was going through a process of political and economic liberalization, and that its ties with Israel were supported not only by the military, but also by large segments of the elites and by the public, he said that it "remained an unstable political system under which changes in the regime...could also produce a major reorientation in its foreign policy, raising the specter of Israel having to deal with a version of an 'Iranian scenario' there."[79]

Reference to the *ancien* peripheral alliance was part of the renewed debate in Israel regarding its regional orientation. In 1958 Israel had had little choice, because no Arab country was willing to be associated with it. In the 1990s, however, Jerusalem appeared to face a dilemma of having to choose between the peace process with the Arabs and its close relations with Ankara. To some extent this mirrored Turkey's dilemma up to the 1990s, when it had to choose between Israel and its strong relations with the Arab countries. But in reality, Israeli decision-makers had no such dilemma in the 1990s. For them, the prospect of rapprochement with Turkey was a dream come true. The dilemmas were expressed mainly by a handful of scholars and some officials in the Foreign Ministry, whose reservations and warnings about the possible impact of warmer ties with Turkey in no way dented the resolve of any Israeli government to continue with them. Here there was a certain difference between Israel and Turkey, at least when the Welfare Party–True Path (Refah-Yol) government held power in Ankara. But even in this short period (July 1996–June 1997), practical relations were not greatly affected by ideological orientation of the Welfare Party leading the coalition. It seems, therefore, that the major breakthrough was achieved when both parties reached the conclusion that their bilateral relations, and their relations with the Arab world, need not be mutually exclusive.

## Israel's Motives and Motivators

In October 1998, Alon Liel commented that: "The handling of Israeli–Turkish relations should be transferred from the generals to the diplomats." Such a statement revealed the continuing centrality of the strategic aspect of the relations and the continued rivalry between Israel's military establishment and its Foreign Ministry. This reflected

the situation in Turkey to a degree, and also harked back to the peripheral alliance, when bilateral military relations overshadowed civilian and
diplomatic ties.

Some commentators have suggested that it was Turkey that approached
Israel seeking rapprochement,[80] but even if so, there was no doubt that
Israel responded promptly because of its own motives. Israel needed
strategic relations with Turkey at that particular time because it had lost
some of its strategic importance to the United States during the Gulf
War (see chapter 1). Israel now sought to compensate for this loss by
forming a loose triangle of relations with Turkey and the United States,
to counterbalance the three radical countries in its neighborhood—
Syria, Iraq, and Iran. This, then, was another difference between the
peripheral alliance and the new alignment. In the former, Israel sought
to prove to the United States its strategic value (together with its new
allies) in resisting Soviet infiltration into the region, while in the latter it
had to confirm its strategic value in a post–Cold War region. Because
the alignment with Turkey was negotiated concurrently with the
Arab–Israeli peace process, there was no doubt that it also played a
role in compensating Israel for an anticipated loss of territories. If the
peace process succeeded, Israel was expected to return the occupied
Palestinian territories of the West Bank and Gaza to the PLO and the
Golan Heights to Syria, a divestment that, following the ceding of Sinai
to Egypt in the 1970s, would have seriously restricted its strategic and
military maneuverability. The Turkish alignment was therefore designed
to help Israel prepare alternative strategic depth, in case its adjacent
regions had to be given up.

The other side of the coin was that if the peace process with Syria
failed, Israel would then be facing three implacable enemies—Syria,
Iraq, and Iran—all of which had vowed to exterminate it. Strategically,
Israel's problem was that it had no common borders with Iraq and Iran,
and hence no direct access to their territories for military operations or
surveillance. An alignment with Turkey could compensate for this, especially as Ankara shared common borders with all three countries, none
of which was eager to confront it militarily. In this sense, Turkey's role
was similar to its position in the old peripheral alliance, except that now
this role was significantly enlarged and much more open, and included
Iran as a target, not a partner.

On another level, Israel had hoped to use Turkey's good offices to
reach into two areas where it had little access: the Muslim world and
Central Asia. As a Muslim nation, Turkey was expected to be a conduit
of goodwill between Israel and Muslim countries, either in promoting

bilateral relations with individual countries, such as Pakistan and Indonesia,[81] or in moderating anti-Israel decisions in Islamic forums. One Israeli official (who wished to remain anonymous) told the author that Turkey was using its influence to promote Israel's relations with Bangladesh, a country with which Jerusalem had no diplomatic relations. Israel also expected to benefit from an open door into Turkey's sphere of influence in the Caucasus and Central Asia. It was hoped that joint Israeli–Turkish ventures in these newly established states, to be done with the blessing of Washington, would draw them into the Western orbit and prevent their drift toward Iran or other states hostile to Israel.[82] This new venture into the lands of the former Soviet empire would not be burdened by the complexes of the past, which had overshadowed the relations of both Israel and Turkey with the Arab world, and promised to be easier to realize than the fading vision of the new Middle East.

The formal Turkish–Israeli agreement was signed in 1996, although military relations had been in the making for more than a decade. The two ministries active in the negotiations were the Defense Ministry and the Office of the Prime Minister.[83] As in the peripheral alliance, the Foreign Ministry was relegated to the background, even advising restraint at times because of considerations in other arenas.[84] As a rule, the Defense Ministry was keen to expand Israel's relations and sell military hardware to as many countries as possible, but it was the Foreign Ministry that ultimately gave the green light to such deals.[85]

According to Ha'aretz commentator, Amnon Barzilai, there were in Israel two calendars documenting the resumption of relations with Turkey. That of the Foreign Ministry linked the revival of relations to the Madrid Conference in October 1991 and the upgrading of Israel's international relations immediately afterward. The calendar of the defense establishment in both countries, however, preferred to date renewed relations from the mid-1980s, when the catalyst was Israel's decision to withdraw from central Lebanon in 1985. The secret relations and mutual visits of the defense establishment of both countries started shortly after this.[86] Also at that time, the strategic concepts and terms of strategic cooperation were conceived. The final impetus was the Oslo Agreement and the subsequent peace treaty with Jordan.

One of the people responsible for forging these relations in the 1980s was David Ivri, who served as director general to the then Defense Minister Yitzhak Rabin, a member of the unity government headed at the time by Shimon Peres.[87] In fact, Rabin and Ivri worked hand in hand during that period and also in the 1990s. Ivri later stated that the

Turkish Air Force became interested in the Israeli Air Force following the latter's achievements against Syria in the Lebanon War in 1982 (indicating once again Syria's linking role between the two countries). As early as 1984 Ivri began a low-profile initiative that won Rabin's support. It culminated in 1986, when Israel entered negotiations to upgrade Turkey's American-made Phantom warplanes. In fact, by 1987 the two parties were on the verge of signing an agreement. But the Palestinian intifada that erupted at the end of that year postponed the arrangement for another decade (links continued, but on a smaller scale).[88]

General Çevik Bir, who played a major role in developing relations on the Turkish side, told the author in 2001 that he had been most impressed by the electronic warfare that Israel had conducted in the Lebanon War, "thanks to which it did not lose a single aircraft." Only later did he learn that David Ivri, the commander of the Air Force, was "the architect of this [technological] achievement."[89] Ivri's air force experience and his position as director of military industry, made him particularly well-suited to approach the Turkish high command and interest them in fields in which Israel excelled, such as the upgrading of aircraft and cooperation in the development of military industry. In the mid-1980s, then, Ivri and Rabin together laid the basis for the rapprochement, and were to reap its fruits during Rabin's term of office as prime minister and defence minister between 1992 and 1995.

The fact that Rabin himself was Chief of Staff during the 1967 Six Day War, which resulted in a stunning Israeli victory, probably appealed to the Turkish military. At the same time, Rabin's military background is likely to have made him especially interested in developing this kind of relationship with Turkey. According to Beni Sheffer, Israel's military attaché in Ankara from 1994 to 1996, the rapprochement was part of Rabin's vision of linking together stable countries in the Middle East. He also entertained the hope to bring Egypt into the alignment, but Cairo's negative reaction scotched the notion. However, another Arab country, Jordan, did enter into the alignment in a low-key fashion. Rabin was also believed to have promoted the idea of the Turkish alignment to Washington on his frequent visits there.[90]

Rabin's involvement in no way diminished the dedication and conviction of the other Israeli prime ministers and politicians active in the Turkish connection, whether they were "civilians" like Yitzhak Shamir, who preceded Rabin, and Shimon Peres and Binyamin Netanyahu who followed him, or former army generals like Ehud Barak and Ariel Sharon, who succeeded Netanyahu. The difference between them was not in substance, but in emphasis and style. For example, during his short-lived premiership between November 1995 and June 1996, Peres put greater emphasis on the peace process with the Arabs, which was consistent with his vision of a new Middle East. In spite of his apparent lack of interest in relations with Turkey, it was nevertheless during his term of office that the agreement was signed and made public.[91]

By contrast, Netanyahu placed greater emphasis on relations with Turkey. In fact, it was said that during his tenure the concept developed that good relations with Turkey could even substitute for those with the Arabs.[92] It is difficult to verify this contention. One thing was certain, however, that even the more hard-line Netanyahu never for a moment considered freezing or downgrading relations with, for example, Egypt, for the sake of closer relations with Turkey. Another politician who contributed a great deal to the Turkish relationship was Yitzhak Mordechai, the defense minister under Netanyahu, who was behind the strengthening of the Israeli–Turkish–American triangle and initiated the joint naval exercises, the first of which took place in January 1998. Interestingly, relations between Israel and Turkey reached one of their high points under the leadership of the most "pro-Arab" Turkish premier—Erbakan—and the most "pro-Turkish" Israeli premier—Netanyahu. If anything, this proved that by that time relations were no longer dependent on one or two people, but involved the political and military establishments of the two countries. In fact, a third country was becoming involved, albeit in a low-keyed way—the United States.

## The United States: The Silent Player

Israel solicited the support of the United States for the new alignment as keenly as it had for the peripheral alliance 30 years before. The differences, however, were significant: the convergence of interests between the three countries—Israel, Turkey, and the United States—was now much more evident; the United States was ready to play a part, albeit minor, in the new alignment; and it was not shy of publicizing this, admittedly at a later date. A spokesman for the State Department, Nicholas Burns, summed up the U.S. position in May 1997:

It has been a strategic objective of the United States that Turkey and Israel ought to enhance their military cooperation and their political relations. Israel is a very close friend of the United States, a close ally of the United States. Turkey is a close friend and ally and it seems to us natural and positive that Israel and Turkey would walk together militarily. The United States is very pleased to *participate* [author emphasis] in that cooperation.

Burns added that this was not a new development: "we've supported this for a long, long time."[93] He did not disclose when this support had begun, but according to David Ivri, it went back to the 1980s. Thus the initial talks between Turkey and Israel in the 1980s for upgrading the Phantoms had been approved by the United States. This was confirmed by the need for the United States to authorize a license for a project on American-made planes. Moreover, Ivri said that all U.S. administrations since the 1980s had regarded the Turkish–Israeli ties as a positive development, and had given them their blessing. Nevertheless, to avoid antagonizing certain other countries, in particular the Arab states and Greece, the United States had been reluctant to publicize this.[94]

In the 1990s, Israeli sources maintained that it was Prime Minister Rabin who, during his visits to Washington, had gotten the Clinton administration interested in the rapprochement.[95] Another source suggested that President Clinton had played a leading role in the Turkish–Israeli military agreement. According to that source, Clinton held a joint meeting with the Turkish Prime Minister Tansu Çiller, Israel's Foreign Minister Shimon Peres, and Jordan's King Hussein following Rabin's funeral in November 1995, where the new strategic concept for the Middle East was articulated.[96]

Another, less visible, player actively promoting trilateral relations was the "Jewish lobby" in the United States, particularly organizations such as B'nai B'rith, the American Jewish Congress, the Conference of Presidents of Major American Jewish organizations, and the Jewish Institute for National Security Affairs (JINSA). Although none of these was a registered lobby (unlike AIPAC, the American Israel Public Affairs Committee), they were all perceived to be such, and all supported Turkey and its close relations with Israel and the United States. Daniel Mariaschin, the director of B'nai B'rith, stated in an interview to the *Turkish Daily News* that "the American-Jewish community has embraced the strong relationship that has been established between Turkey and Israel," and that "we have been quick to promote the importance of Turkey as a friend and ally of the United States after the collapse of the Soviet Union." Later, he said: "we have also made the connection between Turkey as the role model and gateway to central Asia and the Caucasus." The American Jewish organizations wanted to see Turkey's relations with Israel prosper in all areas, including defense and security, agricultural cooperation, trade, academic exchange, and scientific and technical research.[97]

The reasons for the Jewish position were varied, but there was a certain continuity from the time of the peripheral alliance. The Jewish lobby was active in different ways, such as supporting Turkey's cause in

Congress against the Greek and Armenian lobbies (in 2001, American Jewish lobbyists played a key role in blocking a congressional bill in favor of a genocide law, that could have had a direct bearing on Turkey's massacre of Armenians during World War I); urging the U.S. authorities to sanction arms sales to Turkey; obtaining loans for Turkey in the United States and among the G-7 countries, or applying pressure on both the administration and Congress in favor of the Baku-Ceyhan oil pipeline project to bring Caspian oil through Turkey.[98] The role of the Jewish lobby was confirmed by Ivri, who said that in the early 1990s Israel approached various American Jewish groups, which started to visit Turkey and to familiarize themselves with the issues.[99]

The American interest in the rapprochement between its two allies seemed self-evident. The two countries upheld the democratic values so cherished by the United States; they were the two strongest states in the region; they sought to maintain the status quo and stability in the Middle East; they actively opposed religious radicalism and terrorism, and thus formed a counterweight to radical and revisionist elements and countries in the region, chiefly Iraq and Iran. Moreover, the joint operational capabilities of Turkey and Israel could be vital to the United States in any contingency. Even though the separate American alliances with Turkey and Israel went back some 40 or 50 years, it was the first time that a triangle of cooperation was formed, and it had the effect of strengthening each partner separately and all three together.

What areas did the three parties cooperate in? First, as mentioned, U.S. consent was needed for Israel to upgrade Turkey's American-made Phantoms, and this was granted. Second, the United States probably participated in strategic dialogues with the other two, although this was not publicized. Joint exercises were another area of cooperation, first with joint naval maneuvers and then joint air maneuvers. The three also began to develop the mechanism for trilateral antiballistic cooperation (see below). Similarly, the United States reportedly encouraged Israel to cooperate with Turkey in preventing PKK incursions into Turkish territory.[100] On the economic level, there was the beginning of joint enterprises in Central Asia, and politically the United States encouraged Turkey to promote the peace process between Israel and the Arabs, especially the Palestinians. After the outbreak of the second Palestinian intifada in September 2000, the outgoing Turkish President Süleyman Demirel, was called upon to participate in the Mitchell Commission (led by former U.S. Senator, George Mitchell), which had been formed to find solutions to this conflict. Later, in early 2002, the United States proposed Ankara as a venue for peace talks between Israel and the Palestinians (see below).

The other side of the coin, however, was the possibility of a clash of interests or divergent views between the two Middle East states and the United States. For example, it was unlikely that the United States would wish the alignment to become too strong, lest the synergy between Turkey and Israel should get beyond American control. Similarly, the United States did not wish a close alliance to jeopardize its other interests, such as the prospect that the Turkish army might turn increasingly to Israel for its military hardware, instead of buying from American firms. For example, the American ambassador to Turkey, Mark Grossman, fought strenuously against the arrangement for Israel to upgrade Turkish F-4 fighter jets (see below). One of his methods was to infer to the press that the deal was done in a corrupt manner.[101] Another instance was the attempt by the U.S. company, General Dynamics, to undercut Israel's proposed upgrading of Turkish tanks by offering to lease Abrams tanks to Ankara.[102] A further cause of concern to the United States was that it did not want a strong alignment between the two non-Arab states in the region to be interpreted as an anti-Arab axis supported by America, thereby antagonizing pro-Western Arab regimes. In a similar vein, the United States did not wish to alienate other countries in the region that might feel threatened by the alignment, in particular Greece and Cyprus. Another potential obstacle was that the United States did not wish the secrets of certain military equipment that it had sold to Israel to find their way to a third party, even though this party might also be its ally.[103]

The solution to these conflicting interests was that, while the United States encouraged cooperation between the two parties, it put on the brakes whenever it sensed that a project or activity might hurt other U.S. interests or commercial ventures. Similarly, while the United States participated in the joint naval and air maneuvers, it was keen to stress (as did the other partners) that these were for humanitarian purposes alone. The United States also refrained from calling the relations between its two allies an alignment, and, according to the Pentagon, the American military did not participate in the bilateral Ankara–Jerusalem strategic talks (see below).[104] In short, the United States sought to provide an umbrella for the relations, while seeking to prevent them from taking a course independent of its interests. Turkey, however, preferred to deal with Israeli firms over American ones, for they included a technology transfer component.

# Chapter 4

# The Making of the Alignment

Politicians, journalists, and scholars alike have referred to the relationship between Turkey and Israel in various terms, such as alliance, alignment, *entente*, *rapprochement*, cooperation, strategic partnership and agreement.[1] This multiplicity of names indicates that it was not clearly defined, unlike the Saadabad and Baghdad Pacts, but was something more fluid or amorphous. In fact, its designers probably wanted it to appear ambiguous, to be both an alliance, capable of deterring hostile organizations and countries, and a simple agreement that would not antagonize others. Whatever the title, all agreed that it was a major strategic development in the region.

The most intriguing aspect was that a Jewish state and a Muslim state had come together in a rapid, open, and comprehensive manner. It could be argued that this in and of itself was not so unusual, as the peace treaty between Israel and Egypt had preceded the new rapprochement by almost two decades. Yet relations between Israel and Egypt had never gone beyond a cold peace to achieve the sort of intimacy and depth that was to characterize the relationship between Turkey and Israel. Also, Jerusalem's relations with Cairo were not free of rivalry, whereas those with Ankara were.

The coming together of two powerful non-Arab countries was clearly a unique occurrence in the region. To be sure, one could argue that it was not "new," having been preceded by the "peripheral alliance" of the late 1950s. However, the secret nature of the peripheral alliance weakened its deterrent value, and ultimately rendered it more vulnerable. From another angle, it could be argued that Jordan's participation in the new alignment made it essentially benign, and not directed against the Arab world, as many Arab critics feared. But in this regard, Jordan's participation had little attenuating value. Those who continued to wave the banner of "Arab national security" found scant comfort in Jordan's ties with the two non-Arab regional heavyweights. In any case, Jordan was a distinctly junior partner, acting most of the time behind the scenes, especially with Israel.

For Turkey, the alignment signaled some important precedents:

1. This was the first time that Turkey had allied itself with a Middle Eastern country that was not adjacent to it, unlike the Saadabad and Baghdad Pacts.
2. The alignment became the most extensive military cooperation agreement that Turkey had ever had with a non-NATO country.
3. By developing close relations with a Middle Eastern state, Turkey joined the ranks of other NATO members, such as the United States, United Kingdom, and France, which had long been involved in the region's affairs.

For Israel, it was the first time in its history that it had formed an open alignment with a Middle Eastern country, an achievement that reinforced its legitimacy in the region. Indeed, relations with Turkey turned out to be Israel's most important partnership—after the United States—in the realm of security cooperation.[2] So important was it in the eyes of Zvi Elpeleg, Israel's ambassador to Turkey, that he emphasized that without Turkey, Israel was like "a leaf in the wind."[3] Another innovation has been the multidimensional nature of the relationship. Although the military association continues to dominate, the two countries have succeeded in diversifying their ties in a manner that is uncommon for countries in the region. For example, intra-Arab alignments such as the Gulf Cooperation Council, formed in 1981, did not succeed, during their long years of existence, in coming even close to the level of cooperation between Turkey and Israel.

## The Significance of the 1996 Agreement

In contrast to the peripheral alliance, which was concluded in a single night and in response to an immediate threat, the new alignment was the outcome of a long process that took an entire decade to come to fruition. This, and the fact that relations were not limited to the military-strategic sphere, but came to encompass various political, economic, and cultural fields, probably influenced their nature, durability, and strength.

From the start, relations developed along three distinct but complementary tracks: military, diplomatic/political/economic, and intelligence/secret services. Although the third track remained for the most part behind closed doors, there is no doubt that it played a significant role, as it had in the peripheral alliance. According to Beni Sheffer, Israel's military attaché to Turkey from 1994 to 1996, the year 1994 was particularly formative for military relations.[4] In fact, this was true of the other aspects as well. For example, on the diplomatic–political level, 1994 opened with the visit of Israeli President Ezer Weizman to Turkey and ended with that of Turkish Prime Minister Tansu Çiller to Israel. It was true that Weizman had been preceded by President Chaim Herzog, who went to Turkey in July 1992. However, Herzog's visit was unofficial, as he had been invited to participate in ceremonies commemorating 500 years since the arrival of the Jews in the Ottoman Empire, after their expulsion from Spain in 1492. Nonetheless, even Herzog's visit marked a dramatic change in atmosphere, because "the cream of Turkish society" took part in the celebration, including the president, the prime minister, cabinet ministers, army commanders, leaders of academia, and members of parliament. According to Herzog, President Turgut Özal announced that "a new era had begun" and that "constraints had disappeared, barriers had been lifted, and Turkey was prepared to cooperate closely with Israel in every field."[5]

Weizman's official visit, however, was regarded as a turning point between the two countries, as it lifted the veil of secrecy that had long hung over their relations. Senior Turkish officials, who for years had been forced to operate almost clandestinely in Turkey, "rubbed their eyes in amazement to see the flags of the two countries openly flying side by side along the boulevards and on the public buildings of Ankara and Istanbul."[6] The importance that Israel accorded the visit could be inferred from Weizman's decision to make Ankara his first official port of call abroad. Weizman himself must have been of considerable interest to Turkey, especially the military, as he had behind him a brilliant career as Commander of the Air Force.[7] During his stay he achieved concrete results, in the form of mutual agreements "in principle" in the fields "of trade, defense, industry, tourism, security and agriculture."[8] It was also disclosed that the issue of Ankara selling water to Israel had been raised, and Prime Minister Çiller confirmed that she did not "at all fear" the potential reaction of Turkey's neighbors, asserting that "we will do whatever we want with the water we have."[9]

While not going into details, Weizman announced that Israel would cooperate with Turkey "on the subject of terrorism, especially in the intelligence field."[10] Indeed, cooperation in this field was an essential glue in the relationship. In a subsequent interview, Çiller made it clear that she regarded cooperation on terrorism as one of the most important achievements of the relationship.[11] Reportedly, cooperation has centered around annual meetings between senior officials from the intelligence communities of both countries, and guidance from Israeli counterterrorism experts to improve Turkey's handling of the conflict with the PKK.[12] Fighting terrorism was to many Turkish leaders and the media synonymous with fighting the PKK, whose activities were one of the most serious challenges of the 1990s, and they sought to emphasize this aspect of relations. There was therefore a need to publicize perhaps as a demonstration of force *vis-à-vis* the PKK, and perhaps also to better market the rapprochement with Israel to the Turkish public.

Interestingly, Çevik Bir, one of the Turkish architects of the rapprochement, later denied knowledge of any such cooperation. This could indicate either that there was compartmentalization between the military and secret services, or, more likely, that Bir wished to save Israel from embarrassment or complications over Turkey's domestic Kurdish issue. Israel, in fact, sought to keep as low a profile as possible on the subject of the PKK, since it did not wish to unduly antagonize Kurdish communities worldwide and add to its list of potential enemies. Hence the use of the general term, "terrorism." Turkey's interest in publicizing cooperation in this field was made evident when Israeli Police Chief Asaf Hefez visited Turkey in October 1994. The Turkish Interior Minister Nahit Menteşe, revealed that "an agreement on cooperation against drug trafficking, terrorism and organized crime" had been signed with Israel in 1992 and that "great progress" had been achieved since.[13] Later it transpired that Israel had sold Turkey night–vision equipment, as well as the antimissile systems used by helicopters in their attacks against Kurdish rebels. In addition, Turkey adopted a security system on its border with Iraq, similar to that in current use along Israel's borders. This included fences, sensors, armed patrols, and mines. Israel also reportedly helped Turkey to capture the PKK leader, Abdullah Öcalan in February 1999, and a Kurdish terrorist cell of the Turkish Hizbullah group, in January 2000. Prime Minister Bülent Ecevit himself confirmed the latter report.[14]

Military relations took a great leap forward in 1992, when Defense Ministry Director General David Ivri signed a military cooperation agreement between the Israeli and Turkish military industries.[15] In 1993 he came to Ankara at the head of a large delegation of officials and generals, and held meetings that have not yet been made public.[16] The same year, Israel's Commander of the Air Force Herzl Budinger, came on an informal visit to Turkey. In April 1994 it was decided to send an Israeli military attaché to Turkey, after a long period in which this office had remained vacant because of Ankara's decision to downgrade relations in 1980, whereupon the post of military attaché was disestablished in both countries. The man chosen for the job—perhaps not coincidentally— was an air force Squadron Commander Beni Sheffer, who took up his post in July 1994. Two months earlier, in May 1994, Turkey's Commander of the Air Force Halis Burhan, came on a semiofficial visit to Israel to reciprocate Budinger's visit. Indeed, as in the 1980s, ties between the two air forces were both the beginning of and the catalyst for cooperation in other areas.

According to Sheffer, the February 1996 agreement was reached for formal technical reasons: the need of Israel's air force to train in Turkey and of Turkey's to train in Israel. Sheffer maintains that when he first came to Turkey, very little was known in Israel about the Turkish system, and vice versa. But, according to Sheffer, like Israel's military attachés during the era of the peripheral alliance, he soon became a popular diplomat to whom all doors were open, and his personal status surpassed even that of the American military attaché. It was Sheffer who came up with the idea of the air force training exchanges, a proposal that was adopted quickly by the Turks for reasons of their own.

Generally speaking, 1994 was a formative year, because it was during these exchanges and talks with the generals that ideas were canvassed, which would form the basis of all future developments. Sheffer describes 1994 as the year in which the "big delta was formed" and the direction of all subsequent events was laid down.[17] He further confirmed that the Turkish military had decided to go ahead with an alignment with Israel after debates and discussions in January 1995,[18] and that the agreement signed in February 1996 was a mere formality. In this sense, he said, the military was the catalyst for the agreement in Turkey, but that the country's political leaders including both Prime Minister Çiller and Foreign Minister Hikmet Çetin willingly endorsed the move. Initially, he said, there was much debate between the military and the Foreign Ministry, not about the rapprochement as such, but about its tempo. Soon, however, the Foreign Ministry gave way. Initially, the army itself had to go against the trend in public opinion, but this too changed over time.[19]

In the distribution of roles between the two sides, both Ivri and Sheffer felt that the desire for rapprochement was mutual, but on the whole the Israelis came up with the initiatives and new ideas, which found fertile soil with their Turkish counterparts. However, there were also examples of the Turks putting forward suggestions and initiatives. As mentioned, the two leading motivators on the Israeli side were

Prime Minister Rabin and David Ivri, who worked closely and harmoniously together. Overall, Ivri actively cultivated the bilateral relationship for almost fifteen years, beginning in the mid-1980s.[20] On the Turkish side, the four principal motivators and catalysts were the Chief of General Staff Ismail Karadayı and the three generals—Çevik Bir, Deputy Chief of General Staff, Halis Burhan, commander of the air force and Güven Erkaya, commander of the navy.[21] For the outside world, the main event that put Turkish–Israeli relations on the map was the agreement signed on February 23, 1996. In fact, as we have seen, it was just the culmination of earlier developments. Its contents were not as dramatic as might have been assumed from the reactions to it, especially in the Arab world. Its stated objective was "to achieve cooperation in military training between the two countries," as follows:

1. Achieving cooperation on various levels on the basis of the exchange of personnel and their expertise.
2. Exchanging visits between military academies, units, and camps.
3. Application of training and exercises.
4. Sending observers to follow up military exercises in the two countries.
5. Exchanging officials to collect and share information, especially in social and cultural fields that included military history, military museums, and military archives.
6. Exchange of visits by military naval vessels.

Among other important points in the five-page document was "confidentiality of classified security information," which stated that: "all information and expertise exchanged by the two parties to this agreement are governed by the secret security agreement signed on 31st March 1994."[22] The exact contents of the 1994 agreement have never been made public, but apparently it committed the parties to preserving the secrecy of their exchanges.

The 1996 agreement was intentionally general, because at the time of signing neither party had a "grand plan" and neither envisaged that relations were going to become "so deep."[23] Although it was concluded in secrecy, they realized that sooner or later it was sure to be made public. In fact, it is now certain that the Turkish side leaked it.[24] We do not know what moved the Turks to do this, but as the leaks were to continue, it seems likely that there was a mixture of wishing to deter some elements and to allay the fears of others. On the home front, the targets for deterrence were the PKK and the RP. Regionally, this audience was Iran, Syria, Iraq, and most importantly, Greece.[25] On the other hand,

Turkey sought to reassure certain Arab countries, especially Egypt. No sooner did the Egyptians hear rumors of the agreement than they came "hysterically" to Turkey in an attempt to frustrate it.[26] The Egyptians were said to be even more worried than, for example, the Syrians, because they viewed the agreement in geopolitical parameters and not only through the narrow prism of the Syrians.[27] For Cairo, every Israeli gain in the region was deemed a loss for Egypt. It was probably to combat such rumors and to reassure Egypt that Turkey decided to leak the agreement. In fact, al-Safir, which published its text five months later, maintained that it had received it "from Egyptian sources—who are acquainted with developments in Turkey."[28] Israel's attaché, who was in Ankara during the signing of the agreement and shortly afterward, also insisted that it was a Turkish source that had leaked the agreement, since the version that was made public was the Turkish document carrying Çevik Bir's signature.[29]

What, then, is the significance of the agreement, if we know in retrospect that it was preceded by other important agreements and followed by no less important ones?[30] On the symbolic level, it is viewed by the countries of the region as the turning point in relations between Turkey and Israel. In the minds of many, especially the Arabs, there were also lingering suspicions that the agreement contained secret clauses. These were probably magnified by the clause referring to the "secret security agreement" of March 1994. Even so, the two parties continued to insist on the absence of any secret clauses.[31] Whatever the truth, the important question was how the agreement was perceived and interpreted by the outside world.

Many countries in the region, including the Arab states, Iran and Greece, interpreted it as an alliance that was capable of being activated against them. In fact, it is difficult to categorize it as an alliance. On the one hand it was less than this, and on the other, much more encompassing. The kind of relations that had developed did not fit well with typical Cold War alliances, characterized as they were by being formal and straightforward; their partners contributed on an equal footing, they were defensive in nature and purported to employ deterrence without violence. Nor did Turkish–Israeli relations fit the mold of post–Cold War alliances like that against Iraq in 1991, which was notably ad hoc and flexible: The United States provided unique capabilities, while most of the others participated only symbolically, with a token representation. This form of alliance was built not on fixed troop commitments but on an expeditionary force, and required coordination, crisis management, and military operations.

The ramifications of the agreement for the home front were also significant. In Israel, the agreement was broadly accepted and thus occasioned little public discussion. In Turkey, however, while the agreement was controversial it did highlight two significant points: the complexity of the military–political relationship in Ankara, and the overwhelming power of the military when it collided with political opposition, this time the RP. To illustrate the first, it was significant that the agreement was signed by Turkey's Deputy Chief of General Staff Çevik Bir, during a visit to Israel and not by a representative of the Defense Ministry, as was the case with Israel, whose signatory was the Defense Ministry Director General David Ivri.[32] Moreover, although the Turkish constitution stated that all agreements with other countries should be discussed by the Parliamentary Committee on Foreign Relations, this was signed behind the Committee's back, on grounds that it pertained to the security and stability of the state.[33]

The clash of the military with the RP as soon as the agreement was made public in Turkey was also dealt with behind the scenes. Erbakan declared that his party would oppose it in parliament, but did practically nothing. Following the formation of the RP-led government in July 1996, the party's official daily, *Milli Gazete*, published a series of articles accusing Israel of backing terror in Turkey, and suggesting that the only way to prevent anarchy would be to "cut the connecting veins" with Israel.[34] One party official was even more assertive, declaring that: "We shall scrap it" [the agreement].[35] Yet not only did the Erbakan government not rescind the February agreement, it signed that of August 1996 for the upgrading of Turkey's Phantom warplanes by Israel. In playing this down as a mere "technical agreement,"[36] the RP seems to have been under pressure from the military. Chief of Staff Karadayı reportedly told Erbakan not to be "too emotional" and to go ahead and sign the agreement.[37]

## The Nature of Military/Strategic Relations

A high-ranking Israeli official who had played a leading role in the 1958 peripheral alliance maintained that the alignment of the 1990s did not reach the depth of the previous alliance, which, he said, included at a certain point an operational strategic plan against a third party[38] (see chapter 2). This contention cannot be objectively examined, since part of the archives of that era remain closed and because we do not know what secret agreements may be included in the new alignment. Even so, it seems clear to any observer that the openness, diversity, and intensity of strategic relations in the 1990s provided a much more solid basis for long-standing cooperation than did the vulnerable, uncertain ties of the 1950s and 1960s.[39]

The intensity and uniqueness of the new relationship could be gathered from Turkey's decision, in July 1998, to boost the number of its military attachés in Israel from one to three (officers from the air force, navy, and army). This made Israel the fourth country after the United States, Germany, and France to receive three attachés instead of the one that Turkey usually posted abroad.[40] Israel, for its part, sent two attachés. (In one of the exaggerated reports from a Syrian source, Israel intended to expand its military mission from 4 to 400.[41]) Another indication of the close ties between the two armies was the frequent visits of members of the high commands to each other's country, some of which were kept secret for a time, while others were promptly publicized. An example was the visit to Ankara of Israel's Deputy Chief of Staff Major General Matan Vilna'i, on June 3, 1996. Even after Turkey's military headquarters had reported it, the Israel Defense Force (IDF) declined to comment. This continued Israel's traditional downplaying of the growing strategic ties, with most details being released by Turkey, and the IDF disclosing as little as possible.[42] In any case, Vilna'i's semi-official visit was followed by the four-day official visit of Israel's Chief of Staff Amnon Lipkin-Shahak, in October 1997, and that of Defense Minister Yitzhak Mordechai in December. Both occasions were given publicity in Turkey (and Israel) and included a public visit to Atatürk's Mausoleum, which in Turkey is *de rigueur* for any official guest (later, when Prime Minister Ariel Sharon came to Turkey in the midst of the second intifada, he was not invited to visit the Mausoleum, whether for security or political reasons is not known).[43]

These visits were preceded by that of Turkey's Chief of General Staff Ismail Hakki Karadayı, to Israel in February 1997, where he spoke about the "organic, moral and emotional ties between Turkey and Israel" and their "historical togetherness."[44] Karadayı's visit was notable for coming after those of his country's prime minister and president (in 1994 and 1996 respectively), indicating perhaps the high status of the Chief of Staff in the Turkish hierarchy. On the other hand, Karadayı's visit preceded that of his Israeli counterpart, probably because Turkey felt more at ease initiating visits to Israel and only then returning the invitation.

These mutual exchanges by senior officers were supplemented by strategic dialogue, which, according to one scholar, was "the most remarkable element of the security ties," because it allowed for "the development of routine working relations between the two defence establishments at various levels."[45] The decision about these dialogues was taken by David Ivri and Çevik Bir at a meeting in December 1995. The Turks declined to call them strategic, while Israel insisted on this term. Accordingly, each of the parties used its own version.[46] The first strategic dialogue was held in Turkey on November 27, 1996,[47] and was followed by biannual strategic dialogues in each country alternately. In these dialogues, the two parties discussed in particular their common threats and operational plans to forestall them.[48]

Throughout this period, the two sides signed a great number of agreements, but it is sufficient to highlight the main points and their significance.[49] The memorandum of understanding for the training of pilots of both countries in each other's airspace, which had been signed as early as September 18, 1995, was an important development for both air forces, but especially Israel's. The opportunity for Israeli pilots to train over Turkey's vast territory meant that they could overcome the "claustrophobia" that had circumscribed the Israeli air force until the end of the June 1967 War (when the IDF occupied Sinai and could train there), and since the final withdrawal from Sinai in April 1982.[50] A second advantage was the ability of Israeli pilots to become acquainted with areas or countries bordering Turkey, especially those hostile to Israel—Iran, Iraq, and Syria—knowledge that could be crucial in any contingency.[51] In addition, they could practice tactics that they might wish to keep secret from certain enemies. According to the agreement, the training was to take place eight times a year, and by the end of 1999 almost all of Israel's pilots had gained experience in Turkey.[52] For their part, Turkish pilots trained in the Negev desert in southern Israel, using Israel's air combat maneuvering instrumentation training system, including various types of antiaircraft systems that simulated enemy tactics.[53] A Turkish source reported that Turkish pilots at Israel's Shdema air base in the Negev were trained to attack long-range antiaircraft missiles (like the S-300 that Cyprus wanted to buy from Russia), as well as learning radar evasion and jamming techniques.[54]

By early 1998, the two air forces had discussed the possibility of joint training, and in 2000 it got under way.[55] It created a "common language" between them and enhanced the potential of cooperation in case of need.[56] There were also reports that Turkey had built an air base exclusively for Israel in eastern Turkey, in exchange for training Turkish pilots to evade shoulder-mounted surface-to-air missiles, which Kurdish rebels had used to down two Turkish helicopters. Israel's ambassador to Turkey, Uri Bar-Ner, denied these reports. For his part,

David Ivri explained that the air base in question was an existing base not in active use by the Turkish air force, but was made available to Israeli pilots whenever they trained there.[57]

A further development was that in June 2001 the American, Turkish and Israeli air forces held joint air maneuvers over Konya in southern Turkey, demonstrating the joint strategic interests of the three countries and the high level of their cooperation. The degree of intimacy between the Turkish and Israeli air forces could be inferred from the participation of Israeli F-15 planes in the ninetieth anniversary celebrations of Turkey's air force.[58]

The two navies developed close cooperation as well. One of the agreements permitted access by naval vessels to each other's harbors.[59] It probably included a clause allowing Israeli submarine crews to train in Turkey. More important on the demonstrative level were the joint naval maneuvers in the Mediterranean that Israeli Defense Minister Itzhak Mordechai was instrumental in shaping, and in which, for the first time, Turkey, Israel, and the United States took part.[60] Beginning in 1998, the exercises were held annually. Invitations to Egypt and Greece to participate were rejected; Jordan sent an observer to the initial one. The maneuvers were presented as search-and-rescue drills for humanitarian, and not military, purposes. But this explanation failed to satisfy many countries in the region, which regarded the maneuvers of the "trio" as a potential threat.[61] Ankara and Jerusalem, for their part, could only have been pleased with the concern voiced in Arab capitals, particularly Damascus, hoping that the exercises would strengthen their deterrent posture.

In January 1998, Turkish and Israeli warships carried out "a modest joint exercise,"[62] probably the first of many. Then, in April 2001, Israel and Turkey conducted joint maneuvers, without the United States, from the base at Marmaris Aksaz Deniz naval base, which were reportedly not humanitarian but military in purpose.[63] If this information, provided by a Turkish military source, was correct, then naval cooperation had been significantly deepened.

By 1999, the land forces of Turkey and Israel had also initiated a dialogue.[64] One reason for their seeming lag behind the air forces and navies may be that Turkey's army was less open than the other services to cooperating with Israel.

Arms deals between Turkey and Israel were also boosted significantly, especially since Israel did not subject Ankara to the human rights criteria imposed by European countries and the United States. One of the most important and largest deals has been for Israel to upgrade 54 of

Turkey's F-4 jet fighters and 48 of its F-5s. The agreements, signed in December 1996 and 1998, amounted to about $700 m., representing the biggest-ever foreign contract for Israel's aircraft industry.[65] A certain delay in implementing the first deal was caused by the demand of eight Israeli banks for more binding government guarantees to cover the credit lines they were supposed to open, since Turkey did not have to start paying the bill until two years after work on the upgrading had begun. The intervention of Israel's prime minister and finance minister resolved this problem.[66] A bigger stumbling block was Prime Minister Erbakan, who dragged his feet on the contract, but finally agreed to sign. The difficulties illustrated the complexity of the military agreements, and the need for the cooperation and participation of Ankara's political establishment as well. Another agreement was for the joint production of Popeye 1 and Popeye 2 air-to-ground missiles, signed in August 1996 and 1997 and valued at $150 m. and $200 m. respectively.[67]

Turkey's purchase of weapons from Israel was also stepped up. For example, in February 2002 Israel won a $110 m. tender to equip Turkish helicopters with electronic warfare systems.[68] Ankara also considered buying nearly 90 unmanned aerial vehicles (UAVs) to strengthen its surveillance capability in southeast Turkey, as well as reconnaissance, attack, and communication UAVs. Separately from this project, in which the Israel Aircraft Industries was competing with the American General Dynamics Corporation, Turkey was expected to buy from Israel 108 unmanned combat vehicles (UCAV).[69] The military was very keen on purchasing missiles and missile technology, especially because Israel was the only country in the world, apart from the United States and Russia, which was developing an antimissile defense system, the Arrow. Cooperation in this area had been increased in May 1997, during the visit to Israel of the Turkish Defense Minister Turhan Tayan. The idea was to develop a common strategy of joint defense, to forestall threats emanating from Syria, Iran, and Iraq.[70] Indeed, Israel, Turkey, and the United States began to develop the mechanism for a "trilateral antiballistic cooperation." Already in 2000, before President George W. Bush came to power, trilateral theater missile defense talks (TMD) were held. These envisaged the establishment of a regional antiballistic missile defense to deter nations in the vicinity of Turkey and Israel, such as Iraq and Iran, from carrying out ballistic missile attacks. The talks included discussions on how to deal with biological and chemical weapons that could be delivered by ballistic missiles. Israel was able to draw on its "advanced knowledge" of ballistic missiles and of the delivery systems of weapons of mass destruction (WMD), and to brief Ankara.[71]

Nevertheless, one area of technological and scientific know-how seemingly remained closed to Turkey. In the 1960s, Ankara had shown great interest in nuclear technology, but Israel was reluctant to provide information. Now, asked again about the possibility of sharing Israel's technical expertise in nuclear technology, Israeli Prime Minister Binyamin Netanyahu stated: "we have strict regulations in this regard. There cannot be any question of us exporting or transferring nuclear technology to any country including Turkey."[72] In fact, a certain divergence between Turkey and Israel might well have emerged over nuclear weapons, as Turkey would like to see the region free of this nonconventional WMD, while Israel keeps its policy opaque on the issue.

Intelligence sharing was another area of close cooperation. As has been pointed out, there was a long-standing tradition of intelligence exchanges between the two armies and intelligence services.[73] In the 1990s, this received greater impetus because of the convergence of domestic and external threats, especially for Turkey. One example of Israel's contribution to Turkey was, allegedly, that it provided information on the Russian-made Mig 29, the type used by Syria's air force. The report by the Turkish daily, *Hürriyet*, stated that the information had been passed on to Israel by Germany.[74] Israel, for its part, is said to have used its access to Turkish territory to gather information on Iran, Iraq, and Syria, and in return agreed to help train and equip the Turkish army in antiterror warfare emanating from bases in these three countries.[75] Furthermore, according to the UPI news agency, Israel's special forces have taken part in Turkey's regular "incursions" into the Kurdish territories of northern Iraq.[76] This could not be corroborated and it is doubtful that Israelis would take part in the actual fighting. More likely, they contributed in the training of personnel and intelligence. However, the report itself was indicative of how strong and deep the partnership appeared to the outside observer.

## Tanks for Tankers: Anatomy of an Agreement

On March 29, 2002, Turkey signed a secret agreement with Israel Military Industries for the modernization of 170 M-60A1 Turkish tanks, at a cost of $668 m. It was signed after long debates and delays, and was of special interest because it was concluded in the middle of the ongoing Israeli–Palestinian war of attrition, and offers a rare insight into the mechanism of decision-making. On Israel's side, the three key personalities were Prime Minister Ariel Sharon, Defense Minister Binyamin Ben Eliezer, and IDF Chief of General Staff Shaul Mofaz.

All three went to Turkey during 2001 and were said to have lobbied intensively for the tender.[77] In Turkey, the deal was handled by the Defense Industry Executive Committee, consisting of Prime Minister Bülent Ecevit, Defense Minister Sabahattin Çakmakoğlu, and Chief of General Staff General Hüseyin Kıvrıkoğlu. In a Committee meeting on March 8, 2002, at which the decision was taken, Ecevit raised doubts about the wisdom of such a move at that particular time. However, Kıvrıkoğlu convinced him by saying: "our armed forces are in urgent need of tanks." In other words, as on previous occasions, it was the military that held the upper hand on security issues. The deal was leaked immediately after its signing and aroused harsh criticism from some parties in the Turkish Parliament, who called for it to be scrapped, or at least delayed. Ecevit now came to its defense, asserting that it would not be cancelled.[78] Perhaps to silence his critics, Ecevit then offset Turkey's acquiescence to the agreement by stating two days later that Israel was carrying out "a genocide" against the Palestinian people "before the eyes of the world."[79]

Justifications for the deal were not lacking. Israel was "the most appropriate partner," one Turkish journalist explained, because, unlike America, Germany, or other countries, it did not put up a "whole series of political obstacles," of the kind that Turkey was fed up with.[80] Moreover, as Çakmakoğlu stated in parliament, Israel was the only country that had carried out such a comprehensive modernization, and bids made by other foreign companies "had not met the needs of the Turkish armed forces." He further justified the deal by the fact that the modernization would be carried out in a Turkish military factory (in the central Anatolian town of Kayseri); that the payments to be made to Israel would include contracts with Turkish military firms; and that the technological know-how acquired would be used in future projects in Turkey, thus making Ankara "less technologically dependent on the outside."[81] Çakmakoğlu then said that his government was following in the footsteps of its predecessors who had signed modernization deals, and that the urgency lay in the advances made by the Greek army, which had overtaken Turkey in purchasing new tanks: "we needed to make this agreement in order to close the tank gap."[82] Interestingly, Greece was to purchase from Germany 170 Leopard tanks (which Bonn had refused to sell to Turkey), precisely the same number that Turkey wanted to have upgraded.[83] The upgrading was to be done within five years, and the tanks would be operational for another 20 years.[84]

The reasons why Turkey took some six years to conclude the deal were threefold, but none seems to have been political. The first was that

Turkey sought to get optimum price and technical specifications. Initially, Israel offered to upgrade the tanks for $1 bn.,[85] but intense bargaining on the Turkish side, including leaking their wish to end the negotiations, led to a substantial reduction, until the cost reached what Ecevit described as "a suitable price (and quick delivery)."[86] Director General of the Defense Ministry Amos Yaron, who led the talks, said that he told the Turks that Israel was willing to lower the costs, "but we are not ready to subsidize the project."[87] The second reason was pressure on Turkey from the United States to award the modernization contract to American firms,[88] which Ankara finally decided to ignore. Third, was the undeclared linkage that Turkey sought to form between the modernization and Israel's purchase of water from Turkey.

The idea of buying water was mooted as early as January 1994, when Israel's President Weizmann discussed it with his counterpart, Süleyman Demirel, during his visit to Turkey that month. The proposal was to use the surplus from the Turkish Manavgat river, which flows to the Mediterranean, and not the waters of the Tigris and Euphrates, over which Turkey had long-standing conflicts with its neighbors, Iraq and Syria. As if mirroring the tank modernization deal, the water deal also had many ups and downs and took several years to conclude. The main obstacles were the high price demanded by Turkey and the objection from certain circles in Israel to importing such a strategic commodity from abroad; they preferred the cheaper and more reliable option of home-based desalinization.

However, by March 2002, several consecutive years of drought and, even more important, Israel's eagerness to secure the tank deal, brought it to agree to buy water from Turkey. Thus, just a few days before the signing of the tank deal, Prime Minister Ariel Sharon instructed top government officials "to speed up" arrangements for importing some 50 m.–100 m. cubic meters of water a year from Turkey.[89] This amounted to 2.5 percent of Israel's annual needs. The idea was to transport the water by tankers. The discussion on price was postponed to a later date, that is, after the transport company was selected.[90] A Turkish source maintained that the decision to award the defense tenders to Israeli companies "had affected the Israeli cabinet's decision on water imports."[91] As the tank deal was finalized only after Israel's cabinet had decided to speed up the water project, a clear linkage can be assumed between the two. Alon Liel, who was now advising one of the companies competing for the water transport contract, maintained that Turkey had offered the water to offset Turkish arms purchases from Israel. He explained that the defense contracts included clauses requiring Israel to purchase goods in Turkey totaling hundreds of millions of dollars, but that Israel did not buy enough there. Turkey wanted to finance its defense projects by selling water to Israel, among other exports and services. Transportation for ten years was valued at $400 m. This tortuous manner of buying water from Turkey did not end there. A few months later Israel reversed its earlier decision, following which Turkey threatened to drag its feet on the military and other deals if Jerusalem did not fulfill its commitment to buy water. Then, in another U-turn, in August 2002 Jerusalem issued a new directive to buy the water. Two months later, Turkey announced that the modernizing of tanks was going to start. By summer 2003, preparations had been made for the first series of contracts designed to complete the complicated process of bringing Turkish water to Israel by the middle of the decade.

An Israeli official explained that the decision to purchase Turkish water was made for "political-strategic considerations" in the overall relationship with Turkey and not just in view of Israel's need for water.[92] For Turkey, the desire to offset its arms purchases with the selling of water also had a strategic aspect, creating a kind of mutual dependence with Israel, reducing the one-sidedness of the strategic relationship.

In another strategically related enterprise, the Southeastern Anatolian Project (GAP), Liel disclosed that Ankara allowed Israeli companies the sole right to compete for work in eastern Turkey worth $750 m., but complained that Jerusalem did not return the gesture.[93] Israeli companies were involved in water and infrastructure projects in GAP (probably from August 2001),[94] but Turkey's insistence on winning tenders in Israel in return was not always satisfied. For example, Israel did not grant Turkish firms a share in the Construction Project of Ashdod Port. Nevertheless, Turkey decided in July 2002 to award Israel the contract to modernize 300 of its helicopters, at a cost of $110 m.[95] However, it also subsequently froze all Israeli involvement in GAP, along with other countries. The reasons may have been varied, but it also perhaps indicated that Turkey would not indefinitely tolerate such imbalanced relations over the long term.

## People-to-People Relations

Israel, much more than Turkey, was eager from the start to achieve diversification in their bilateral ties. Past experience had taught it that unless relations were open and diversified, it was very easy to cut them off in a single stroke. In other words, it hoped that diversification would help the relationship to endure. Also, for a country that was isolated and lacked legitimacy in the eyes of its neighbors, it was of the utmost importance to extend the hand of friendship to the different strata of Turkish society, and establish empathy on the people-to-people level as well. Indeed, strong ties with a Muslim people was considered by Israel to be one of the most important goals of bilateral relations,[96] because it could provide a model for other Muslim peoples. In many respects, the same goal had motivated Israel in its relations with the Arab countries with which it had signed peace treaties—Egypt and Jordan. However, the pace there had been very slow and subject to fluctuation, remaining on the whole limited to government-to-government contacts, without reaching the wider community. Because Israel was engaged in the peace process with the Arab states concurrent to developing its strategic relations with Ankara, it was in even greater need of expanding its ties with Turkey into more diverse political and civilian spheres, so as to deflect Arab attention from the strategic aspect and focus on the more benign ones.

From Israel's perspective, developing friendly political relations was no less important or effective than the military exchanges. The frequent public visits to Israel of Turkish officials, including heads of state, were unprecedented in the history of their association. Nor could these be compared to relations between Israel and any other country in the region, even Egypt and Jordan, with which Jerusalem had peace agreements. Equally important were the public visits by Israeli officials to Turkey. The most significant were those of Prime Minister Ehud Barak, who during his short 18-month term went to Turkey no fewer than three times. These visits came much later than that of the Turkish prime minister to Israel, probably because Turkey considered Barak's predecessor, Binyamin Netanyahu, to be a hard-liner toward the Palestinians, and was reluctant to invite him. Barak's much more dovish stance on the Palestinian question was welcomed in Turkey. His peace overtures to Syria were most probably not. The result was a Turkish need for frequent consultations with Barak. The visit by Prime Minister Ariel Sharon in August 2001 was particularly noteworthy, because of his hawkish stance in Turkey's eyes[97] and because it took place in the midst of the second Palestinian intifada, which started in September 2000. So was the visit by Israeli President Moshe Katzav on July 8–9, 2003, notwithstanding the advent of an Islamist government to power in Ankara. Once Turkey had crossed the Rubicon, moving forward had become easier.

As in the peripheral alliance days, Israel now endeavored to strengthen economic ties with Turkey and put relations on a more solid footing, since economic activity was bound to impact larger segments of the population than military cooperation did. This was expedited by the complementarity of the two economies—Israel had advanced technological know-how and Turkey had cheap labor. Turkey was also the largest economy in the eastern Mediterranean, and offered huge potential as a market and a source of supply.[98] From Turkey's perspective, Ankara was now much freer to develop economic relations with Israel than it had been, for example, in the 1970s, when it was very conscious of the Arabs' oil weapon and hoped to enlist their financial support in combating its economic problems (see above and below). It was true that by the end of the 1990s, Turkey's economic and financial problems had become, if anything, even more acute, but given the Arab countries' own economic difficulties and Ankara's frustration at their lack of support in the past, it could now develop economic relations simultaneously with Israel and the Arab states without the specter of an Arab boycott hanging over its head. Moreover, Israel could be helpful in lobbying in the United States and Europe for assistance to resolve Turkey's severe financial and economic crisis, which came to a head at the beginning of 1991. The idea that relations with Israel and the Arab countries should not be mutually exclusive was best expressed by Turkey's Foreign Minister Ismail Cem, who said:

Turkey's relations with Israel are not subject to negotiation. In the same way, our relations with Arab countries cannot be used against us as a trump card . . . we cannot restrict our relations with Israel just so that our relations with the Arab countries could improve.

Cem also recalled that 19 of the 32 member countries of the Organization of the Islamic Conference had *very close* [emphasis added] commercial ties with Israel.[99]

Israeli Prime Minister Binyamin Netanyahu, speaking on the economic relationship, stated in January 1997:

It is very important to develop cooperation in economic and technological spheres as much as in the security sphere . . . Israel is going through a technological revolution. There are more than 1,000 venture firms in Israel possessing high-technology. This figure puts Israel second after the United States. Turkey could benefit from this.[100]

In the Arab world, such declarations aroused deep suspicions and fears of an Israeli "colonization" of the Arabs, hence their resistance to cooperation. In Turkey, however, there was greater openness toward cooperation. Even Erbakan, during his premiership, made overtures to

the Governor of the Bank of Israel Jacob Frenkel, for advice on infla-
tion in Turkey.[101] That Turkey had no problems benefiting from Israeli
technological know-how was clearly demonstrated on the military
level, but it was also true of civilian and business relationships. At the
end of 2001, for example, Israel participated in the Informatics 2001
CEBIT Fair in Istanbul, with the aim of establishing commercial relations with Turkish companies and extending its network in information
technology. Such commercial links would draw on Israel's expertise
in telecommunications products, which made up roughly 20 percent of
its exports.[102]

Although lagging behind military relations, economic and trade links
also surged ahead. During the visit of the Turkish Foreign Minister
Hikmet Çetin, to Israel in 1994, it was decided to establish the legal
framework for economic and commercial relations. A major advantage
was that, unlike other Middle Eastern states, the two countries enjoyed
free market economies, which made any exchanges much easier.
Analyzing Turkish–Israeli economic relations, Israeli economist Paul
Rivlin spoke of two models. The first was what he called the Middle
East model, in which trade and economic development were usually
subordinated to politics. An example was the economic relationship
between Egypt and Israel, which Egyptians considered as a zero–sum
game: if Israel gained, they lost. Such thinking, Rivlin maintained, has
been behind the very low intra-regional trade in the Middle East. The
second was the economics-led model that guided thinking and action
in the United States and Europe. Here, politics was subordinated to economics: anything that stood in the way of economics was gradually
shunted aside. Rivlin's view was that economic relations between
Turkey and Israel were closer to the American European than the
Middle Eastern model.[103]

According to one source, negotiations were sometimes difficult.
However, the parties managed to overcome this and to sign some
important agreements. These included free trade; economic, commercial, technological, and scientific cooperation—the first that either side
had had with another country in the Mediterranean; a treaty to prevent
double taxation; and an agreement for mutual encouragement and protection of investment; all were signed in 1996–97. Other agreements
covered cooperation in telecommunications and postal services, health
and medicine, transportation, energy, tourism, agriculture, education,
and training and construction.[104]

Trade made an important stride forward as well. Speaking on the
subject, Turkey's ambassador to Israel, Barlas Özener, confirmed in

June 1999 that the legal infrastructure of economic relations had been established and that many companies were making use of it.[105] In February 2000, a meeting of Turkey and Israel's Joint Economic Commission signed a memorandum of understanding on free trade zones. These were to enable the two countries to export goods to the United States without custom duties and quotas. Israel's officials promised to launch efforts to obtain the support of the United States for the zones that were planned in Turkey. The memorandum aimed at increasing the annual volume of trade between Turkey and Israel from $900 m. to $2 bn. By the end of 2002, trade between the two countries amounted to $1.2 bn., with Israel's exports to Turkey reaching $383.1 m. and its imports $813.7m.[106] A consensus was also reached about undertaking joint investments in third countries.

In trade terms, reciprocity grew, with Turkey exporting even more than it imported from Israel,[107] but the same cannot be said of tourism. Israeli tourists far outnumbered their Turkish counterparts. In 1995, one of the peak years, Israelis visiting Turkey reached 287,000, while only 11,767 Turkish tourists came to Israel.[108] The reason for this imbalance is that Israelis flocked to Turkey because it was nearby and cheap by Israeli standards. Gambling was also an attraction when this was permitted in Turkey. For Turks, Israel was both expensive and not as easy to reach. For example, the need to fly there made it much less attractive than Europe. Other reasons were security problems and Israel's lack of tourist promotion in Turkey. Consequently, people-to-people relations had a greater chance of developing in Turkey than in Israel.

Israel had two other important opportunities to demonstrate its goodwill to the Turkish people. The first was in early July 1997, when a large fire broke out in an ammunition factory in the Turkish town of Kırıkale, 60 km. east of Ankara. The blast completely destroyed the ammunition factory, injured several police officers, soldiers, and civilians and caused extensive damage to a hospital. There was a danger that it would spread to the main ammunition storage, where hundreds of bombs were kept, each containing 800 kg. of TNT.[109] Turkey approached Israel's air force to send special helicopters to help put out the fire. Initially the air force was reluctant, because to do so risked leaving Israel without any *extra* helicopters in case of an emergency. At that point, Defense Minister Yitzhak Mordechai decided to take the risk and sent a message to Çevik Bir to this effect. According to Mordechai's military secretary, Ya'acob 'Amidror, Israel's prompt support helped lift relations to a new level, because it proved that Israel was willing to stand by Turkey at a high cost. This also contrasted sharply with the reaction of the United States and other countries, which failed to respond to Turkey's appeal.[110]

The second opportunity, also considered a landmark in the relationship, came after the severe earthquake in Turkey in August 1999. The spontaneous outpouring of concern and assistance from Israelis, coupled with the subsequent rescue efforts by the IDF and Israel's construction of a village at Adapazarı to house the homeless, were reportedly "praised and appreciated by all," and boosted Israel's image in the eyes of the Turks. The village, which cost 25 m. new shekels (about $6 m.), included 312 houses for 2,500 people and was given the name "Turkey–Israel." Prime Minister Barak, who came to Turkey to inaugurate it, was received by Ecevit's warm words: "you give us an outstanding human lesson. The Turkish people will never forget your deeds."[111]

Another contribution to people-to-people contacts was in the area of cultural exchanges. The coverage in each country's media of events in the other was historically unprecedented. It must be remembered, however, that coverage of Israel and Israeli issues in the Turkish media, including opinion pieces, was twice as much as Israel's of Turkey[112]— probably because in Turkey the issue of Israel remained, on the whole, controversial. Indeed, even in the 1960s, when coverage of Israel was very low, pro- and anti-Israeli articles could still be found, indicating the deep rift in Turkish public opinion on the subject. The more extensive attention to Israel in the 1990s and 2000s, especially in the electronic media, helped to bring its affairs—for better or worse—into every Turkish home. Understandably, Israel's image on the popular level has not remained static, fluctuating from the very positive, after the support to Turkey in the earthquake, to the more negative, during the renewed conflict with the Palestinians. One symbolic example was the attitude to Haim Revivo, an Israeli football player who joined Turkey's Fenerbahçe team. Because of his success, Revivo was considered, during the good times, as Israel's best ambassador to Turkey. However, when Israel's conflict with the Palestinians intensified, he became the subject of anti-Israel verbal attacks.[113]

On the whole, however, cultural and scientific exchanges expanded significantly, including exhibitions, bands, concerts, and student exchanges. A particularly important contribution was made by the Süleyman Demirel program, which was established at the Moshe Dayan Center at Tel Aviv University in 1999 and endowed with $500,000 annually by the Turkish Council of Higher Education, a figure matched by Tel Aviv University. The program sponsors various cultural, scientific, and academic exchanges between the two countries. Similarly, the exchange of students and scholars encouraged by the Foreign Ministries of both countries covered areas of study from languages to history and medicine. Direct links were also established between universities. To enrich the mutual understanding between the two peoples, some translations were made from the literature of one to the other. For example, Orhan Pamuk's novel *The Black Book* was translated into Hebrew, and novels by Israel's Amos Oz were translated into Turkish (from English, not Hebrew).

## Potential Obstacles

This idyllic picture of flourishing relations should be qualified by mentioning certain issues which, although not yet problematic, could become so under certain conditions. This is especially true regarding the Kurdish problem. On the one hand, this appeared to facilitate the rapprochement between the two countries (see above). On the other, it also had the potential to complicate relations. In spite of reports about Israel's support to Turkey in its conflict with the PKK, there were lingering suspicions both on popular and governmental levels in Turkey that Israel was assisting, or was likely to assist, the PKK or the Kurdish Turkish movement in general in their demands. These stemmed from the existence of a Jewish Kurdish community in Israel sympathetic to the Kurdish cause, as well as from Israel's support of the Kurds of Iraq in the 1960s and early 1970s. It was of little help to Israel to stress, time and again, that this belonged to the past and, more importantly, that it made a clear distinction between the Kurds of Iraq and those of Turkey. As a consequence, any incident was liable to blow Ankara's suspicions out of all proportion.

Indeed, this happened when Turkey captured the PKK leader, Abdullah Öcalan, on February 15, 1999 in Kenya (see below). Reports to the effect that Israel had assisted Turkey in the capture[114] resulted in Kurdish demonstrations outside of Israel's diplomatic posts in Europe. The most serious incident was an attack on the Israeli consulate in Berlin that resulted in the death of four Kurds. Israel's fears that this incident might turn Israel into a target of PKK attacks in Europe prompted Prime Minister Netanyahu to send, via the Mossad, a calming message to Kurdish leaders in Europe that Israel was not involved in the capture and indeed sought to remain neutral in the conflict.[115] Even though this was not sent directly to the PKK, in deference to Turkish sensitivity to any Israeli contact with a "terrorist" group, Turkey warned Israel not to continue with such contacts. Jerusalem thereupon informed Ankara of "its commitment not to have any contact with the

Kurdish rebel movement,[116] and President Weizman assured Hikmet Çetin, speaker of the Turkish Parliament, who came to Israel shortly afterward, that Israel had no plan to establish ties with the PKK and that it "supports Turkish struggle against terrorism."[117]

The extent to which Israel was willing to defer to Turkish sensitivities could be seen in a minor incident. Yaşar Kaya, one of the leaders of the banned Kurdish Democratic Party (DEP) and speaker of the "Kurdish Parliament in Exile," was invited to Israel by a local non-governmental group. Turkey's immediate message of its "sensitivity on the invitation" caused the invitation to be withdrawn.[118] The incident proved that for Israel, the Turkish–Kurdish issue could be a two-edged sword, and that, in regard to terrorism, Israel needed to take into account Turkey's sensitivities, even though this was not reciprocated by Turkey on the Palestinian issue. On the contrary, Turkey did not consider breaking off relations with the Palestinians for their terrorist attacks against Israel, and, as we have seen, Prime Minister Ecevit described Israel's reaction to these as genocide.

Another dispute a year later followed the declaration by two Israeli politicians, Yossi Beilin, the Minister of Justice and Yossi Sarid, the Minister of Education, to the effect that Turkey's massacres of the Armenians during World War I constituted a "genocide." Sarid also called for the history of this alleged genocide to be inserted into Israel's high school curriculum.[119] Israel, cognizant of Turkish sensitivities, has always been cautious on this subject and has refrained from making official statements about it. In 1997 an Israeli professor, Ehud Toledano, who was a candidate for the post of Israel's ambassador to Turkey, was rejected by Ankara because of his alleged reference to the matter. Now, the announcements of the two ministers caused a stir in Turkey. Israel was called on to clarify the issue. It failed to convince Ankara that these were merely personal opinions, and Turkey sent a strong message to Israel by instructing cabinet ministers as well as senior generals not to attend Israel's Independence Day celebrations in May 2000.[120] However, further clarification by the Israeli ambassador and other officials helped to defuse the mini-crisis. In all probability, the main reason behind Turkey's burying the hatchet was Israel's past help, through the Jewish lobby in Washington, to obstruct the Armenian lobby's attempts to pass a resolution calling the massacres a genocide, as well as to establish a museum for the American "genocide" in Washington.[121]

On another level, Turkish newspapers reported from time to time that Israelis were involved in irregularities, or even bribes, in pursuit of the modernization contracts on the aircraft and tanks.[122]

These allegations, which could well have originated from the U.S.-based General Dynamics Land Systems, a competitor with Israeli firms, were picked up by the parliamentary opposition, especially the Islamists, who were opposed in principle to any deal with Israel or with General Dynamics, for that matter. Tarnishing Israel's image was a way of obstructing or even preventing such a deal. As it turned out, these reports failed to achieve their objective.

A more serious potential obstacle came from neighbouring governments. Many of them, particularly among the Arab states, were extremely disturbed by the warming of Turkish–Israeli ties, and hoped to impede and even reverse the process. The following chapter analyzes these reactions in detail and their ultimate lack of success.

# Chapter 5

## Implications and Reactions

Unlike the peripheral alliance, which caused no reaction because of its secrecy, the new alignment brought immediate and sharp responses from countries in the region. These varied from one country to another, or from one group of countries to another, but only one Arab state—Jordan—welcomed it, and most perceived it as a serious threat to themselves or to the region as a whole. The questions that need concern us here are: What impact did the alignment have on the region's stability? Did the Turkish–Israeli alignment bring about the formation of a counter-alliance or any other alignment in the region? The greater part of this chapter is devoted to examining the reactions of Arab states, for several reasons:

1. In the past, their attitude was the main stumbling block to close and open relations between Turkey and Israel.
2. Their numerical strength gave them leverage that no other neighboring country, such as Greece or Iran, could compete with.
3. Any counter-alliance was likely to include this huge bloc, or at least parts of it.

In this discussion, Turkey's relations with the Arab states are paramount, both because of their love–hate nature and because only by pressuring Turkey (and not Israel) could the Arab world hope to frustrate the alignment.

## The Reaction of Arab States

The alignment caused great concern and even alarm among many Arab countries. Some viewed it as Turkey's second betrayal of the Arabs in 50 years—the first being its recognition of the state of Israel in 1949. The 1996 agreement looked especially threatening because it caught the Arab world in one of its weakest moments, when it was suffering the fragmentation caused by the 1991 Gulf War, and because the new alignment was interpreted as anti-Arab to the core. These fears were, in fact, fourfold:

1. The alignment would increase the strategic threat to the Arab states in general and to the more vulnerable ones—Syria and Iraq—in particular.
2. It would marginalize the Arab world in the international arena.
3. It would further fragment the Arab world by drawing an Arab country, Jordan, into the alignment.
4. It would jeopardize the Arab–Israeli peace process, or at least weaken the bargaining power of the Arab partners, by providing Israel with new strategic depth, as it were, thus strengthening its hand and its intransigence at the negotiating table.

Relations between the Arab world and Turkey were ambiguous through and through. On the one hand, their cultural and religious affinities should have formed a powerful bond, but on the other, a number of barriers and problems eclipsed the strength of these cultural ties and even threatened to turn them into a source of friction by the end of the century. Interestingly, both parties pointed to the existence of psychological barriers, which were the outcome of mutual negative images and perceptions formed over time, and believed that these had to be overcome as a precondition for improved relations.[1]

The negative image that Arabs had of Turks was demonstrated in a study by a Turkish academic, Ekmeleddin İhsanoğlu, of Egyptian history textbooks from the years 1912 to 1980. The texts were found to emphasize the militaristic and oppressive aspects of the Ottoman Empire, and to accuse it of having controlled the Arabs by harsh measures and of deliberately isolating them from Western civilization. A source book from the 1950s about Turkey and the Arabs that had influenced school texts, described the Ottoman occupation of Arab lands as "the worst tragedy that has befallen the Arabs and Muslims throughout their history" and held it responsible for "defects" in the Arabs.[2] These images were considered to be valid even in the 1990s.

The counter-image that Turks had of Arabs was revealed by an Arab scholar, Ibrahim al-Daquqi, who examined cultural and linguistic influences, school textbooks, the image of Arabs in Turkish newspapers, and a poll of Turkish intellectuals. After analyzing ten historical texts from 1931 to 1990, he concluded that in spite of changing times and circumstances, all without exception presented a negative image of Arabs as traitors, who had "stabbed the Turks in the back" during World War I by joining the British enemy. This image of treachery, Daquqi said, has remained "as a Damocles sword hanging over the head of the Arab–Turkish relationship."[3] He also surveyed Turkish newspapers for three months in 1993–94, finding a very low coverage of Arab events (2.4 percent) and a perception that Arabs interfered in Turkey's internal affairs; "used Islam to hurt Turkish national security"; "coveted" Turkish lands and water; incited the Kurds and supported terrorist acts against Turkey. There was a recurrent negative image of the Arab, especially the Palestinian, as backward and a terrorist.

Although these historical stereotypes on both sides have not been dispelled, a scholarly trend began in the mid-1980s aimed at revising relations between Turks and Arabs by an examination of these images. As one Turkish scholar put it: "Turkish and Arab decision-makers are as affected as are the masses by the mutually created negative images about each other. The psychological uneasiness with which the Turks and Arabs view each other proves to be detrimental to both sides, reducing the possibilities of harmonious co-operation between them."[4]

Beyond these images, perceptions were, of course, determined by political, economic, and strategic factors, and it is instructive to analyze relations between the Arab world and Turkey up to the February 1996 rapprochement with Israel.

## The Ebb and Flow in Relations Until the Late 1980s

When analyzing the history of the relationship between Turkey and Arab countries in the twentieth century, Arab scholars and journalists tend to generalize and speak of Turkey and *the* Arab world, as if the latter related to Turkey with a single voice or as a collective. Similarly, they tend to interpret Turkey's behavior to a particular Arab state as if it were toward the entire Arab world. While on a certain emotional–psychological level this generalization might be justified, the reality was far removed from such a monolithic picture. In fact, as I argue, these relations were much more varied, complicated, and nuanced, and reflected among other things the rivalries and tensions within the Arab world itself. One example stands out—Turkey's role in the Baghdad Pact. It has been customary to portray this Pact, the defense treaty signed in 1955 between Turkey and Iraq (later joined by Iran, Pakistan, and Britain), as "anti-Arab" or aimed at "the encirclement of the Arab homeland."[5] This portrayal disregards the fact that an *Arab* country was a partner and that the Pact itself both reflected and reinforced the prevailing rivalries between pro-Western and pro-Soviet camps in the Arab world.

Arab scholars identify four major phases in Arab–Turkish relations up to the end of 1980: 1923–45, the years of alienation; 1945–65, estrangement and clash; 1965–75, relative improvement of relations; and 1975–85 "dramatic change" for the better or the "Arab era of power."[6] At the end of the 1980s a new phase began, which again changed mutual perceptions and attitudes and is discussed in greater detail below. While accepting this periodization, the following observations need to be made. First, even at their lowest point, relations never reached the level of armed conflict or war, as was the case between Iran and Iraq. Second, even in what was described as the period of "estrangement and clash" there was no rupture of ties between Turkey and "all Arab countries." In fact, in all periods good relations were maintained with individual Arab countries. For example, in the first phase (1923–45) Turkey maintained links with Iraq, Jordan, Saudi Arabia, and Egypt. With regard to Saudi Arabia, Turkey was the first country to officially recognize Riyad—in May 1926—and to send an ambassador there. Moreover, the two states had signed a treaty of friendship in 1929.[7] The variety and complexity of relations was even more pronounced in the second period (1945–65). Not only was Turkey linked to Iraq in the Baghdad Pact from 1955 to 1958,[8] thereby antagonizing Egypt, but Ankara further incurred Cairo's wrath by recognizing Syria after the latter's withdrawal from the UAR (the unity with Egypt) in September 1961. So furious was Egypt that it broke off relations with Turkey for two years.[9]

Having clarified these points, it is important to examine the historical areas of friction between Arabs and Turks, because many of these issues would recur at the end of the century. Arab scholars identify a cluster of four or five such areas: cultural, territorial, political, ideological, and strategic. The problems pertaining to the different levels tend to overlap and sometimes to reinforce one another. Some are general, relating to all Arab countries, while others are more specific and concern only one or two of them. Yet the tendency of any individual country has been to portray its bilateral problem with Turkey as an all-Arab one, so as to mobilize Arab support for its cause.

The one issue that bedeviled all Arabs was the cultural rift that developed between them and Turkey after World War I. There seems to be unanimity among different ideological and political commentators, both Islamist and secular, in identifying modern Turkey's "original sin"—its severing of cultural bonds with the Arab world—as a main cause of the estrangement. As mentioned in chapter 3, Atatürk's triple move of secularization, changing the alphabet from Arabic to Latin, and cleansing the Turkish language of Arabic (and Persian) words, was interpreted as an anti-Arab move and was one of the "most bitter and severe" actions in creating the psychological barrier between the two parties.[10] Much as they would have liked it, the Arabs were fully aware that Turkey was not going to turn back the pages of history and readopt the Arabic alphabet or reintroduce the Arabic lexicon. Still, there was great hope that Islam could become the main channel for strengthening relations with Turkey. In the past, the Ottoman Empire had come under criticism because of its attempts, in its final phase, to contain nascent Arab nationalism, but it was applauded for maintaining strong cultural ties with the Arabs nevertheless. As one scholar noted: "Relations had been strong in the shade of Islam, but they became weaker and weaker with the decay of the Islamic bond."[11] This yearning for the revival of Islam's historical role proved to be quite problematic, because in Turkey itself Islam was to become a two-edged sword.

Indeed, Islam played an increasingly paradoxical role in the relations between Turkey and the Arab world. On the one hand, their common religious bonds could have been the best way of cementing relations between them, hence the Arab desire to see Islam grow stronger in Turkey. On the other, the mainstream of Turkey's intellectual, military, and political elites perceived in the rising power of political Islam during the 1990s the gravest danger to the state, hence their least desire was that it become the main catalyst for strengthening relations with Arab states.[12] Accordingly, they viewed with great suspicion the deepening ties between Turkish and Arab Islamists. Another paradox was that while certain Arab governments, such as those of Egypt, Syria, or Iraq, were fighting their own Islamists and seeking to contain political Islam in their own countries, they nevertheless wanted this radical form of Islam to gain ground in Turkey, and thus further antagonized the staunch supporters of secularism in Turkey, chief among them the military. In short, Islam could no longer fulfil its simple role of past centuries as the primary cultural bond between Turks and Arabs.

The second layer in the complexity of relations was the territorial disputes. Although directly concerning only two Arab states, Syria and Iraq, these touched some raw nerves in other Arab states as well, either because of what might be called instinctive emotional Arab solidarity, or an amorphous fear of Turkish designs elsewhere in the Arab world, or even latent negative memories of the Ottoman Imperial era. Both disputes in question were the legacy of European imperialism: the Mosul Vilayet area had been allocated to Iraq in 1925 as a result of pressure and maneuvering by Britain, then the mandatory power in Iraq; and Alexandretta was given to Turkey a decade later (1938) following an agreement with France, the mandatory power in Syria. While the latter dispute was constantly hammered in the Syrian and other Arab media, Britain's role in the Iraqi exchange had been completely forgotten. Herein lies the big difference between the two disputes: in the Iraqi case, Baghdad had harbored fears, although latent, of Turkish revisionism; but in the Syrian case, Turkey came under constant pressure from Syrian revisionism.[13]

These differences go a long way to explain the divergence in relations between Turkey and Iraq, on the one hand, and Turkey and Syria on the other. Iraq, which was weaker than Turkey and lived in the shadow of possible Turkish revisionism, did everything to accommodate Turkey, even allying itself with Ankara in the Saadabad (1936) and Baghdad Pacts and increasing cooperation in all fields, including the Kurdish issue. Indeed, up until the Gulf crisis in 1990 Turkey enjoyed close relations with Iraq, stronger than with any other Arab country. The opposite was true for Syria. Like Iraq, Syria was weaker than Turkey, but it nevertheless attempted to challenge the status quo from time to time—such as encouraging a proxy war on the border through the Turkish Kurds.

Nonetheless, the balance of power between Turkey and the other two countries remained essentially the same, until the eruption of the Gulf crisis in 1990. From that point on, Iraq was increasingly concerned with possible Turkish territorial claims. The territorial issue was further complicated by the other, closely related, disagreement between Syria and Iraq, on one side, and Turkey on the other, regarding water sharing. Both disputes are discussed at length below. What should be emphasized, however, is that once they flared up, the two Ba'thi regimes in Damascus and Baghdad attempted to give them an all-Arab flavor and to turn them into bones of contention between Turkey and the Arabs.

Another issue that concerned all Arab countries without exception, at least on the emotional–ideological level, was Turkey's recognition of the state of Israel and its position on the Palestinian issue. Turkey's behavior was perceived as a betrayal of the Arabs, by joining hands with their archenemy, Israel. As one commentator put it:

not only did Turkey not content itself with the passive crime of alienating itself from the problem of Palestinian Arabs, but it took one active step further by recognizing Israel. It then took another active step in helping it survive and consolidate itself, and another hostile one [against the Arabs] by attempting to break the economic embargo that the Arabs had imposed on Israel. Thus, it was the only state [in the world?] which had interfered in a war which was still going on between the Arabs and Israel, by taking the Israeli side.[14]

This move was sometimes explained as a kind of Turkish reprisal against the Arabs' "betrayal" of it during World War I, and at other times as pure anti-Arabism. In fact, Turkey's recognition of Israel and its "abandonment" of the Palestinian cause was compared adversely with "the Ottoman state" (*dawla*), which had been wholly opposed to Zionism and never agreed in any way that Palestine should be turned into a national home or a state for the Jews. This was especially true of Sultan Abdül Hamid II (1876–1909), who rejected the Zionist project in spite of Theodor Herzl's attempts to "seduce" him "by proposing huge financial support to rescue the Ottoman state from the financial crisis from which it suffered." Abdül Hamid insisted that he would never give up "one inch" of the land that belonged to the "Muslim nation," and was quoted after his deposal as saying (quite anachronistically) that he refused "to stain the Ottoman state and the Muslim World with this eternal disgrace by allowing them [the Jews] to establish a Jewish State in the holy land."[15]

Najda Fathi Safwat, the Iraqi consul to Turkey in the years 1956–58 and author of the aforementioned quotation, asserted that "Turkey's recognition of Israel has remained a painful memory in the annals of the Arab–Turkish relations and a stumbling block before a real development of these relations." He further compared Turkey's relations with the Arabs and Israel to a kind of balance, "whose scales cannot go up simultaneously," that is, Turkey could not have good relations with Israel and the Arab countries at one and the same time. Rather, it should choose between the two, for the Arabs would continue to consider "Turkey's relations with Israel as the real touchstone for Turkey's stance toward the Arabs."[16]

This is indeed the crux of the matter. To what extent does this metaphor of scales correspond to reality, and to what extent is it merely a myth? Although there is some truth in it, the reality is much more nuanced and complicated, and Israel was undoubtedly only one of many factors influencing the relations between Turkey and the Arab states. It is interesting to note, first, that no Arab country broke off relations with Turkey after its recognition of Israel, whereas Egypt did so after Ankara recognized Syria in 1961. Second, Baghdad even signed a pact with Ankara without conditioning it on the latter's severing relations with Israel. Similarly, when Ankara, from the mid-1960s onward, sought to strengthen relations with the Arab countries, they welcomed this without conditioning it on cutting off relations with Israel. This is not to say, of course, that they did not try to make Ankara do so, in the belief that they could use "the weapon of material enticement to apply strong pressures on Turkey to cut its relations with Israel."[17] In any case, this weapon had lost much of its effectiveness following the peace agreement between Egypt and Israel in 1979, as Safwat himself lamented: "If Turkey's stance on the Palestinian issue is not satisfactory to Arab countries what do they wish Turkey to do? Do they wish it to fight on the Arabs' side against Israel or do they wish it to be more Arab than the Arabs themselves when it perceives an Arab state reaching understanding with Israel and exchanging relations with it?"[18]

Another area of friction was Turkey's Western orientation. Turkey's eagerness to belong to the West, or to be considered Western, was interpreted at best as a Turkish attempt to alienate itself from the Arabs, and at worst as out-and-out anti-Arabism. Conceding that "Westernism" had been "a divisive factor" between Turkey and the Arabs, the head of the Middle East department at the University of Ankara suggested that "a rapprochement between Turkey and the Arab Middle East could take place only when there was a "fissure ... in its relations with the West."[19]

In addition to the cultural aspects referred to above, Westernism touched on various other domains, such as the political system, foreign policy orientation and alliances, and ideology. In theory, the different political systems in Turkey and the Arab states could have been a source of friction between them. Yet even though many Arab countries may have felt threatened by the spillover effects of a democratic regime to the north, the issue was too sensitive to be aired publicly. It was only in the 1990s, when concern about "Turkey's designs" in the Middle East increased significantly, that Turkey's "fake" democracy came under attack from Arab commentators. The urge to criticize Turkey on this point was nourished by Ankara's alignment with Israel and the two countries' portrayal of themselves as the only democracies in the Middle East.

Much more serious, in the view of some Arab states, was Turkey's pro-Western orientation and alliances. For one thing, Turkey's attempts to ally itself with the West were considered by the Arabs (on Ankara's own admission) to be the main motive in its recognition of Israel.[20] For another, Turkey's alliance with the West and its membership of NATO in 1951 came at a time when certain Arab states, in particular Egypt, were at loggerheads with Western imperialism, in the form of Britain. Thus Turkey's Western orientation became the major cause of friction with Egypt during the 1950s and early 1960s. Accordingly, Egypt rejected the plans proposed by the United States and Britain in 1951–52 to establish a regional defense scheme that was to include the United States, Britain, France, and Turkey.[21] These were rejected by the other Arab states as well and came to nought.[22] The main explanation for this failure was Egypt's refusal to join as long as Britain continued to occupy the Suez base.[23] In retrospect, however, it is possible that other motives were involved; including suspicions and fears regarding Turkey's real intentions, nourished by centuries of Ottoman rule, as well as the latent rivalry between Turkey and Egypt—the two leading states in the Middle East.

Egypt's fierce opposition to the Baghdad Pact was yet another facet of these fears and rivalries. In addition to stirring up intra-Arab competition, the Pact brought about the polarization of the Arab world during the 1950s, a process that Turkey inevitably became part of. Perhaps not surprisingly, during the Suez War of 1956 Egypt accused Turkey of participating in the tripartite hostilities against it, on the grounds that Ankara was a comember with Britain in the Baghdad Pact.[24] Another aspect of this polarization was, of course, the ideological–political stance of the Arab countries toward the two superpowers, with Iraq and Egypt representing the two poles. While Iraq belonged to the Western camp (Britain, the United States) until the late 1950s, Egypt belonged to the Eastern camp (the Soviet Union) until the early 1970s. These roles were reversed in the early 1970s: Egypt moved increasingly toward the Western/American camp, and Iraq gravitated toward the Soviet Union/Eastern one.

The fact that Turkey and Iraq, and then Turkey and Egypt, belonged to the same Western camp at least for a certain period, demonstrated that Turkey's Westernism could not automatically be interpreted as anti-Arabism.

Since Turkey's Westernism was perceived to be a main stumbling block in the development of strong relations between the Arab states and Ankara, the need arose on both sides, especially during the 1970s, to define the areas that could facilitate their rapprochement. A Turkish analyst defined three such areas as anti-Westernism, Islam, and economic interests.[25] The problematic nature of the first two has already been referred to, and according to many Arab analysts the economic factor was anyway the most important, or even "the decisive one in Turkish–Arab relations."[26] In practice, the economic factor has played two roles: enhancing political relations with Turkey, and serving as a means of pressurizing Ankara to adopt pro-Arab positions, especially in regard to the Arab–Israeli conflict. As one Arab observer put it: "Inasmuch as Turkey's economic relations with the Arabs are vital and important, they could be used politically to pressurize Turkey with a view to moving it to adopt balanced policies towards its Arab neighbors."[27] Potent as the economic factor could have been, it nevertheless carried its own limitations and weaknesses: it was quite limited in time and scope; it was most effective only when accompanied by other political factors or developments; and it threw into relief the imbalance between Turkey and the Arab states, something that Ankara tried to redress.

It is well established that economic relations between Turkey and the Arab states improved significantly during the 1970s, when Turkey's economic crisis coincided with the world oil crisis, which turned oil into the key element in the relationship.[28] Yet it must be stressed that, important as they were, these relations were limited to only three Arab oil states: Saudi Arabia, Libya, and Iraq (until 1991, when the United Arab Emirates (UAE) took Iraq's place). In 1992, for example, 91 percent of Turkish imports from the entire Arab world originated from these three states. Similarly, 99.3 percent of Turkish workers in Arab countries were based in Libya, Saudi Arabia, and the UAE.[29] However, since oil was the key to these relations, they were subject to the fluctuations and changes of the world oil market. Hence, when in oversupply, oil lost its effectiveness as a political weapon against Turkey. Also, while Arab countries could use the oil weapon against Turkey until the end of the 1980s, after the Gulf crisis Turkey could use it in a different way against one of them—Iraq—by closing the twin oil pipelines crossing its territory. In addition, as we shall see, Turkey's dependence on oil from Arab countries induced it to try and balance the situation from the mid-1980s by developing a "strategic fluid" or weapon of its own—water.[30]

An Arab analyst once described the period that followed the 1973 War between Israel and the Arabs as the Arabs' "era of power" *vis-à-vis* Turkey. This was made possible by "the rise of the Arabs as an economic power," a status based mainly on oil, which gave them worldwide clout.[31] Turkey's recognition, in June 1975, of the PLO as the sole legitimate representative of the Palestinian people, and its vote in November of the same year in favor of the UN resolution equating Zionism with racism, were seen as the "fruit" of "this era of power." However, this era was quite short-lived, lasting only one decade. Indeed, in analyzing the economic factor it should be borne in mind that it was effective because it coincided with other internal and external developments that made Turkey vulnerable or more amenable to such pressure.

Internally, some ideological changes began to be apparent, most importantly the rise of the pro-Islamic trend, which advocated, among other things, the revival of political Islam in Turkey and closer ties with the Muslim Arab world.[32] Externally, the Cyprus crisis, which reached its height with the Turkish occupation of the northern part of the island in July 1974, came to be regarded by most Arab and non-Arab analysts as a major watershed in Turkish foreign policy. The subsequent rebuff by the West and the arms embargo by the United States encouraged Turkey to strengthen its relations with the Arab East, by attempting, among other things, to win the support of Arab states on the Cyprus issue at the United Nations (see chapter 2). (It may be observed that the West's rebuff of Turkey in the 1990s would at this later time and context lead Turkey to strengthen its relations with Israel to the level of alignment.) By the mid-1980s, this combination of internal economic and ideological pressures and external constraints began to give way to new developments, which once again changed the balance of power between Turkey and the Arabs.

Domestically, the establishment of the PKK and its protracted fight against the central government from 1984, persuaded the political Left in Turkey to gradually modify its pro-Arab stance—and to approve Turkey's relations with Israel. This came about because of Syria's backing for the PKK and the PKK's own links with the PLO. According to Turkish security officials, these ties had been established at the end of 1979 through a PLO official in Ankara. Subsequently, the PKK transferred a considerable number of its fighters as well as its leadership to Palestinian camps located in Lebanon. There, the PKK was able to receive professional training, and even participate in PLO-armed operations against Israel. This lasted until June 1982, when Israel destroyed a number of guerrilla training camps during its massive military offensive against Palestinian and Syrian forces. Approximately two dozen PKK personnel were killed in the attacks. Subsequently, Syria permitted the PKK to train in Syrian territory.[33] The involvement of Syria and the PLO in what Ankara considered as its internal affairs, cooled relations with the PLO and created a new area of friction with Syria.

Externally, after the mid-1980s the oil weapon was no longer available because of global changes in the oil market. The Cyprus issue, while not solved, began to subside and in any case Turkey gave up hoping that the United Nations would settle the dispute in its favor, in which case the Arab vote would have been critical. The Arab–Israeli conflict, which on one level was a major cause of contention between Turkey and the Arab states, lost much of its salience, both because of the signing of the peace agreement between Egypt and Israel in March 1979 and the rise of another conflict, the Iraq–Iran War, which lasted from 1980 to 1988. Taken together, these developments put an end to the Arabs' era of power and ushered in a new era from 1990, one in which Turkey was increasingly seen by the Arabs as a direct threat. It must be stressed that initially these threat perceptions were not related to the Turkey–Israel relationship, even though by early 1990 some Arab writers were pointing to the "collusion" of these two states against the Arabs.

## The "Sick Man" and the "Wealthy Man": Turkish–Arab Relations in the 1990s

In a conference held in May 1991 on "Turkey's relations with the Arab East in the 1990s," the Arab participants pointed to the Arabs' "extreme weakness" vis-à-vis Turkey, which turned them into the "sick man" of the region, a stigma once associated with the Ottoman Empire.[34] Conversely, Turkey's position was likened, in another conference, to "a man who woke up one morning and found himself in a possession of a big treasure."[35] These images of the "sick man" and the "wealthy man" symbolized the exchange of roles between Turkey and the Arabs, or at least the changed perceptions of the Arabs in the 1990s compared to the 1970s. In fact, much Arab comment during the 1990s emphasized this imbalance, the economic, strategic, and political threat emanating from Turkey and the different ways of coping with the situation. What, then, influenced this changed perception? How much of it was myth, and how much reality?

Arab perceptions were related to diverse regional and international developments as well as to Turkey's direct links with certain states, and together these put into relief its new role in the region. For portions of the Arab world and particularly Iraq and Syria, the end of the Cold War signified the loss of a patron—the Soviet Union—and the disappearance of a superpower that could restrain other regional and international powers. The 1991 Gulf War brought to the surface the severe divisions among the Arab states, thus affecting negatively the balance of power between them and their non-Arab neighbors. Finally, George Bush's newly proclaimed New World Order and the Arab–Israeli peace process legitimized, as it were, the encroachment of non-Arab players on the Arabs' sphere of influence.

The Arabs' loss appeared to be Turkey's gain. The end of the Cold War and the collapse of the Soviet Union removed an immediate and persistent security threat from Turkey, and opened up new horizons in Central Asia and the Balkans. The Gulf War reinstated Turkey's importance in the eyes of the West and laid open northern Iraq to Turkish incursion, or at least placed it within its sphere of influence. In Arab perceptions, the New World Order assigned Turkey the role of the region's policeman, while the Arab–Israeli peace process removed the last obstacles to Turkey's relations with Israel.

Besides these regional and international developments, other issues concerned Turkey and certain Arab countries more directly, the most important of which was water. This issue became acute during the 1990s for various socioeconomic and political reasons, and raised fears among many Arab states, and not only the two directly concerned— Syria and Iraq. Put bluntly, the fear was that the Arabs' oil weapon would be overwhelmed by Turkey's water weapon. The cause of this concern was two Turkish projects, "the peace pipeline" and the GAP, with its massive dams and irrigation.

In mid-1987, Turkish Prime Minister Turgut Özal proposed during a visit to Damascus the concept of "peace water" (*Barış suyu projesi* in Turkish, *miyah al-salam* in Arabic), or the "peace pipelines" (*anabib al-salam*) for selling water to eight Arab countries. The project envisaged establishing two water pipelines to carry the surplus from the Seyhan and Ceyhan rivers. The western pipeline was to provide water to Syria and Jordan, and the Gulf pipeline to the six Arab countries of the Gulf (except Iraq). The idea of the peace pipeline was proposed to Özal by the director general of the Israeli Foreign Ministry, Abraham Tamir, who held a series of discreet talks in Ankara in 1986–88, which included different strategic, economic, and political issues. Arab objections to Israel's participation in the plan led Turkey to exclude it—while still retaining the name "peace pipelines." Even so, the Arab states rejected the project out of hand.[36] A second attempt in 1991 to revive the project also met with failure.

There are a number of explanations for the rejection, twice over, of this project, which theoretically could solve the acute water problems of these countries. One was that, economically speaking, the project was too expensive for the countries concerned to be worthwhile. Another was that dependence on Turkish water would hinder or slow down progress in their own national projects for self-sufficiency, such as desalinization or the pumping of ground water.[37] It seems, however, that the weightier reason was that such a project would put Arab states at Turkey's mercy. The threefold fear was that it would enhance Turkey's regional weight at the expense of the Arabs, threaten "Arab national security" (*al-amn al-Qawmi al-'Arabi*) by providing Turkey with a strategic asset, and, if Israel were included, would bring about the collusion of these two states against the Arabs. Thus it was maintained that the project represented "a strategic threat to all the countries of the region," as it would bind them economically and strategically to Turkey's vital interests, and would be a "new economic imperialist project" aimed at exchanging the "surplus of oil with the deficit of water."[38] Another claim was that the inclusion of Turkey in any vital Arab project, such as water energy or the defense industry, "might "jeopardize the economic basis of the hope for Pan-Arab regional system."[39]

Over time, regional energy and electricity projects that included Turkish participation were established. However, even those Arab parties who benefited from these projects rejected the concept of the peace pipeline. One commentator explained that the pipeline would cause a "problem of dependence" that could not be balanced, "since the Arab partners in the project would find themselves depending on Turkey more than Turkey would depend on them."[40] Turkey's closure of the Iraq oil pipeline from 1990 to 1996 during the Gulf crisis was given as a case in point, demonstrating Ankara's ability to use the "water weapon" as a means of pressurizing Arab countries "in the service of Turkish, American and Western interests." Little wonder, then, that those Arab or Turkish circles which opposed the project turned its name from the "peace pipelines" into the "dream pipelines" (*anabib al-ahlam*). Indeed, so far the project has remained a mere dream.[41]

Much more realistic and threatening was the GAP project, which Turkey began developing in the late 1970s. The project envisaged the damming of the Euphrates with 14 dams with a view to generating energy and irrigating new vast lands in southeastern Turkey.[42] Here the fear was, first, that Turkey would become an economic powerhouse or "water giant," with less and less incentive to pursue economic relations with Arab countries; second, that it would marginalize even further the agriculture in Arab countries, by turning Turkey into the main source of food in the region; and third, worst of all, that it would enable Turkey to control the supply of water to its two neighbors, Syria and Iraq. When Turkey halted the flow of the Euphrates to Syria and Iraq for one month in January 1990, in order to fill the giant Atatürk dam, this substantiated their fears. One analyst went as far as to describe it "an act of war," carried out at a time when the two countries affected were unable to respond—Iraq had just come out of its war with Iran and was unable to take on a new confrontation, and the deep rift between Iraq and

Syria precluded their coordinating a response to Turkey.[43] Echoing, as it were, these fears Prime Minister Özal stated: "They [Iraq and Syria] would now be doing their utmost to prevent us from building this dam had we not started its construction during this period [the war]."[44] What really alarmed Syria and Iraq was that Turkey took this action unilaterally,[45] without consulting them, and that they were without recourse. Indeed, the incident also brought to the fore a crucial problem—just how to share the water—and up till today this has remained the main bone of contention between Turkey and both Syria and Iraq.[46]

It is beyond the scope of this book to enter into details of this dispute. Suffice to say that it had far-reaching political and strategic ramifications, most important of which was Syria's escalation of its support of the PKK's war against Turkey, to try and force a solution to the water problem. Another outcome is the tendency to give this incident an all-Arab slant by linking it to the Arab–Israeli conflict, among other issues. It was alleged that the Turkish action deliberately intersected with the Arab–Israeli conflict, for three reasons: water issues had been at the heart of the Arab–Israeli conflict "in the last four decades"; engaging "the Arabs or part of them" in the water issue would distract their attention from the main issue of the Arab–Israeli conflict; and dissipating the Arabs' energies on one front, Turkey, was likely to impact negatively on the other front, Israel. Accordingly, some opinion leaders called on the Arab states to adopt a unified collective stand against Turkey by using economic relations to try to force it to take more balanced positions, since it was asserted that "Turkey could not be the friend of some Arabs and the enemy of others."[47]

The water issue was but part of the overall Arab perception of the strategic threat presented by Turkey in the 1990s,[48] a threat that they felt was intensified as a result of other concurrent regional and international developments, and by the new role in which Turkey cast itself, which took full advantage of these developments. This new role was taking a leading part in the New World Order, together with the revival of old imperial dreams and the establishment of "Greater Turkey." One commentator held that "the rulers of Ankara are dreaming of reviving the Turkish empire . . . [erecting it] on the debris of the Communist empire in Asia" [referring to Turkish speaking Central Asian states] and by "subjecting the Muslim minorities in Eastern Europe" [the Balkans].[49] Another opined that Ankara's new strategy since 1990 was aimed at turning Turkey into "a state of the first order in the region," by assuming the leadership in a region extending "from the Balkan to the borders of China and from the Black Sea to North Africa." This was made possible, he said, by the collapse of the Soviet Union and Yugoslavia; the establishment of six Muslim states in Central Asia; the breakdown (*inhiyar*) of Iraq and the fragmentation in the Arab world. In short, it was intended to endow Turkey with the role of America's "policeman in the region."[50] Others spoke of a "new Turkish imperialism," "neo-Ottomanism," "Pan-Turanism" [the ideology of a unified state of Turkic nations], or the formation of the "Turkish bloc" or a Turkish "world" consisting of Turkey and the Turkish states of Central Asia, which together approximate to the size of the Arab world. This development, it was feared, was likely to increase the rivalry between these two "worlds" and upset the balance of power in the region.[51]

Indeed, what disturbed many Arab officials and analysts most, was not so much Turkey's aspirations in Central Asia or the Balkans as its "return" to the Middle East and its perceived ambitions there. Of special concern were Ankara's pretensions to present itself as a model of a democratic and secular state that Arab and Muslim countries could emulate, and to serve as a bridge between East and West.

Nor was Turkey's proposal to play a facilitating role in the peace talks between the Arab states and Israel, after the Madrid Conference in 1991, any more welcome to the Arabs. Theoretically, Turkey could have been an ideal mediator, because it had ties with both parties, was part of the region and not an outsider, and represented a multicultural identity of both Western and Eastern/Islamic, tendencies. In practice, however, the Arab partners concerned were adamantly opposed to granting Turkey any such role,[52] either because they were suspicious of its pro-Israeli bias and Western leanings, or because they did not want to strengthen its standing in the region, or were fearful of two rivals aligning against them.

The Arabs equally rebuffed Turkey's attempts to participate in the new security system (*nizam amni*) or regional system (*nizam iqlimi*) that was envisaged after the Gulf War. In fact, even those who advocated strengthening relations with Turkey on all levels were wary of its inclusion in any regional security system. The arguments against this were that non-Arab countries, such as Turkey or Iran (or Israel), should not be allowed to use the "security and strategic vacuum" created in the Arab homeland after the Gulf War, "to interfere in one way or another in Arab security arrangements," and that the security system should remain a purely Arab one. Furthermore, as the Arabs were caught in a weak position that had been further exacerbated by the Gulf War, they were now hardly able to defend themselves against the encroachment of non-Arabs. Hence, only after uniting their forces could they allow non-Arabs to join the system.[53]

Closely related to this was the reasoning that any new regional Middle Eastern system (*sharq awsatiyya*) that included non-Arabs would not benefit the Arabs themselves in any way, but would rather put them at a disadvantage, since it would "leave the cards in the hands of other parties which are hostile to the Arabs." Such a system, it was maintained, would neither stop Turkey from diverting water from Syria and Iraq, nor prevent Israel from attacking Arab countries.[54] Another implied objection to Turkey's inclusion was its membership of NATO—the only Middle East state to belong—and its perceived loyalty to this military pact, which turned Turkey into the Western-American logistical base in the region. By joining NATO, Turkey was felt to have demonstrated its ultimate preference for "the Atlantic alternative" over a "Muslim Middle Eastern" association.[55] Above all, there was fear of Turkey's growing military capabilities, which were enhanced significantly after the 1991 Gulf War, making it the second power in NATO after the United States.

Thus, after having suffered a strategic crisis because of the end of the Cold War, Turkey suddenly assumed not only a leading position in the region, but also that of a patron.[56] Some argued that this pushed the Turkish military into taking a leading strategic role, a tendency that was buttressed by "the Turkish army's complex of power which made it willing to fulfill any military mission outside the borders of Turkey."[57] All these concerns made Turkey appear more of a strategic threat than a partner in any regional security system—which in any case never materialized. In fact, this rebuff was a replay of a similar move in the early 1950s. Interestingly, the 1955 Baghdad Pact was still considered to have been a mistake, precisely because it allowed the inclusion of marginal (*hamishi*) states in the Arab regional system.[58] Turkey was thus not only unwelcome as a strategic partner in the Arab system, but was increasingly viewed as an immediate and direct threat to Arab security. Ankara was perceived as bent on "harming the Arabs" by escalating its stands against Syria and Iraq, "especially at a time when the Arab system was in its weakest point." It was accused of interfering in Arab internal affairs, in particular on the issues of water and minorities, as well as supporting the partitioning of Iraq.[59] The intention behind such activities, it was alleged, was to "escalate the problems with the Arab countries with a view to exhausting their forces," thereby distracting their attention from the real issues of Arab destiny and weakening their capabilities to face "the real threats which prevent them from attaining their lofty goals."[60] In summing up, it should be stressed that (a) Arab anxieties regarding Turkey's "expansionist" role in the region predated its alignment with Israel; and (b) the Arab rejection of any strategic partnership with Turkey also preceded the alignment, and might even have contributed to Ankara's decision to upgrade its relations with Israel.

## The Turkish–Israeli Alignment—The Baghdad Pact Redux?

The February 1996 agreement between Turkey and Israel came as a shock to many Arab states. Some even termed it "the 1996 Baghdad Pact," betraying their fears of this "new pact." These "political and security fears," it was observed, engulfed Arab capitals in general, and those that stood to suffer its negative impact in particular.[61] Many Arab politicians and commentators regarded the agreement and its consequences as a quantitative change in the triangle of Arab–Turkish–Israeli relations. First, Turkey appeared to have abandoned its traditional policy of balancing the Arabs against Israel in favor of a clear-cut alliance with the latter. Second, although the two countries were known to have had different military and security cooperation agreements in the past, these had never reached such a scope and depth, or attracted such wide publicity, as the February 1996 agreement; the main restraints on Ankara had, in fact, been precisely its consideration for Arab sensitivities. Third, the alignment both reflected the weakened status of the Arab world *vis-à-vis* the two other sides of the traditional triangle and took it even further, so that the Arabs now had to contend with two non-Arab forces acting, as it were, in unison against them rather than acting separately.

Herein indeed lies the big difference between the Baghdad Pact of 1955 and the Turkish–Israeli alignment of 1996. While in 1955 Israel was excluded from the Pact,[62] in 1996 it became the main partner with Turkey. In 1955 the Arab states opposed to the Pact could count on Soviet rivalry with the West to thwart, or at least to significantly weaken, the agreement, but in 1996 no such option existed. Because of the American unipolar system that developed after the Gulf War, it was doubly difficult to thwart the alignment. As one commentator said, Washington "relies on its bilateral ties with Arab governments and the dependence of some of them on its protection to ensure that they do not oppose its regional policies."[63] Furthermore, the 1955 Pact was largely defensive in nature, aimed as it was against the inroads of the Soviet Union in the region, while that of 1996 seemed to have the potential of becoming offensive, at least in the view of such countries as

Syria and Iraq. For Iraq, this was indeed the key difference: from being a partner in an alignment, it had now become a potential target.

Invoking the Baghdad Pact had yet another aim: sending a message to the Turkish government that the alignment would collapse in the same way as the Baghdad Pact had, and that any such agreement forged at the expense of the Arabs was doomed to failure. However, futurology apart, two points should be stressed: first, the Baghdad Pact was not designed against one common threat, but against several—Turkey against the Soviet Union, Pakistan against India, and Iraq against Nasserism—a structure that had seriously weakened the alliance. Second, the Pact collapsed not because of differences on security or foreign relations issues between its members, but because of domestic developments in one of them—the fall of the monarchy in Iraq in 1958 and its consequences.

Speaking on the significance of the alignment, Syria's Vice President 'Abd al-Halim Khaddam, described it as "the greatest threat to the Arabs since 1948," giving Israel and Turkey "a free hand in the region under US cover."[64] Indeed, the threat was perceived on several levels— ideological, political, and strategic. On the ideological level, it was the first time in modern history that a Muslim country had *openly* allied itself with the Jewish state. This was all the more disturbing because Islam should have served as a fundamental obstacle to such an event. For the Syrian leadership, an alliance between its Muslim neighbor to the north and the Jewish state was particularly galling. Syrian Foreign Minister Faruq al-Shar' asked: "How can those who believe that secularism is against religion and want a non-religious Turkey agree to set up a military alliance with a state ruled by fanatics?"[65]

Accordingly, there was a need to delegitimize the Israeli–Turkish relationship. One way to do so was to blame it on the rich Jews of Turkey, the *dönme* (Jews who had ostensibly converted to Islam but secretly practiced Judaism).[66] No less troubling was that it was an alignment between two non-Arab countries, hence its perceived aggressive character against the Arabs as a whole. Most disturbing of all was that it was between the two militarily strongest states in the region, with grave strategic implications for individual Arab countries and for the Arab world in general.

As a threat to the Arab collective, the alignment seemed to have implications in three areas: Arab security, the balance of power in the region, and the Arab–Israeli peace process. The "grave dangers" to Arab national security (*al-amn al-qawmi al-'Arabi*) derived from the "crisis" that this was undergoing due "to Arab fragmentation, the upsetting [of the balance of power] and the exposure (*inkishaf*) to pressures from

regional and international forces." Hence the fear that the Turkish–
Israeli alignment would replace the "Arab regional system" by a larger
one—"the Middle East system" (*sharq awsatiyya*)—in which the two
non-Arab states would play the leading role, supported by the United
States,[67] while the Arab states would be confined to a marginal or a subordinate role.[68] Worse, the new alignment was bound to upset the balance of power in the region, by "setting into motion the process of
polarization and axis-building," like that of the 1950s; by according
Turkey a leading regional role that might encourage it "to revive the
Turkish empire" in the Middle East; and by enabling Israel to "maintain
its absolute military superiority" over the Arabs through its "monopoly
of the nuclear weapon."[69] Israel's enhanced military position, it was
argued, was likely to have "negative effects" on the peace process with
the Arabs, because the Jewish state would be less inclined to make "any
concessions" to them, but would rather attempt "to pressurize the Arabs
in the peace negotiations and impose its conditions for peace by force."[70]

Among the Arab states, Egypt, Iraq, and Syria felt especially threatened
by the alignment and led the opposition to it. Although invited to join the
alignment or at least its security aspects, Egypt, as on past occasions (1952,
1988)[71] was extremely reluctant to do so.[72] Egypt's reaction was probably
motivated by its latent historical rivalry with Turkey and by fears that
Ankara was intruding on its sphere of influence in the Mediterranean.[73]
Regarding itself as the guardian of Arab security, Egypt was concerned by
the strategic hegemony that the alignment might confer on Turkey and
Israel over Arab states. Ever present, too, were intra-Arab rivalries and animosities, such as Cairo's anger at Amman's "independent" policy of joining
the alignment and its futile attempts to prevent this.

Compared to Egypt, the threat to Iraq appeared to be much more
tangible and immediate. A series of developments in the bilateral sphere
added to Baghdad's anxieties. These were Ankara's month-long blocking of water flow to Iraq (and Syria), and its closure of the Iraqi oil
pipelines in 1990 after Iraq's occupation of Kuwait; Turkey's backing of
the anti-Iraq alliance during the 1991 Gulf War by allowing its bases to
be used for attacks on Iraq, and for surveillance on northern Iraq after
the war; the support, albeit half-hearted, given by Ankara to the Iraqi
Kurds after the establishment of their semiautonomous zone in northern Iraq in 1992; and the occasional incursions of the Turkish army into
Iraqi Kurdistan to fight the Turkish–Kurdish PKK.[74]

These developments were coupled with occasional hints by Turkish
officials about Turkey's "historical rights" to the Vilayet of Mosul area.
President Özal himself considered having the Mosul and Kirkuk areas

occupied by the TAF. (Chief of Staff Necip Torumtay, who disagreed with the plan, resigned in protest.[75]) For Iraq, Turkey's interest in Mosul signified a drastic change, one that could lead to Ankara's encroachment on Iraq's sovereignty and even open the way to a revival of its historical demands on the Mosul region. The alignment thus appeared to have a direct bearing on Iraq in three areas: enhancing Turkey's military superiority over Iraq, which could be used to realize what Baghdad perceived as Ankara's latent ambitions on Mosul; allowing Israel virtually direct access to Iraq by facilitating different forms of surveillance, or even attacks, such as that on the Osiris nuclear reactor in 1981 (which was carried out through the airspace of Jordan and Saudi Arabia); and finally, establishing a tripartite Turkish–Israeli–Kurdish anti-Iraq axis, on the lines of the tacit one that had existed between Iran, Israel, and the Kurds from the mid-1960s to the mid-1970s.

Syria's situation was the most difficult of all, because the alignment appeared to impact it on both military and political levels. Militarily speaking, Syria feared the scenario of a pincer movement from north and south by the two strongest armies in the region. The fact that those two countries had for a long time controlled what Damascus regarded as Syrian territory—Hatay, now in Turkish hands and the Golan Heights, now in Israel's—only compounded Syria's concerns about the alignment. Syria's enmity at that time with its eastern neighbor, Iraq, and its strained relations with its southern neighbor and partner to the Israeli–Turkish alignment, Jordan, further exacerbated Damascus's sense of encirclement.[76] Politically, Syria again appeared to be the main casualty. Unlike the other two Arab partners in the Arab–Israeli peace process—the PLO and Jordan—which had made important progress by 1996, Syria lagged behind and remained stuck in the early stages of negotiations. Syria thus suspected that the alignment would further strengthen Israel's bargaining power in these negotiations, or discourage it altogether from moving forward in the peace process.[77]

## "The Smart, Strategic Way for Arab States to Handle Turkey"[78]

The Arab world's immediate reaction to the alignment was to try to convince Turkey to abandon it. These efforts were directed, quite naturally, at Turkey rather than Israel, since there was still a hope of persuading Ankara to change its mind. In addition, although some Arab papers portrayed Israel "as the only real beneficiary"[79] of the alignment, a closer reading reveals that the greater concern was the alignment's significance for Turkey and the leverage Ankara had now gained *vis-à-vis* the Arab world, and that there was less concern about its significance for Israel. It was clearly understood by Arab observers that while the alignment might have enhanced Israel's bargaining power, mainly in its negotiations with Syria, it had undoubtedly strengthened Turkey's strategic standing in regard to Iraq and Syria and even Egypt, thereby identifying Turkey as the greater and more immediate threat.

For many years, but especially since the 1990s, there has developed in the Arab world what may be called two approaches or schools of thought about the most appropriate way to address Turkey: the first preached conciliation and alignment; the second, containment and isolation. It must be emphasized that these schools of thought were by no means clearly defined, and that sometimes the views of both were expressed at one and the same time even by the same writer, politician, or government—illustrating the complexity of Turkish–Arab relations. The conciliation school believed in building bridges with Turkey and bringing it, as it were, back into the Arab fold. This would be achieved, among other things, by strengthening political, economic, and cultural relations, and stressing the common historical, religious, and cultural heritage. The need for both parties to change their negative historical images of the other was placed high on the agenda.

The most outspoken representative of this approach has been Saudi Prince Khalid bin Sultan bin 'Abd al-'Aziz, who published a lengthy article in the leading pan-Arab daily, *al-Hayat*, entitled "Friendship is Temporary; Enmity is Temporary [and only] Interests are Everlasting," in which he analyzed Arab–Turkish relations and proposed ways of managing them so that Israel would not "win another round" against the Arabs. Describing the Turkish–Israeli alignment as a "crisis," Ibn Sultan blamed the Arabs for "mishandling" it. After neglecting Turkey for years, believing it would stay on their side forever, they now accused it of "betrayal" and "treachery." The prince maintained that the Arabs failed to understand the complexities of Turkey's domestic situation and that it had a right to pursue its national interests, which in this case had dictated the "accord" with Israel. This accord, he pointed out, offered Turkey "a number of advantages," such as improving its military capabilities, which would enable it to put pressure on Syria and to have the upper hand with the PKK. Ibn Sultan then suggested better ways for coping with the situation:

1. The Arabs should be sensible and realistic, rather than impulsive and emotional; threatening or challenging Turkey would not serve any interest.

2. They should put mutual economic interests first in their relations and aim for full economic partnership in all spheres—agricultural, industrial, and commercial.

3. Cultural, social, and media cooperation should be equally important, including the elimination from textbooks of the mutually offensive references that shaped the ideas and opinions of the younger generation.

4. Gulf Arab states and their Islamic neighbors—Egypt, Syria, Turkey, and Pakistan—should come up with a joint defense plan and hold joint training exercises. As a member of NATO, Turkey could then play "a significant role" as a channel of communication between the region and the West.

Concluding on a more pessimistic note, the prince quoted the following saying: "Someone was asked how the glory of the Umayyads was lost. He replied: They drove away their friends, believing in their friendship and drew their enemies close, seeking to win their affection. And so they lost their friends while failing to win over their enemies."[80]

The other school of thought continued to stress the negative heritage of Kemalism and its three pillars of Westernism, secularism, and democracy. Ridiculing Turkey's democracy as a farce and a "democracy of tanks," its proponents maintained that Turkey could not present itself as a model for the Arabs.[81] Turkey's attempts to tie itself to the West were similarly ridiculed on account of their meager results. Indeed, Turkey's alliance with Israel was portrayed as part of its futile efforts to overcome once and for all its mental schizophrenia. One of the most vocal members of this school of thought was Najib al-Rayyis. In a lengthy article in *al-Nahar* he attacked the Turkish people for being "a fickle people in politics and language," "a boorish nation, unable to express feelings of friendliness and appreciation," racists especially against Arabs, schizophrenic in their relations between East and West, and driven by "Pact-o-mania," the most recent being that signed with Israel.[82] Losing confidence that secular Turkey would make a *volte-face* toward the Arabs or at least be more "balanced," Rayyis demanded the exclusion of Ankara from any regional security system and bringing collective Arab pressure to bear on Turkey to change its stance toward the Arabs.[83]

At the same time, however, differentiating between the "pro-Arab Muslim Turkish masses" and the ruling regime, especially the army, this school of thought called on these masses to come out against their government's policy. In short, it advocated driving a wedge between the Turkish people and their government, while emphasizing Islam as the most important bridge between the Arab and Turkish peoples. According to this view, the more Islamized the Turks became, the greater the possibility of strengthening the bonds between them and the Arab world. Accordingly, this view—and that of many Arab countries—pinned great hopes in the Welfare Party—True Path Party (Refah-Yol) coalition government that came to power in July 1996 and that was, for the first time in Turkish history, a government under Islamist leadership.[84] However, these hopes were quickly dashed because the government was short-lived, surviving for only 11 months, and because Necmettin Erbakan, the prime minister and head of the Islamist Welfare Party, failed to bring about the expected change in direction and even pushed the secularist–military establishment into further boosting Turkey's relations with Israel.[85]

Having failed to extract Turkey from the alignment, various Arab states attempted to use the *fait accompli* it presented to reap some benefits for themselves, or at least to minimize the damage. Thus Jordan sought to join the alignment to strengthen its position toward Iraq, Syria, and the Palestinians; Egypt, to enhance its role as a mediator between Turkey and the other Arab countries; Iraq, to mobilize all possible Arab support for its cause and break out of its isolation; and Syria, to reduce the Turkish threat to itself and lobby for Arab support for its position on the Arab–Israeli peace process, all of which demonstrated that the alignment had impact on inter-Arab relations.

Jordan's decision to take part, as an observer, in the Turkish–Israeli naval maneuvers held on January 7, 1998 incurred the wrath of certain Arab states, especially Egypt and Syria, which depicted it as a return to the 1955 Baghdad Pact. They further described it as "a conspiracy against Arab and Islamic countries," and "a blatant and aggressive act" seeking "to disturb regional security and stability, to return the region to the policy of alliances and axes and to provide facilities to the enemy of the Arabs and the Muslims."[86] Syria, which felt that the alignment was directed mainly against itself, saw in the Jordanian move an act of provocation against Damascus, and attempted to dissuade Amman by launching a propaganda campaign against it, among other things. Egypt, which itself had been invited to participate in the maneuvers but had refused to do so, also attempted to pressure Jordan not to join in, but without success. Yet this opposition clearly put the Jordanian government on the defensive with regard to its critics and opponents, both at home and in the Arab world at large.[87]

Defending the move, the Jordanian Foreign Minister Fayiz al-Tarawina asserted that Jordan was "invited by Turkey and not any other party [Israel]"; that the invitation had already been accepted by the outgoing government; that Jordan's participation was symbolic, as it sent only one observer; and, most important, that "these maneuvers are not against any party."[88] A more assertive tone was struck by Jordanian journalist Fahd al-Fanik, who had previously objected to Jordan's participation in the maneuvers, but, once the Syrian propaganda campaign was launched, started to counterattack. Blasting Syria for its anti-Jordan campaign, Fanik maintained that Jordan's "sin" of sending an observer paled against Syria's alliance with a non-Arab country—Iran—against Iraq [during the Iraq–Iran war] and its alliance with the United States [during the second Gulf War]. Ridiculing Syria's alarm calls, he said: "All of a sudden, this Jordanian officer appears on the scene to tip the balance in favor of the aggressors who are plotting to attack Syria."[89] In spite of Syrian and Egyptian pressure, Jordan continued to quietly carve a role for itself in the alignment, stressing, in the words of Fanik, that it was an independent and sovereign state and "nobody's protectorate," hence it had "the right to establish ties with Turkey or other countries in line with its interests."[90]

From the outset, Egypt attempted to don the mantle of the guardian of Arab security. Cairo used its relations with Ankara—significantly improved some time after the 1979 peace treaty between Egypt and Israel—to try and convince or pressure Turkey to abandon the new alignment, which, in Egypt's view, harmed Arab security.[91] However, its failure to break up the alignment moved Cairo to assume the role of mediator between Syria and Turkey. The first opportunity was at the Arab Summit of June 1996, where the Turkey–Israel alignment was on the agenda. While Syria sought to have the summit condemn the alignment, it was Egypt that pushed for a more moderate statement, calling only for Turkey to reconsider "the Pact" "in a way that preclude[d] any encroachment on the Arab countries," and expressing the hope that "traditional Arab–Turkish ties and mutual interests" would continue as before.[92] On the other hand, following the massing of Turkish troops along the Syrian border and extensive maneuvers by the Turkish army's second corps in border areas in May 1996, Egypt appealed to Turkey to halt the escalation of "anti-Syrian acts."[93] Egypt was to assume an even more active mediatory role in the crisis of October 1998 between Syria and Turkey. All in all, Egypt sought to keep open its own lines of communication with Turkey, while preventing an increase in tension between Damascus and Ankara.

Iraq, too, attempted to use the alignment for its own purposes, with three aims in mind. The first was to mobilize Arab support against the repeated incursions of the Turkish army into northern Iraq, which had the declared objective of fighting the Kurdish–Turkish PKK. Indeed, it was particularly after the Turkish incursion of May 1997 that Iraq started to sound the alarm about the alignment, blaming the whole idea on Israel and its model of a security zone in south Lebanon, and calling for a halt to the occupation of Arab territory. Second, Iraq hoped to bring about a rapprochement with its archenemy, Iran, and its long-standing rival, Syria. The reasoning was that the alignment endangered all three, hence the need to mend fences and unite forces against it. The third aim was to end Iraq's isolation in the Arab world and obtain the removal of the UN sanctions imposed on it after the invasion of Kuwait in August 1990. Here, the reasoning was that only with a free and strong Iraq was there a chance to counterbalance the Turkish–Israeli alignment. As one pro-Iraqi commentator put it: "the most effective move the Arab countries threatened by the Turkish-Israeli alliance can do to offset it is to rehabilitate Iraq and bring it back to the fold."[94]

The case of Iraq, best illustrates and even epitomizes the duality and ambivalence that prevailed in Arab–Turkish relations. The ambivalence arose from Iraq's increased dependence on Turkey, together with Baghdad's fears of a growing threat from Ankara. The oil–for–food deal initiated at the end of 1996 by the United Nations permitted the reopening of the Iraq–Turkey twin pipelines, making Turkey an official outlet for Iraq to the outside world. This, together with the tense relations with Jordan—Iraq's sole outlet for seven years—promised to turn Turkey into a formidable partner for Iraq. Indeed, economic relations have been on the ascendance ever since. Yet the closure of the twin pipelines since 1990, because of the Gulf crisis, served as a reminder of Iraq's vulnerability and its dependence on Turkish goodwill.

Parallel to the reopening of the oil pipelines were two developments that increased Iraq's anxieties: the Turkish army's incursions into Kurdistan and the deepening alignment between Turkey and Israel. The opposing trends of conciliation and containment go a long way to explain Baghdad's harsh rhetoric toward Turkey on the one hand, and its attempt to curry favor on the other. Thus Iraq launched a propaganda campaign against Turkey that was unprecedented in its intensity and harshness. The main themes that recurred in speeches and the media were Turkey's Western orientation; its policies in Iraqi Kurdistan; the water issue; the alignment with Israel; and Turkish domestic and foreign policies in general. In one of his speeches, President Saddam Hussein accused Turkey of doing everything "to keep the [Iraqi Kurdish] region outside the control of the Iraqi state," by hosting and aiding the armies of the United States, Britain, and France and by facilitating the task of Western and "Zionist spies" to "roam" in that part of Iraq. Speaking in the name of the Arabs, Saddam then warned against the conspiracy that he claimed was being hatched against Iraq and the Arabs, "by making Turkish policy clash with Arab interests." This policy, he said, "would lead to the building of relations of military cooperation with the Zionist entity, including air activities close to Iraq and Syria." Finally, he called on Turkey to rectify its mistakes toward the Arabs and Iraq and to build sound relationships with them instead.[95]

Iraq's sense of vulnerability and weakness in regard to Turkey was reflected in many newspaper articles, which attempted at the same time to appeal to Arab countries and to Iran. Warning about the "strategic partnership" between Turkey and Israel, a series of articles in al-Jumhuriyya, for example, maintained that its "main objective" was to prevent Iraq from breaking the blockade and to "force Arab states to submit to the regional Turkish–Zionist leadership and start the process of containing Iran." The danger emanating from this partnership was the strategic encirclement of the Arab states, especially Syria and Iraq, by turning them "into a new kind of desert," dependent on the United States for all their needs. In short, the overall aim was to antagonize all the Arab and Islamic states.[96] Other articles spoke of "a hundred years" of Turkish enmity toward the Arabs and evoked the Turanian dream of controlling not just the Arab region, but the Caucasus and Central Asia as well.[97]

At the same time, other articles sought to appeal to Turkey, calling on it to weigh the economic and other benefits it received from the Arab countries, especially Iraq, against the disillusion it reaped from the West—and to opt for the Arabs. There were only two alternatives: either the "Western lap" or a return to friendly relations with the Arab world.[98]

Iraq's warnings against Turkey touched a sensitive chord in many Arab states, as well as in Iran, and they were quick to condemn the Turkish incursions into Iraq and the alignment with Israel. Although a thaw in relations took place between Iraq and some of these countries, solidarity with Iraq was not translated into any tangible action capable of changing Turkish policies.

The Turkish–Syrian crisis of October 1998 can be taken as a case study for assessing the alignment, its impact on the Arab world, and the different reactions it aroused. During the first three weeks of October 1998, Turkey put pressure on Syria to end its support of the PKK and its leader, Abdullah Öcalan. Leading Turkish military and political figures threatened war, and backed up their warnings with a military build-up along the Turkish–Syrian border. The crisis ended with Syria's consent—for the first time in 16 years—to Turkish demands, including the expulsion of Öcalan from Damascus. Iran and Egypt played important mediating roles between the two parties, helping to defuse the crisis.[99]

Not surprisingly, Syria itself perceived this Turkish "renewal of threats" in the context of Ankara's military alliance with Israel. As one official pointed out: "Military alliances are generally formed against a particular party and Israel has left no room to doubt that it is forming and directing this alliance against Syria and Lebanon."[100] Interestingly, the Syrian reaction was conciliatory and low-keyed, "as Syria was determined to avoid hostilities and had not sent a single soldier to the border with Turkey."[101] Even the Syrian media kept quiet on the crisis. In addition, Syria sought to put the blame on Israel, so as not to antagonize Turkey unduly. Although Israel signaled its noninvolvement in the crisis,[102] Damascus continued to point to the alignment itself as the source of all evil. Propaganda aside, Syria seemed to have genuinely felt that Turkey's strong-handed policies were a direct outcome of the alignment.

Theoretically, the Turkish–Syrian crisis was the ideal moment for the formation of a counter-alliance. In fact, Syria was incapable of initiating such a move and may also have been unwilling, and its agreement to Egyptian and Iranian mediation efforts was evidence of a sober and realistic assessment both of its own power and that of Arab solidarity. Iraq, which feared that the crisis might have spillover effects on itself, and yet sought to use it to improve its credentials with Syria, vehemently attacked Turkey's move in its media, describing it as a threat not just to Syria and Iraq, but to Arab security as a whole. Furthermore, it accused Turkey of having devised "a multi-phased strategy," the aim of which was to "antagonize the Arabs" and "break ties with the Arab nation."[103] In addition, it claimed that the "alliance" sought "to turn the Turkish lands into a base for spying, and for terrorist and Zionist activity against the Arab nation," the ultimate goal of which was "to create more than one military, political and geographical belt of aggression to weaken the Arabs."[104] Meanwhile, Tariq 'Aziz, Iraq's deputy prime minister, declared Iraq's absolute solidarity with Syria.[105] But beyond these verbal attacks on Turkey and vows of solidarity with Syria, Iraq did little; the last thing it wanted was to antagonize Turkey. Accordingly, in the same breath Baghdad advised settling "the problems between any two neighborly countries ... through dialogue and understanding and not through threats," explaining that "advice and caution" should not be interpreted as "signs of weakness."[106] Indeed, the Iraqi case illustrates the yawning gap between rhetoric and politics, as well as the duality in the relationships between Turkey and certain Arab countries.

In contrast, Egypt, a potential leader of such a counter-alliance, opted for the mediatory role that had become customary under President Husni Mubarak. But this angered some radical Arab commentators, one of whom went as far as to accuse Egypt of trying to block the most effective step that could be taken to deter the Turkish–Israeli alliance, namely, "the formation of a counter-alliance comprising Syria, Iran and Iraq." Another, ridiculing Cairo for engaging in inconclusive diplomatic contacts and consultations in response to the threat, maintained that: "Turkey is massing troops on the Syrian border and all we (Arabs) do is consult."[107] Undeterred by such criticism, Cairo even sought to use the momentum of its newly assumed role of mediator to boost its bilateral relations with Ankara and bring about a "constructive rapprochement" between Turkey and the Arabs. President Mubarak came on a two-day visit to Turkey in early December 1998, which was described by *al-Ahram* as extremely successful and turning "a new page in Arab–Turkish ties." In addition to the bilateral economic agreements in various areas, the visit was said to have put "a final end to the stage of mutual suspicions between the Arabs and Turkey." While raising questions about Turkey's past behavior, an apologetic tone was not missing, as commentator Ibrahim al Nafi'i expressed: "Mubarak's achievements compensated for the shortcomings in Egypt's and the Arab world's foreign policy *vis-à-vis* Turkey over more than three quarters of a century, i.e. since the disintegration of the Ottoman empire, during which time Arabs and Turks either ignored each other or harbored mutual suspicions."[108] Setting aside Mubarak's aggrandizement, there is no doubt that the Turkish–Syrian crisis exposed Syria's great vulnerability as well as the Arab system's general weakness, and that this moved the Arab countries, especially Egypt, to court Turkey rather than form alliances against it.

To sum up this particular episode, then, the following conclusions may be drawn:

1. The alignment survived its first possible challenge from the Arab world and Iran; it did not collapse, and nor did the crisis trigger a counter-alliance.
2. Rather than weakening Turkey's position with regard to the Arabs, as they had repeatedly warned, the alignment strengthened Turkey even more: not only did Syria climb down over the PKK—the most

important card in its hand against Ankara—but other Arab states, and not just Egypt, began to court Turkey and attempt to mend fences with it.

3. It was ironic that the one seemingly effective weapon that Syria had against Ankara, the PKK, turned out to be a double-edged sword. Not only did the PKK threat become a *casus belli* for Turkey against Syria, but it was an important factor in further cementing the alignment between Turkey and Israel.

4. Relations between Turkey and Syria improved significantly following the episode, starting with the Adana agreement of October 20, 1998 in which Syria agreed to stop unconditionally any support to the PKK, continuing with the signing of a military cooperation agreement in June 2002 that spoke of future joint military exercises, and a number of subsequent high-level visits to each other's capitals.[109]

## The Special Case of the Palestinians

If there is one single issue that had an impact on Turkish–Israeli relations, it is that of the Palestinians. Theirs was a special case, which on the one hand attracted Turkey's genuine domestic affinity, solidarity, and identification with their cause, but on the other, provided the Arabs with their most effective tool for applying pressure on Turkey to disengage from Israel. As a result, it can be said that in the first two decades of the PLO's existence—from the mid-1960s to mid-1980s—the high points in Ankara's relations with the PLO were also the low points in its relations with Israel (hence the juxtaposition of Turkey's recognition of the PLO in 1975 with its pro-Arab vote on the UN resolution equating Zionism with racism). True, this development resulted from the different internal and external pressures at play in Turkey, but there is no doubt that sensitivities toward the Palestinians within the different strata of Turkish society also played an important role.

In any case, from the end of the 1980s onward this negative correlation began to change. Turkey's relations with the PLO no longer stood in the way of its desire to improve with Israel. In fact, Turkey now saw the two relationships as complementing one another. Accordingly, Turkey upgraded relations with both parties in 1988.[110] From the Israeli side, conciliatory moves toward the Palestinians eventually brought a flourishing of its relations with Turkey.

One of the initial factors accounting for the Turkish shift was its unhappiness with certain PLO policies—primarily its relations with the PKK, but also its position on Cyprus. The PLO, besides supporting the

Greek side on this issue, complained after the Gulf War about the double standard toward Turkey and Iraq, saying that while the international community did nothing to push Turkey out of northern Cyprus, they readily allied themselves against Iraq to oust it from Kuwait, a comparison that greatly alarmed Turkey.[111]

The 1993 Oslo Agreement between Israel and the PLO brought about a quantum leap in relations between Turkey and Israel. Certainly, Turkey was only one of many countries to which the agreement afforded this opportunity. But in its case, the agreement provided both an umbrella and a shield against the constant attacks that it had betrayed the Palestinian cause. This positive correlation could also work the other way round: because there are no antagonistic relations between Turkey and the Palestinians, such as existed with Syria, Ankara could use its alignment with Jerusalem as a means of mediating between Israel and the Palestinians.[112]

The second intifada between the Palestinians and Israel, which erupted in September 2000, provided an important test of the strength of Turkish–Israeli relations and of Ankara's ability to draw a clear line between its common strategic interests with Israel and its emotional identification with the Palestinians. Unlike the first intifada of 1987, which led to the blocking of a military deal between Turkey and Israel, the second intifada caused nothing of the kind. On the contrary, as we have seen, Turkey signed an important military agreement with Israel at the height of serious clashes between the Palestinians and Israel.

Officially, Turkey found appropriate justification for its move. Referring to developments in the region (the intifada), the deputy under-secretary of the National Defense Ministry said that the situation in the Middle East had existed for some 55 years and it was not known for how long it would continue. Hence, "it is not possible for the Turkish armed forces to define its necessities by developing concepts according to an unknown [variable] and [be able] to maintain its quality of deterrence."[113] It is true that on the popular and declaratory level there was in Turkey strong criticism of Israel, but it seems that two parallel lines developed whereby the two stances could coexist. Because of its special relations both with Israel and the Palestinians, Ankara endeavored to play a certain go-between role, for example, in the participation by former Turkish President Demirel in the Mitchell Commission, formed in November 2000 "to investigate violence in the Palestinian territories";[114] the joint visit in late April 2002 of Turkish Foreign Minister Ismail Cem and Greek Foreign Minister George Papandreou to mediate between the parties; and the suggestion (which did not materialize) of turning Ankara into a venue for peace talks between the Israelis and Palestinians. Notwithstanding the considerable empathy in Turkish public opinion and political circles for the Palestinian issue, this could not of itself turn the clock back and cause the freezing of the alignment. By the year 2003, Turkey's own interests overwhelmed all other considerations.

## Old Conceptions, New Realities

In developing its relations with Israel, Turkey had consistently been guided by the premise that improved relations with the Jewish state would lead automatically to estrangement with the Arabs, hence the need to keep certain aspects of these relations (security–military) strictly secret, or to play a very delicate and intricate balancing act between them. However, as we have seen, Israel, although important, was not the decisive factor in Turkish–Arab relations. Rather, these were the outcome of various bilateral considerations; historical legacies that had scarred their mutual images and perceptions; various shared economic and political interests, which at times turned into a weapon in the hands of one of the parties against the other (oil, water); and different ideological and territorial disputes that marred relations with one Arab country or another. Indeed, it must be stressed that Ankara's relations with the Arab states were not monolithic, and existed at different levels with different countries at different times. Occasionally, they even reflected inter-Arab relations and rivalries. For example, Egypt's relations with Ankara between 1955 and 1965 were more a reflection or outcome of Egypt's intra-Arab relations, initially with Iraq and then with Syria, than of Ankara's relationship with Jerusalem. The disparity between the myth and the reality of Israel's role was best illustrated by Egypt's decision not to cut off relations with Turkey after the latter's recognition of Israel in 1949, whereas it did so when Ankara recognized Syria in 1961 (following Syria's secession from the UAR with Egypt). It was notable that not a single other Arab country broke off relations with Turkey because of its recognition of Israel, although, whenever possible, they put pressure on Ankara to downgrade this relationship.

As in the 1950s, Arab concerns in the early 1990s regarding Turkey (until the signing of the agreement with Israel in 1996), were not necessarily connected with its relations with Israel, but rather to Ankara's changing role in the region and the resulting shift in Arab perceptions. Turkey's ambition to play a new role in the Middle East, its perceived use of the water weapon, its occasional military incursions into Iraq and threats to do the same to Syria, were all interpreted as a significant change in the balance of power between Turkey and the Arabs. These perceptions were further reinforced by the loss in effectiveness of the economic leverage that some Arab oil states had had over Turkey, while the Islamic bond—in theory the most "natural" and important of any between the two parties—became even more problematic during the 1990s.

Against this background, the Turkish–Israeli alignment, which was both public and far-reaching, was disturbing, even traumatic for many Arab countries. Paradoxically, rather than causing estrangement or weakening Turkey's standing among the Arabs, as they had repeatedly warned, it yielded some important dividends for Ankara. Finding itself in a weakened strategic position and facing a Turkish army determined to force its hand, Syria finally acceded to Turkey's demand to cease its nearly two-decade-long support of the PKK. Other Arab countries, most importantly Egypt, courted Turkey even more energetically. Indeed, there was a yawning gap between rhetoric and politics, reflecting on the one hand the ever-ambiguous relations between Ankara and many Arab states, and on the other, the need to strike a balance between the urge to mobilize Arab public opinion against Turkey's move and the concern not to antagonize Ankara. In the final analysis, the alignment not only reflected but also reinforced Turkey's freedom of action or independence in regard to Israel.

## The Changing Role of Iran

Iran's reaction to the alignment was noteworthy because of its past role in the peripheral alliance (see chapter 2) and its new role as the implacable enemy of Israel. Like the Arab states, Iran felt threatened by the alignment, and like them considered that any chance of overturning it would be via Turkey and not Israel—a nation over which it had no leverage whatsoever. If the Arab countries had failed to torpedo the alignment in the name of Arabism, could Iran fare better and do so in the name of Islam? Iran did attempt to use Islam for the double purpose of pressurizing Turkey directly to leave the alignment and persuading other Muslim countries to do likewise. But the weapon of Islam in the hands of Iran turned out to be two-edged when applied against Turkey. In appealing to Islam, Tehran touched on the very dichotomy that divided Turkish society and political culture, in the range of attitudes toward Islam and secularism, identity, self-image, and perception of the outside world. On the one hand, since the 1960s Turkey had wished to draw nearer to the Islamic world and even to join the Islamic Conference Organization, which it did in 1969.[115] On the other, since the Islamic Revolution in Iran, Turkey had sought to present to the world a different Islamic model, one that could coexist with democracy, Westernism, and, most importantly, with secularism.[116]

Not only was there a vast difference between the two Islamic models that set them worlds apart, but the perceptions they shared of threat from the other's ideology increased significantly during the 1990s. In spite of the passage of more than two decades since Iran's Islamic Revolution, as late as summer 2002 a Turkish National Security Council document identified the greatest danger to Turkey as emanating from the East (Iran).[117] The fourfold threats that (among other things) helped to cement the Turkish–Israeli alignment in the first place, were: the ongoing threat of Iran's export of its Islamic model to Turkey; Iran's suspected support to the PKK; fear of Iran's long-range missiles and its growing nuclear capability; and its rivalry with Turkey in Central Asia. For its part, Iran had deep-seated fears and suspicions in regard to Turkey—its membership in NATO; its large army; the frequent Turkish military incursions into Iraqi Kurdistan and increasing Turkish influence there, which in many ways supplanted that which Iran used to have during the three previous decades; the growing interdependence between Turkey and the United States; and finally, above all, the alignment with Israel and all its implications, including flights by Israeli pilots that now ventured close to Iran's borders.

Iran used different methods to try and convince Turkey to break off its alignment with Israel. On the rhetorical level, Tehran repeatedly focused on the subject of Islam, which should have inhibited such relations. The general tone was to warn Turkey that "while the Zionist regime has much to gain from this concession, Ankara will get nothing but [will] whip up the anger of its own Moslem people and create a gap between Turkish people and the government." The alignment also "creates distrust among Moslem countries of the region and causes them to distance themselves" from Ankara.[118] On the whole, Iran described Turkey as a victim of the Zionists and Americans, whose "plots" and "conspiracies," and not Turkish free will, had brought about the alignment. The words were accompanied by deeds. Iran sought to take advantage of the Welfare Party–True Path Party (Refah-Yol) advent to power in Turkey in summer 1996 to strengthen its relations with Turkey, among others, as a means of distancing it from Israel. During Prime Minister Erbakan's visit to Tehran in early August 1996 (with a delegation of 250 officials and businessmen), Iran's spiritual leader,

Ayatollah Ali Khamenei, reminded Erbakan that he had come to power "in the name of Islam and for Islam," and called on him to break the recent links with Israel, for, as he said: "The Zionist regime is a very dangerous entity that only looks after its [own] interests."[119] However, to Iran's great disappointment, not only did Turkey not break its ties with Israel, but a few days later it signed a second military agreement, hence Iran's conclusion that "the countries of the region should revise their early optimism regarding the election of Mr. Erbakan."[120]

Iran also tried to incite Turkish public opinion against Israel. This was demonstrated in the Sincan affair, which took place in February 1997 and included "A night for Jerusalem." The mayor of Sincan, a Welfare Party member, held special activities in a big tent resembling the al-Aqsa mosque and decorated with posters of members of Hamas and the Lebanese Hizbullah. The guest of honor, Iranian Ambassador Muhammad Riza Bagheri, delivered a speech in which he challenged "those who sign agreements with America and Israel every day," asserting that Turkish youths "will deliver them God's punishment."[121] This led to a diplomatic crisis, which ended in the (brief) recall of the Iranian and Turkish ambassadors to their respective countries. In response, during a visit to the United States, Turkey's Deputy Chief of General Staff Çevik Bir, harshly attacked Iran—"the registered terrorist state"—and accused it of "exporting the Islamic revolution to Turkey," "supporting the PKK," and "producing weapons of mass destruction." Bir went as far as calling on the United States to list Iran as "a terrorist state."[122]

The next encounter came during the Islamic Conference, held in December 1997 in Tehran. Fifty-five Muslim countries participated, and a resolution was proposed criticizing the military relations of "Muslim countries" with Israel. Its three main backers were Iran, Syria, and Iraq. Turkey's delegate, President Demirel, defended his country's military accords with Israel, saying that the agreement was bilateral and did not pose a threat to a third country. Failing to convince his critics, however, Demirel left the Conference early. This, and the visit to Turkey of Israel's Defense Minister Yitzhak Mordechai, at the very time the Conference took place, was considered a Turkish snub to the Muslim world as a whole.[123] In a last attempt to put an end to the alignment, Iran and Egypt sent urgent messages to Ankara on December 20, 1997 calling on it to adhere to the charter of the Group of Eight Islamic Developing Countries (known as the D-8: Turkey, Iran, Egypt, Pakistan, Malaysia, Indonesia, Bangladesh, and Nigeria), which had been formed in Turkey earlier that year and "forbade" the conclusion of a military or strategic alliance with any country that threatens "the security of the member states of D-8." Tehran and Cairo reportedly suggested freezing Turkey's membership in the D-8 and transferring the group's headquarters from Istanbul to Cairo if Turkey did not withdraw from the alignment,[124] but nothing came of these threats.

Meanwhile, signaling to Turkey its stern response to the alignment, Tehran tried to improve relations with its archenemy, Iraq, and to further upgrade relations with Turkey's main rivals, Greece and Syria. At the same time, Iran tried to mediate between Ankara and Damascus during the October 1998 crisis, and to strengthen economic relations with Turkey. However, neither the stick nor the carrot would budge Turkey from the alignment. It was indeed a sign of changing times that Iran, which had been central to the peripheral alliance of the 1950s and 1960s, should now find itself fighting tooth and nail against another alignment between Turkey and Israel. In taking such a position, Islamist Iran seemed to be trying to compensate for what its predecessor, the Shah's regime, had done in allying itself with Turkey, and especially Israel.

## Greece and Cyprus: Ambivalent Reactions

In evaluating the impact of the alignment on the region, it is not enough to consider the Arab and Muslim world alone. Two non-Arab, non-Muslim countries, Greece and Cyprus, should also be taken into account

While Israel did not have to fear the impact of the alignment on Iran, it did need to consider the effect on Greece and Cyprus, whose foreign policies had long been intertwined. Until 1991, when relations between Israel and Greece (and Cyprus) were extremely cool, even hostile, with Greece at times treating Israel as negatively as did the Arab countries, Israel was quite indifferent to the Greek position.[125] However, the decision by Athens (and Nicosia) to establish full diplomatic relations with Jerusalem in 1991 began to make a certain difference. Just as Turkey had been concerned about the possible impact of its relations with Israel on the Arab world, Israel too had some anxiety with regard to the effect on Greece and Cyprus.

Initially, both Greece and Cyprus attempted to put a bold face on the Turkey–Israel alignment, declaring that it was an interstate agreement that should not affect their relations with Israel.[126] Little by little, however, they began to express their concern about its consequences for themselves. As with the Arab states, Israel's laconic answer was that the agreement was not against either Greece or Cyprus.[127] Such declarations, however, failed to put to rest these fears, which only increased with the growing closeness between Jerusalem and Ankara.

Cyprus was concerned that the alignment would strengthen the Turkish sector of the island and embolden Turkey in its policies toward the Greek sector. A case in point was Turkey's strong reaction to the Greek Cypriot plan, in summer 1998, to deploy on the island some S-300 antiaircraft missiles it had purchased from Russia. Turkey's objection caused the plan to be cancelled (the missiles were deployed in Crete instead), but not before strong suspicions had been aroused in Cyprus that Turkish pilots were being trained in Israel in missile evasion tactics, or even to destroy the antiaircraft missiles. In an attempt to dispel these suspicions, Defense Minister Yitzhak Mordechai stated that Israel would "never interfere into the affairs of Cyprus and side with Turkey against Greece over the missile issue in Cyprus."[128] In November 1998, Israeli President Ezer Weizman came on a first official visit to Cyprus, where he again reassured the Cypriot government that Israel's cooperation with Turkey was not directed against Cyprus or, indeed, any other third party.[129] These assurances received a blow when, shortly afterward, two Mossad agents were arrested in Cyprus for spying. According to rumor, they were gathering information for Turkey. Whatever the truth, it was indeed ironical that the Cyprus issue, which had been such a big hurdle in Turkish–Israeli relations in earlier periods, now came to enhance relations between the two—or at least was suspected of doing so.

Like Cyprus, Greece too was greatly disturbed by the alignment, calling it on one occasion "an alliance of wrongdoers."[130] Greece's concern was that the alignment would further strengthen the position of its traditional rival, Turkey, with which it had several other points of conflict during most of the 1990s.[131] However, in spite of the alignment—or perhaps because of it—by the end of the decade Greece had improved relations with both Turkey and Israel. The particular relevance of Greece–Israel relations is that in this case Israel was the focus of the attempts to apply pressure to give up the alignment. When the criticism intensified, Israel revealed that in 1994 Greece and Israel had signed a pact similar to that between Israel and Turkey, but that Greece had never implemented it.[132] In January 1997 Israel's Air Force Commander Eitan Ben Eliyahu, had visited Greece to discuss implementation but nothing came of it. Then, in May 1997, there were talks of holding joint naval military maneuvers, the first of their kind, near the island of Rhodes,[133] but nothing came of this either. Throughout, Greece warned Israel about going ahead with cooperation with Turkey because, as the Greek Foreign Minister Theodore Pangalos, put it: "Turkey isn't an ally you can count on," since it "had traded with Nazi

Germany during World War II."[134] He also asked: "who is threatening Turkey for it to need such a defence programme?" The Greek Ambassador to Israel described Israel's relations with Turkey as a "malaise."[135] On similar lines, the Greek Defense Minister Akis Tsohatzopoulos, warned that "the rationale of axis in today's strategies leads to the counter-rallying of all the others," adding that the security of Turkey and Israel could not be strengthened except in the context of the collective security of the entire region.[136]

By the end of 1999, relations between Greece and Israel began to improve rapidly for three interrelated reasons: the realization by Athens that it should no longer ignore the alignment and that its interests would be better served if it strengthened military relations with Israel; a rapprochement between Greece and Turkey, against the background of the earthquake disaster in both countries in mid-1999; and finally, a change of position on Israel's part as well. It turned out that not only Greece was dragging its feet on relations with Israel, because of its traditional pro-Arab policy, but that Jerusalem also was unenthusiastic about such a rapprochement, to say the least. Israel's main concern was that a negative reaction from Turkey could endanger the alignment, and there was also tension between Israel's Defense Ministry and Foreign Ministry on the question of how to proceed with Athens. While the Defence Ministry, headed by Mordechai and Ivri, was adamant about not doing anything that could jeopardize relations with Turkey, the Foreign Ministry aimed at more balanced relations between its two important, but rival, friends in the Mediterranean. But with a change of personnel in the Defense Ministry in 1999, when the Barak government came to power, and the conviction of the new administration that they could do business with both Turkey and Greece, military and political relations with Athens were stepped up. These included the posting of three Greek military attachés to Jerusalem (but no Israeli attaché to Athens), the visit of the Greek defense minister to Israel in October 1999, and the decision to increase defense cooperation. Greece now perceived a new defense partnership with Israel as a way of offsetting Jerusalem's alliance with Ankara.[137] Thus, not only did the alignment with Turkey not mar Greek relations with Israel, it even led to Athens courting Israel. But for Israel, relations with Turkey remained its most important and crucial alliance, as one defense official stated: "The relationship with Greece will never take on the same scope as our alliance with Turkey, not on the strategic level and not on the business level."[138]

## Alliances and Counter-Alliances

Conventional wisdom has it that alliances bring about the formation of counter-alliances. Indeed, Egypt's Foreign Minister 'Amru Musa, warned shortly after the military agreement between Turkey and Israel was made public that the Arab countries would have "to do something to counter the alliance," since "for every action there is an equally powerful reaction in the opposite direction."[139] 'Amru Musa probably expressed the expectation of many in the Arab world and elsewhere that the Turkish–Israeli "move" would produce a counter-reaction in the region. However, no such counter-alliance materialized. As one commentator said during the Turkish-Syrian crisis: "we would have expected the countries of the region who are directly threatened by the alliance, such as Egypt, Syria, Iraq and Iran, to get together urgently at summit or Foreign Minister level to discuss ways of confronting it practically and effectively. But our expectations and those of many concerned people remained unfulfilled."[140] The question, therefore, is why was a counter-alliance not formed?

Single-factor explanations must clearly be ruled out. Multiple internal, regional, and international developments combined to block the initial impetus to collectively check, and eventually attempt to roll back the Turkish–Israeli alignment. As a result, the alignment became an unchallenged *fait accompli*. Taking the Baghdad Pact as a precedent, it must be stressed that in the bipolar world of the 1950s the Soviet Union played a key role in encouraging the counter-alliance to the Pact—the formation of the UAR between Egypt and Syria. But in the unipolar world of 1996 there was no Soviet Union, and Russia was either unwilling, or too weak internally and externally, to mobilize the countries of the region against this "pro-Western" alignment. In the Arab world, it was true that in both instances the accords were interpreted as a threat to the Arab security system. However, in the 1950s the Arab system, or at least a leading member of it—Egypt—could gather the support of certain Arab countries to counter the Baghdad Pact, while in the 1990s this system was too weak and fragmented for such a grouping.

Looking more specifically at individual countries that could lead or join a counter-alliance, reveals similar difficulties and inhibitions. Theoretically, the most natural candidates for a counter-alliance were the countries that felt most threatened by the alignment—Syria, Iraq, Iran, Egypt, and even Greece. In practice, however, neither Syria nor Iran could trust Saddam Hussein's Iraq as a partner in such a concerted move. Asked why Syria and Iraq would not come closer, Syria's Information Minister Muhammad

Salman, said at the time: "you should not respond to a misguided alliance by another misguided alliance."[141] Indeed, the eight years of war between Iran and Iraq and the 30 years of mutual suspicion and animosity between Syria and Iraq, rendered the process of reconciliation—let alone the formation of an alliance among the three—uniquely tortuous. Curiously, Iran's overtures to Syria, its ally since 1980, to expand their ties into a strategic alliance were rebuffed by Damascus, which was afraid of increasing its isolation in the Arab world or of antagonizing the Arab Gulf states, which remained wary of Iran's expansionist ambitions.[142]

Egypt was yet another country that felt weakened by the alignment and could have been a potential leader of a counter-alliance.[143] Here, however, there was a big difference between the Egypt of the 1950s and the 1990s. Unlike the regime of 'Abd al-Nasser's era, Egypt did not perceive the alignment of 1996 as an imminent danger. Nor did it consider Jordan, the tacit partner of the 1996 alignment, to be a rival in the struggle for Arab hegemony, as it had perceived Iraq in the 1950s. Similarly, for all its tense relations with Amman, Egypt did not wish to be in conflict with Jordan.[144] The other significant differences were that Egypt was now on good terms with Turkey and had established full diplomatic relations with Israel. Most important, and closely related to the above, was that Egypt was now in the American orbit, so to speak, and all these factors reduced its incentives to lead a counter-alliance.

Greece, too, felt threatened by the alignment, but apart from strengthening relations with Syria and Iran (as well as with Russia and Armenia),[145] its anxieties did not drive it to seek a counter-alliance with these two states or, indeed, with any other country in the region.

If a counter-alliance did not materialize, this is not to say that the region remained indifferent to or unaffected by the alignment.[146] By far the most interesting development was the rapprochement between Syria and Saddam's Iraq, which started shortly after the signing of the Turkish–Israeli agreement. Initially, this was quite slow and cautious, mainly because of Syria's reservations, but picked up speed following Bashshar al-Asad's rise to power in Syria and increased concern in both Baghdad and Damascus over American intentions in the region following the events of September 11, 2001. Indeed, Syria aroused America's wrath by extending succor to Iraq during the U.S.–Iraq war in spring 2003. The overthrow of Saddam's regime, America's occupation of Iraq, and Iraq's indefinite disappearance from the regional order as an independent actor, created a situation unprecedented in the post–World War I Middle East. How this would affect regional dynamics, the calculations of individual regimes, and internal political developments remained to be seen.

# Conclusion: A New Regional Order?

In the last decade of the twentieth century, four competing visions vied for influence in the Middle East: George Bush's vision of a New World Order, Saddam Hussein's New Arab Order, Turgut Özal's New Turkic World, and Shimon Peres's New Middle East. This profusion of visions emerged after the collapse of the Soviet Union, and with it the Cold War regime that had dominated the region—and indeed the world—for a large part of the twentieth century. In the Middle East, the catalyst was Iraq's invasion of Kuwait and all its ramifications, and perhaps another impetus was the approaching end of a turbulent millennium and the beginning of a new one, with its aura of apocalyptic visions and expectations—not least in the Middle East.

In the end, not one of these visions was realized. President Bush's dream, and that of his successor, Bill Clinton, of bringing peace and democracy to the Middle East remained illusory. Worse, by the beginning of the third millennium America itself, for the first time in its history, became a victim of the lack of democracy and peace in this region. The attacks on the Twin Towers and the Pentagon on September 11, 2001 were carried out by Islamists motivated by extremist ideologies that had been nurtured in some Middle East countries. Similarly short-lived was Saddam Hussein's vision of the new Arab order, lasting a mere seven months—the time needed to oust him from Kuwait. Özal's all-embracing vision of a "Turkish Century" was replaced after his death in 1993, by a more sober and pragmatic policy toward the region and Central Asia. Peres's benign vision of a new Middle East was also nipped in the bud by its own naiveté and the unanimous rejection by the Arab world of the proposed embrace, which was interpreted in no uncertain terms as an Israeli–Zionist cultural invasion of the Arabs.

Still, there was no denying that the region looked different from its pattern of the previous four decades. The difference lay in three key developments in the final years of the century: America's emergence as the sole superpower in the region, thanks to its global triumph in the

Cold War and accompanying success in building an international coalition in 1990–91 to counter Iraqi revanchism; the Arab–Israeli peace process, which began in 1991, and the open alignment between Turkey and Israel five years later. Although not conforming to Peres's vision, the peace process, one of America's three policy pillars in the region, was significant in several ways. First, at one point it included three potential Arab partners—the Palestinians, Jordan, and Syria—and not the sole Arab partner of the Israel–Egypt peace treaty in the late 1970s. Second, it granted much-needed legitimacy to Israel in certain parts of the region. Third, it paved the way for the alignment between Turkey and Israel in the 1990s. But the peace process itself was to prove volatile. The Syria–Israel track did not even take off. The Palestinian track, after a few promising years, devolved into another round of conflict, one of the most destructive in the battle-scarred history of the two sides, and only the 1994 Jordan–Israel peace treaty remained viable. Indeed, peace with Jordan illustrated the continuity in relations between the two countries, and was the culmination of the back-channel ties they had developed over the years. But Jordan's position also embodied the changed times, in that Amman became a silent partner in the new alignment between Turkey and Israel, thus differentiating it from the peripheral alliance of nearly forty years before, which had been composed solely of non-Arab members.

Even before the peace process had broken down in Fall 2000, the second of America's three policy pillars—the dual containment of Iraq and Iran—had proven to be a thin reed. Only its third pillar—the Turkish–Israeli alignment, had proven to be durable.

From its very beginnings, the alignment was controversial, and different critics, skeptics, and prophets of doom spoke forcefully against it. In Turkey, they came from various walks of political life rather than the corridors of power, and argued along traditional lines that the agreement was bound to mar relations between Turkey and the Arab world, and indeed with the entire Muslim world.[1] More specifically, they warned that it would cause a rupture of Ankara's relations with Damascus. Some saw it as a betrayal of the Palestinian cause, and predicted that as soon as the peace process between Israel and the Palestinians crumbled, so too would Turkey's alignment with Israel.

In Israel, critics and skeptics were far fewer and less influential than in Turkey. Still, some argued that the alignment would damage the peace process with the Arabs, undermine Israel's relations with Greece and Cyprus, drag Israel into conflicts that were none of its business, such as Turkey's conflict with its Kurdish minority, and that Israel's technical and military secrets might be leaked by Ankara. Most of all, it was feared that the secular regime in Turkey might be overturned and Israel would be left empty-handed and facing a stronger, unfriendly Turkish army, as had happened with Iran after the fall of the Shah.

The Arab countries, Iran, Greece, and Cyprus were genuinely alarmed by the alignment on their own account, and also raised the specter of it seriously destabilizing the Middle East by increasingly polarizing the region into competing axes.

In retrospect, none of these predictions came true, and in some cases the very opposite happened. Not only were Turkey's relations with the Arab countries not impaired, but in many instances they improved significantly, most obviously with its archenemy, Syria. Similarly, the assumed linkage between the Palestinian issue and the quality of Ankara's relations with Jerusalem proved to be overblown. The renewed fighting between the Palestinians and Israel from 2000 had but little impact on the alignment. Indeed, at the time of some of the worst clashes Turkey signed an important new agreement with Israel. On the whole, the single "Arab political collective" that in the past had seriously affected the political calculations regarding the region proved to be a mere phantom. Similarly, the myth of an inevitable interconnectedness in the triangle of Turkish–Israel–Arab relations, which had dominated Turkish foreign policy for more than four decades, was shattered once and for all, and relations between Turkey and Israel could now develop independently of the Arab factor. In other words, Turkey was no longer captive to these self-imposed shackles, and relations with Israel and with Arab countries were no longer mutually exclusive, however deep the bonds of Muslim brotherhood. Overall, Turkey's regional stature and freedom of maneuver had increased substantially.

Nor did the warnings of negative consequences for Israel turn out to be valid. The alignment did not bring a rift in Israel's relations with the Arab states, or cause the peace process to flounder. When negotiations with Syria and the Palestinians failed, this was in no way due to the relationship with Turkey. The breakdown was rooted entirely in the age-old conflict between Israel and the Arab countries, or more precisely in the unwillingness of some of them to accept Israel's existence in the region. Israel's relations with Greece, on the other hand, benefited from the alignment. Just as certain Arab states began to court Turkey because of the new alignment, so Greece made similar overtures to Israel. Further, Turkey is not known to have leaked any of Israel's secrets to a third party, and Israel, for its part, took precautions not to be drawn into a conflict between Turkey and any third party. As for those who feared an

Iranian-style Islamic Revolution in Turkey that would lead to a repudi-ation of the alignment, they underestimated the influence of the mili-tary in Turkish society and politics, and, more generally, the extent to which Turkish society has absorbed Western ways. Moreover, they failed to sufficiently understand the profound differences between the Iranian and Turkish Islamist models.

The alarm bells which had been set off in the region regarding the likely fallout from the alignment—namely, that it would cause new ten-sions, trigger new conflicts and wars, and generate polarizing counter-alliances—all proved unfounded. If anything, the deterrent strength of the alignment led Syria to the decision to "go to Canossa" in order to turn the page in its relations with Turkey. Genuine counter-alliances were slow to emerge, because there was no superpower to back them, because of hostile or tense relations between potential partners, and, his-torically speaking, perhaps because the region had never managed to produce any strong and enduring alliance, with the exception of the Turkish–Israeli alignment.

The Turkish–Israeli alignment became in time a *fait accompli* that the countries of the region have, if reluctantly, learned to live with. On the whole, the alignment and the weak political response to it demonstrated the multipolarity in the region and the lack of unity among its members—especially among the Arab countries, where collaboration might have been expected. Rather than a new regional order imposed from above, as in the past, there has been a significant intra-regional reordering of relations or forces.

How, then, should the alignment be assessed? Without doubt, the alignment has proved its resilience: it survived the Erbakan Islamist-led government in Turkey and three fragile coalition governments in Turkey and Israel, as well as the renewal of the Israeli–Palestinian con-flict. Its durability derived in no small measure from its multidimen-sional character, expanding from the military/strategic sphere to include political, diplomatic, economic, and sociocultural relations. The absence of any counter-alliance made the continued deepening of relations that much easier. Most important, the alignment has demonstrated that Turkey has freed itself from the Arab spell.

On the face of things, two dramatic developments could have been expected to negatively affect the Turkish–Israeli alignment: the over-whelming electoral triumph of the Adalet ve Kalkınma Partisi (AKP) Islamist party and its advent to power in Turkey in November 2002, and the 2003 U.S. war against Saddam Hussein's Ba'thi regime in Iraq. Observers speculated that Turkey's new Islam-oriented government might seek to weaken its relations with Israel in favor of closer ties with its Arab-Muslim neighbors. Moreover, the balance of power within Turkey was now shifting, as the civilian political sector began to assume increasing control at the expense of the military's previously unchallenged dominance. With the military having been the leading advocate of closer ties with Israel during the 1990s, it seemed possible that the Ankara–Jerusalem relationship would be affected accordingly.

The other potential dark cloud for the Turkish–Israeli partnership appeared in early 2003, via Iraq.[2] Turkey's last-minute decision not to allow American troops to cross its territory to attack Iraq occasioned the severest strain ever in the 60-year-old Ankara–Washington alliance, and seemed likely to create considerable fallout in the Israeli–Turkish sphere. Washington had assumed that the Ankara–Jerusalem duo would deepen its own standing in the region, building on its long-standing strategic ties with each. But Turkey's rejection of American entreaties in a time of war demonstrated anew the inherent limitations on the U.S.-centered regional order, whose central pillar was the Turkish–Israeli–Washington triangle. To put matters in even broader perspective, the Middle East had fallen under the dominance of a single great power for the first time in 200 years. Nonetheless, one of America's primary local allies, Turkey, proved capable of independent action that placed serious limitations on its U.S. patron. As for the other local ally-client of the United States, Israel, its unswerving support for the war, and Turkey's unbridled opposition to it, suggested that the Turkish–Israeli alignment would, at best, undergo painful adjustments, and at worst, be fundamentally undermined over the longer term.

In addition, Turkish threat perceptions had now changed dramatically from the early 1990s. Syria had been neutralized, and even embraced; Iran was deemed a neighbor whom one could, and must do business with; Iraq had already been contained in the American "box" for years; hence for Turkey, the earlier urgency of a close military-strategic alignment with Israel had disappeared. The real threat appeared to stem from the enhanced standing and aspirations of Iraq's Kurdish minority bordering Turkey, which had aligned itself foursquare with the U.S. war. Here, as well, Turkey's interests appeared to diverge significantly from those of the United States and Israel: Ankara feared that Washington's declared opposition to a Kurdish independent state would not hold up to Kurdish pressures, and that Israel would follow Washington's lead.

Another, no less powerful factor deemed likely to impinge on the Ankara–Jerusalem partnership was the widespread perception in Turkey that Israel and the American Jewish community were principal catalysts behind the American decision to go to war in Iraq. The broad popular opposition in Turkey to the war stained Israel's image there, and could have been expected to negatively affect the partnership.

As it happened, the relationship weathered the storm. According to a knowledgeable high-ranking Israeli official,[3] not only did the AKP government not seek to lower the profile of Turkish ties with Israel, it even improved upon the previous Ecevit government's links, in some cases. One reason for the AKP's benign stance toward the Jewish state was to prove to European skeptics that it was genuinely interested in constructing a new type of Islamic state, both internally and in foreign affairs, which would be conducted according to the principles of Western, enlightened democracies. The issue was hardly philosophical: Turkey fully understood that the success of such a model would ease its path to joining the EU. Another reason for the AKP's openness to Israel may have been its desire to avoid creating additional friction with Turkey's military establishment, which viewed the party's ascent to power warily, at best. In broader terms, Turkish–Israeli relations had in any case ceased to be based in the military-strategic domain only, having come to encompass significant components of civilian society, particularly in the economic sphere.

Ironically, the rift between Ankara and Washington not only did not harm relations between Turkey and Israel, but laid the basis for additional cooperation. The severe damage done to Turkey's image and status in the corridors of power in Washington necessitated rapid damage control. Notwithstanding its eagerness to be accepted into the EU "club," Turkey could hardly afford the loss of its former pivotal geopolitical status in U.S. eyes and transformation into a marginal country. Mending fences with Washington in such circumstances, therefore was crucial. In Turkey's eyes, backing from Israel's supporters in Washington could only help its lobbying efforts. Jerusalem was quick to comply, encouraging its backers to take up the cause of repairing the torn fabric of Turkish–American ties.

In any event, Turkish–Israeli links were reinforced after the war. They included talks on new arms sale, and the visits of Turkey's Chief of Staff to Israel and high-ranking Israeli officials to Turkey. To be sure, as of February 2004, neither Foreign Minister (and briefly, Prime Minister) Abdullah Gül nor Prime Minister Tayyip Erdoğan had yet visited Israel, in contrast to Gül's numerous trips to Arab capitals and Iran. The official explanation for such visits was that Turkey needed to coordinate its activities with these countries in order to try and prevent the U.S.–Iraq war. As for abstaining from visiting Israel, their rationale was said to be twofold: They wanted to avoid clashing with Israel and the United

States over their preference to visit Palestinian Authority President Yasir 'Arafat, who was being isolated in his Ramallah compound by Israeli forces, and; they preferred to avoid drawing public attention to their intimacy with Israel at a time in which public opinion was inflamed against the American war in Iraq.[4] Substantive progress in U.S.-sponsored "road map" designed to reactivate the Israeli–Palestinian peace process was likely to remove this potential irritant between Ankara and Jerusalem.

Echoing, as it were, General Gürsel's recommendation for a secret *amour* between Turkey and Israel, Alon Liel warned in 1997: "We are allowed to love Turkey and we should be glad if the Turks love us too. But making love in front of a jealous and hostile public means shortening the days of the love affair."[5] Seven years on, the Turkish–Israeli embrace had withstood the glare of public light, continued to be durable, and had even favorably affected Turkey's relations with its Arab and non-Arab neighbors alike. In this regard, Turkey had successfully developed a "dual orientation" toward Israel and the Arab states. Nadav Safran had used this term to describe America's policy shift in the 1970s toward Israel and the Arab states, in which "the pursuit of [crucial] interests [regarding both sides] requires it to endeavor to cultivate good relations with the ones as well as the other and to seek to accommodate their principal respective concerns." For the United States, advancing its interests in the Arab world in those years "rested decisively on its especially close relationship with Israel."[6] For Turkey in the 1990s, embracing a strategic and economic partnership with Israel had significantly enhanced its regional standing. Substantial improvement in relations with erstwhile foes (e.g., Greece, Syria) was achieved, economic links in the Arab world were preserved and developed further, and its image at home and abroad as an important Muslim state was burnished. Turkey's serious setback with the United States in 2003 promised to reverberate for some time to come. Nonetheless, both Ankara and Washington were keen on repairing the U.S.–Turkish "leg" of the triangular relationship. As for Israel, the partnership with Turkey had borne even more fruit than could have been hoped for: militarily, strategically, politically, and economically. To be sure, the renewed violent conflict with the Palestinians damaged Israel's standing among Turkish public opinion as did its close affiliation with the United States in the Iraq war. Yet the Turkish–Israeli alignment has remained firm, and the likelihood of *regional* pressures forcing a return to the nadir of the 1970s and 1980s appeared remote.

# Postscript

Under the AKP government, Turkey's foreign policy toward the Middle East has undergone profound changes, which were, in turn, the outcome of various domestic and regional developments. These changes altered Turkey's threat perceptions, its new understanding of its role in the region, and a redefining of who its appropriate regional partners were. The two most important determinants of the change were the advent of the AKP to power in 2002 and the 2003 Iraqi war. The fact that the two events occurred almost simultaneously contributed significantly to Turkey's evolving new vision regarding the Middle East.

The main guiding principles of Turkish policy under the AKP toward the Middle East, however conflicting they may be at different times, are the following:

1. Playing a pivotal role in the region, or what Turkish analysts have termed as Neo-Ottomanism or the Turkish grand strategy in the Middle East.
2. Multilateralism, which meant courting Arab and Muslim countries of the region while keeping its ties with Israel.
3. Engaging its neighbors for the sake of insuring "zero conflicts" with them.
4. Playing the role of mediator in different regional problems.
5. Attempting to strike a new balance between its European and Middle East policies.
6. Setting a model of a democratic Muslim state for Arab and Muslim countries, in contrast to Iran.

The most important transformation is that the AKP turned Islam into a platform for advancing its bid for regional leadership. As long as nationalism was the dominant ideology in the region, Turkey and major Arab countries were frequently at loggerheads. Now with its advent to power, the AKP used Islam as a glue between the three major nationalities in the region, Turkish, Arab, and Iranian.

In an attempt to enhance its stature in the Muslim world, the AKP engaged Hamas and granted it legitimacy, rather than ostracize it as most world countries did. The invitation to Hamas's senior personality in Damascus, Khalid Mash`al, to visit Ankara in early 2006, was a harbinger for things to come.[1] Second, unlike Egypt, Saudi Arabia, or Jordan, for example, Ankara did not raise the specter of Shi`i Islam, allowing it to pose as neutral party in the Sunni-Shi`i conflict raging in the region and thus enhance its stature in the Muslim world. Accordingly, it managed to keep on good terms with Shi` Iran as well as with both the Sunnis and Shi`is of Iraq. Similarly, in the last few months and especially after the war in Gaza, Turkey has sought closer ties with Arab and Muslim countries due to domestic political and economic considerations in advance of approaching local elections, and in order to obtain aid from Arab oil-rich countries at a time of economic crisis. At the same time, it continued its attempts to play the role of mediator, using both its European and its Middle Eastern credentials.

Turkey's threat perceptions continued to emanate from the support which the neighboring countries—Iraq, Syria, and Iran—might grant the PKK, hence the special importance it attached to its relations with them. But by the turn of the century one could notice a change in the role of these neighbors. While in the 1990s Ankara perceived Syria and Iran as the main source of threat, following the Gulf war in 2003, it came to assign this role to Iraq.

Turkey's relations with Israel should be seen against this background, as well as the sea changes that have occurred in the region since the AKP's advent to power in Turkey in 2002

## The Changing Strategic Map of the Region

Most of the factors that helped bring about the rapprochement between Turkey and Israel in the 1990s have been drastically altered. For example, the 1991 Gulf war was an important trigger for the rapprochement.[2] Turkey and Israel were in agreement on the necessity of the war and on their support for the United States. The Turkish military, which was at its apex of political power, played a leading role in the rapprochement. Turkish-Syrian hostility provided another motive for rapprochement, as Damascus was considered a common enemy that needed to be checked. Similarly, Iran's Islamic Republic was perceived as posing a common threat. On the positive side, the Palestinian issue appeared to be on its way to resolution, removing a severe stumbling block in Ankara-Jerusalem relations.

In recent years, all of these common denominators had disappeared. Moreover, a number of potentially damaging developments had emerged: For example:

1. The concurrent strengthening in Turkey of ultra-nationalist and Islamist currents posed a potential threat to relations with the Jewish state.
2. The Turkish military elite, the chief architect of Turkey's close links with Israel, lost of its hold over the political system and thus its ability to dictate foreign policy lines. Moreover, the growing friction between this elite and the AKP government, manifested in the still-unfolding Ergenekon scandal, only added to the ambiguity toward Israel.
3. The 2003 U.S.-Iraq war sparked deterioration in Ankara's relations with Washington and also had negative effects on Turkey's perceptions of Israel's role in the region, especially regarding Iraqi Kurdistan and the Kurdish Regional Government (KRG).[3]
4. Turkey has developed close relations with Syria, thus lessening Turkey's need for a strong ally in the south to counterbalance Damascus.
5. For the ruling AKP, the Islamic Republic of Iran appeared much less threatening than it did to previous governments.
6. The ongoing conflict between Israel and the Palestinians, particularly the outbreak of the second *intifada* in Fall 2000, and the more recent conflict with Hamas in Gaza severely damaged Israel's image in Turkey. Ankara's tilt toward Hamas, which the EU considered a terrorist organization, could be noticed from Turkey's invitation to Hamas leader to visit Turkey, as well as the harsh attacks by Turkish officials on Israel following the Israeli offensive on Hamas in early 2009.

Capping these changes is the fact that the long-standing, inherent asymmetry in Turkish-Israeli relations became even more pronounced under the AKP.

## Asymmetry and ambiguity in Turkish-Israeli relations

The asymmetry in Turkish-Israeli relations exists on a number of levels—declaratory, diplomatic, and political. Israel is usually the courting partner—the needy party, politically speaking—and thus the one that initiates actions to maintain good relations. For Israel, relations with Turkey are a source of pride and legitimacy; for the Turkish government, on the other hand, they sometimes serve as an embarrassment or pose a dilemma. For example, notwithstanding the fact that Israel has been considered Ankara's strategic partner, it does not exist on the map of the weather report broadcast by TRT1, a Turkish national television station. Damascus, Amman, and the rest of Arab capitals do appear on the nightly weather map displayed to viewers, but Jerusalem and Tel Aviv do not.

Turkish politicians have no qualms about vehemently attacking Israel because of its policies toward the Palestinians, yet Israeli politicians tiptoe around any issue that touches on Turkish sensitivities.[4] Thus, for example, they refrain from even mentioning Turkey's policies regarding the Kurds, let alone criticizing them.[5]

As for the Turkish media, most of its reports on the Palestinian problem are one-sided and biased against Israel. Israeli attacks against Palestinians are always reported, but the Turkish media rarely dwells on Hamas terrorist attacks against Israel.[6] By contrast, the Israeli media reports on the fighting between the Turkish army and the PKK mainly from the Turkish point of view, and rarely shows any sympathy to the PKK.

There is no doubt that Israel has lost the battle to receive fair treatment from the Turkish media, which may reflect negatively on Turkish politicians' decision-making.[7] On the other hand, it should be noted that the media at times takes its cue from the politicians. Thus for example, Prime Minister Tayyip Erdoğan declared in June 2004 that "Jews were the victims [in Spain]. Today Palestinians are the victims and the people of Israel are treating Palestinians as they were treated 500 years ago"[8]. Even if unintentionally, such declarations certainly contribute to the spread of anti-Israeli and anti-Semitic expressions in the media and among the Turkish public.

Indeed, there are signs of growing anti-Semitism in Turkey in recent years. Thus, for example, *Mein Kampf* (*Kavgam*) was for a time a best seller in Turkey.[9] The immediate causes for the rise in anti-Semitism are not very clear. It could be the result of the strengthening of ultra-nationalist trends, or that the very ascent to power of an Islamic party has legitimized it. One thing is certain: the Turkish government has not done enough to fight this phenomenon. Whereas Germany and other states forbid the publication of *Mein Kampf*, the Turkish government did not do so on the flimsy pretext of protecting democracy. And although Prime Minister Erdoğan declared time and again that Turkey was against anti-Semitism his other declarations seemed to tip the balance in the Turkish street (see below).

By contrast, official Israel has done its best not only to take into consideration Turkish sensitivities on the Armenian issue but also lobbied hard in Washington against any attempts to achieve U.S. recognition of the Armenian massacres as genocide.

## What keeps Turkish-Israeli Relations Going?

Having said all this, we need to put things in proportion. My main argument is that notwithstanding the sea changes that occurred in the region after the second Gulf war in 2003 as well as the far-reaching changes in Turkey's foreign policy, still both states have had vested interests in maintaining the good relationship, even at times of crisis. One of the most important explanations for their longevity is that the two states have no serious problems on the bilateral level. They have never engaged in a war against each other, nor do they pose any sort of strategic menace to one another. Quite the opposite. Similarly, the generally positive historical bonds between the two nations have also contributed to this longevity.

Thus, the strength and depth of the Turkish-Israeli bilateral relationship had been without parallel anywhere else in the Middle East. By way of comparison, Israel's peace with Egypt is still a cold one, thirty years after the signing of their peace treaty. President Husni Mubarak has never visited Israel on an official visit, nor did Egyptian intellectuals and journalists find it easy to be associated with Israel or even visit it. The same was true for Jordanians, with whom official relations were established much later.

By contrast, since the upgrading of Turkish-Israeli relations to the ambassadorial level in 1991, bilateral ties have been quite cordial, and even intimate. Visits by high level officials, including heads of state, to each other's capitals have been frequent. Under the AKP governments alone, most of Turkey's top officials, including Prime Minister Erdoğan and President Ahmet Necdet Sezer, have traveled to Israel.[10] For their part, Israeli officials have been only too eager to reciprocate. Thus, all Israeli prime ministers, presidents, and defense ministers have visited Turkey during the last decade.

With regard to the increase of anti-Semitic expressions in Turkey, one cannot ignore the efforts by a number of Turkish intellectuals and the more liberal-leftist media to oppose it.[11] As a balance to *Mein Kampf,* one should also mention that a Turkish novelist, Ayşe Kulin, wrote a novel about Turkish diplomats' endeavors to save Jews from the Nazi horrors.[12] Such a phenomenon is almost impossible to find in the literature or the media of

Arab countries, including those which have diplomatic relations with Israel. On another level, Israelis have flocked to Turkey, but generally shunned Egypt and Jordan. In 2007 the number of Israeli tourists to Turkey exceeded half a million, totaling 511,435.[13] Thus, unlike Israel's relations with Arab countries, which are mainly on the official, governmental level, Israeli–Turkish relations have had a significant societal dimension.

## The bonds of common interests

Since the 1990s, the strategic map and the strategic challenges in the region have changed dramatically for both Turkey and Israel. For Turkey the challenge shifted to Iraq and the Kurds, for Israel to Iran and the Palestinians. Yet Turkey and Israel still have common threat perceptions. Both states have common interests in fighting terror. Although there might be differences between Turkey and Israel on the definition of what constitutes terror and who exactly is a terrorist, the two are likeminded in perceiving the seriousness of the threat being posed, their common interest in combating it and the importance of developing the proper military means to do so. Thus, Turkish Prime Minister Erdoğan and Israeli Prime Minister Ariel Sharon signed in early 2005 an agreement for establishing a "hot line" for the exchange of intelligence on terror between their two offices.[14]

The fact that Israeli Defense Minister Ehud Barak visited Turkey just days before the onset of large-scale Turkish military operations against PKK bases in Iraq at the beginning of 2008 is itself telling. Indeed, Turkey's Defense Minister Vecdi Gönül subsequently revealed that Turkey had benefited from Israeli military know-how in its actions against the PKK.[15] Such revelations are greeted uneasily in Israel, which is concerned with possible PKK revenge acts, as occurred after the capture of Abdullah Öcalan, the leader of the PKK, in 1999. However, Israel generally refrains from complaining about them, in order not to ruffle Turkish feathers.

Iran is another cause of concern for both states. It is true that on the face of it, high-ranking Turkish officials seem to support the Iranian stance on the issue of its nuclear program, but in fact both the government and the military in Turkey dread the day when Iran will possess a nuclear weapon, and the possible dramatic alteration in the regional balance of power.[16] Thus, in many ways Israel is doing the dirty job that Ankara is unable, or unwilling to do because it wishes to remain on good terms with Tehran. That strategic relations have remained strong between the two military establishments is proved by the fact that the Turkish Head of National Security visited Israel in May 2005, the first such visit in the history of the relationship.[17]

Notwithstanding conspiracy theories regarding Israel's allegedly malevolent role in northern Iraq, the Turkish and Israeli governments share concerns regarding the possible negative consequences of the disintegration of Iraq and its splitting into three states. In their view, such a development would not only further destabilize the region, but would also be likely to encourage the Kurds in Turkey and Palestinians in Israel to take the Iraqi Kurdish case as a model for their own activities.

With regard to Turkish-Arab relations, the AKP government has made significant efforts to forge closer ties with Arab countries for ideological, political, and economic considerations. Indeed, in a most important *volte face* Ankara has established strong relations with Syria, its one time arch rival in the region.[18] Still, mutual suspicions and antipathies have not entirely dissipated. As in the Iranian case, Israel serves as bulwark against real or imaginative threats emanating from Turkey's Arab neighbors.

Cognizant of the danger of putting all of its eggs in the military basket, Israel sought from the start to diversify its links with the Turkish state and society. Economically, Israel sought to further deepen the links that have been flourishing since the early 1990s and which reached a peak in 2008. Thus, in the first part of 2008, Israeli exports to Turkey grew by 56% compared to the first part of 2007, totaling $821m, while Israeli imports also grew by 30%, totaling $1bn.[19] On another level, Israel acquiesced to Ankara's desire to play a role as a facilitator or a mediator between Jerusalem and Damascus. Israel's acceptance of Ankara's diplomacy served to acknowledge the legitimacy of Turkish ambitions to play a leading role in the Middle East.

For Turkey the move highlighted its pivotal role in the region. Thus, while the Bush administration was reluctant to mediate between Israel and Syria, and with Egyptian-Syrian relations too antagonistic for Cairo to fulfill such a role, Ankara was only too eager to do so. Generally speaking, Turkey was of the opinion that one should engage Syria, Iran, and Hamas rather than isolate them, and in this it was at odds with the Bush administration. Turkey's mediation, as long as it went on, added another important dimension to Turkish-Israeli relations in that it deepened the bonds of mutual confidence and diversified ties by adding diplomacy to the existing links in the military, economic, and political spheres.

## Turkey's New Role as a mediator

Turkey's new role as a mediator between Israel and Syria is intriguing. This is indeed a 180 degree change compared to the situation that existed during the mid-1990s. While in that period Turkey moved to forge the alignment with Israel for fear, among other things, that the latter would conclude peace with Syria, now that Ankara has settled its differences with Damascus, it has emerged as a peace broker between Israel and Syria. In fact, what might have pushed Syrian President Bashshar al-Asad to negotiations with Israel could be the urgent need to get back the Golan Heights after he had given up on Alexandretta/Hatay to Turkey as a price for rapprochement with Ankara.

Indirect peace negotiations between Israel and Syria resumed in May 2008 after eight years of deadlock, this time under Turkish auspices. The Israeli representatives to the negotiations Turkey were Shalom Turjeman and Yoram Trubovitz; their Syrian interlocutor was Riyad Dawudi. Four rounds of meetings took place in Istanbul and Ankara during the spring and summer, in which the Turkish mediator played the role of messenger since the negotiators neither met face to face nor resided in the same hotel. In a statement issued by Israeli Prime Minister Ehud Olmert on May 21, 2008, on the day of the first meeting, he revealed that preparations for that move had begun a year earlier and that it was Israel which approached Turkey asking it to mediate.[20] Describing the opening of the negotiations as an exciting event, Olmert emphasized that it was "a national duty" and that he was walking on the path of his predecessors in office.[21]

Turkey's new role gained great support at home. Newspapers of different political convictions described the move in superlative terms. Sami Kohen, writing in the centrist *Milliyet*, stated: "As a result of the intensive efforts of Turkish diplomacy, Israeli and Syrian representatives have come to Turkey and begun the process of proximity talks. Turkey is trusted by both sides. In fact, it might be described as the only country of its kind. The fact that Turkish diplomacy has assumed such a role is a development that gives Turkey credibility in the international arena." Erdal Şafak, in the centrist *Sabah*, emphasized that "Turkey, as the only country trusted by both parties, has acquired power in the Middle East, a card in the EU and prestige in the world. And in case the talks result in a peace agreement that will change the balances and dynamics in the Middle East, Turkey's power and prestige will reach an extraordinary and amazing degree." Ibrahim Karagul also highlighted Turkey's new role in the liberal pro-Islamic *Yeni Şafak*: "Turkey, which has not been included in any talks in the Middle East for years and whose influence has always been kept limited, has become the sponsor of a great initiative for the first time, and in the most difficult arena. This means that Turkey, which has been trying to open to the region for about 10 years, has now become a key country."[22]

Another phase in Turkey's mediation efforts took place on December 22, 2008, when Prime Minister Olmert came to Turkey to discuss the issue with Prime Minister Erdoğan. Concurrent with Olmert's visit, President Bashshar al-Asad declared his readiness to hold direct talks with it. However, not much came out of the mediation, as Olmert himself had less than two months left in office before the February 2009 Israeli general elections, and as Asad decided to call off the negotiations due to the Israeli offensive on Hamas in early 2009. For Prime Minister Erdoğan, the Israeli offensive which cut his mediation efforts was like a slap in the face.

## The Gaza Setback

The Israeli three week offensive in Gaza in January 2009 had negative impact on Turkish-Israeli relationship. And the questions that need concern us are: why was it so? Will this alter the basics of relations? What is the long-term significance of this episode?

The Turkish harsh reaction to the offensive was both on the official and popular level. PM Erdoğan led the way by warning Israeli leaders that history will judge them for the black stain they are leaving on humanity. He even went as far as to declare that the blood of the dead Palestinian children would not be left on the floor, and that Israel's deeds were "a crime against humanity." Worse still, he demanded the expulsion of Israel from the United Nations for ignoring the organization's call to stop the fighting in Gaza.[23] Then came the Davos incident at the end of January in which Prime Minister Erdoğan demonstratively walked off the stage during his debate with Israeli President Shimon Peres. No wonder, then, that Erdoğan came to be considered a hero by Gazans, Iranian, and Syrians. Taking their cues from him, the media and the Turkish street escalated their anti-Israeli and at times even anti-Semitic attacks to a point which surpassed sometimes those voiced in Arab countries. Huge anti-Israeli demonstrations flooded the streets of Turkey's major cities and towns[24] in which demonstrators burned Israeli flags and waved anti-Israeli and anti-Semitic slogans. One of the placards read: "Jews and Armenians cannot enter, but dogs can."[25] In another incident, someone wrote on the door of one of the biggest synagogues in Izmir "We will kill you," which led to the closing down of synagogues.[26] The reaction on the popular level was partly spontaneous and partly officially organized, including even the mobilization of school children, which points to a political hand acting behind the scenes.

Evidently, there was clear sympathy toward the Palestinians among the Turkish people. At the same time it was also evident that the government was attempting to manipulate this sympathy for different purposes: mobilizing support for the AKP in the Turkish local elections in March; deflecting attention from the domestic PKK problem; challenging the military, the architect of the relations with Israel; and finally, enhancing Turkey's role among Arab and Muslim countries.

For all of these rhetorical and emotional reactions, it should be pointed out that, practically speaking, the Turkish government did not initiate any punitive move against Israel. Thus for example it did not recall its ambassador to Ankara as it had done on an earlier occasion. Moreover at the very time that Prime Minister Erdoğan was lashing out at Israel, media reports suggested that an arms deal worth 167 million U.S. dollars was signed between Ankara and Jerusalem.[27]

## Overview

Under the AKP government, relations between Turkey and Israel have witnessed a lot of ups and downs that had to do not with any direct difficulties in bilateral relations between Ankara and Jerusalem but mainly with the stance of either of the two toward third parties. These included the Kurds of Iraq, Israel's second war against Lebanon in 2006, and its offensive on Hamas in Gaza in January 2009. Yet, notwithstanding these myriad changes in recent years, Turkish-Israeli relations have remained on the whole quite solid. Turkey benefited from certain military know-how and other strategic matters while Israel enjoyed the official recognition and legitimization by a Muslim country. The price was the anti-Israeli lip service that Erdoğan and other Turkish officials had to pay to appease public opinion or buy its goodwill at home as well as in the Arab and Muslim world. At the same time, the attacks against Israel also reflected a genuine inner conviction among certain Turkish politicians.

One should note that the correlation between progress in the peace process with the Palestinians and the Turkish-Israeli relations, first apparent in the early 1990s, continued to hold. The collapse of the peace process in October 2000 and the ensuing violence caused considerable damage. On the other hand, Israel's withdrawal from Gaza in summer 2005 engendered a flood of visits by high-ranking Turkish officials. Already in May, in anticipation of the withdrawal, Prime Minister Erdoğan traveled to Jerusalem. In contrast with his harsh attacks on Israel a year earlier, he now praised Israel's Prime Minister Ariel Sharon for his decision to withdraw. However, the Israeli attack on Hamas in

2009 has once again brought new tensions into relations. Yet while Prime Minister Erdoğan called the attack "a crime against humanity" he also attempted to play the role of mediator for the conclusion of a ceasefire between the two parties.[28] Thus, the quality of Israeli–Turkish relations will undoubtedly continue to be affected by the course of the Israeli–Palestinian conflict.

To sum up, asymmetry and ambiguity continue to characterize the relationship, and it seems that both Turkey and Israel have accepted the rules of the game. Israel keeps its complaints to itself, for the sake of political and strategic considerations. Thus, Israel demonstrated that it had learned the lesson of the past: It avoided repeating its mistake of 1956, when it recalled its ambassador in protest against similar move by Turkey, only to find that it would take more than thirty years to return. For its part, the Turkish government, with an eye to Arab and Muslim sensibilities, sticks to its ambiguous pronouncements and attitudes, while also pointing to its good relations with Israel in order to curry favor in Western capitals, to enhance its role of mediator in the region as well as to placate the Turkish military. Finally, although Turkish–Israeli relations under the AKP governments have lost much of the intimacy of the 1990s, still the bonds of interests are strong enough to enable the two partners to overcome occasional crises.

# List of Abbreviations Used in

# Notes and Sources

| | |
|---|---|
| AFP | Agence France Press |
| DR | Daily Report |
| IDF (Radio) | Israeli Defence Forces |
| INA | Iraqi News Agency |
| JP | *Jerusalem Post* |
| IISS | International Institute for Strategic Studies |
| MECS | *Middle East Contemporary Survey* |
| MERIA | Middle East Review of International Affairs |
| MESA | Middle East Studies Association Bulletin |
| SWB | BBC Summary of World Broadcasts |
| TDN | Turkish Daily News |
| TRT (TV) | Turkish National Television |
| USIS | United States Information Service |

# Notes

## Introduction

1. Israel State Archives, 3348/24, Meeting between Morris Fischer and General Gürsel, August 16, 1960.

## 1 After the 1991 Gulf War Earthquake

1. *Los Angeles Times*, January 30, 1991.
2. Ibid.
3. For Wilson's Fourteen Points, see *Encyclopedia Britannica* (Internet version). For his doctrine of self-determination, see James Gelvin, "The Ironic Legacy of the King-Crane Mission," in David W. Lesch, *The Middle East and the United States: A Historical and Political Reassessment* (Boulder, CO: Westview Press, 1996), pp. 11–27.
4. *Los Angeles Times*, January 30, 1991.
5. See Haim Bresheeth and Nira Yuval-Davis (eds.), *The Gulf War and the New World Order* (London, New Jersey: Zed Books, 1991). See pp. 1–10, and more specifically Noam Chomsky's essay, "The US and the Gulf Crisis," pp. 13–26. For a different kind of critique, see Lawrence Freedman and Efraim Karsh, *The Gulf Conflict 1990–1991* (Princeton, NJ: Princeton University Press, 1993), pp. xxix; 3–19.
6. On this, see Lawrence Freedman, "The Gulf War and the New World Order," *Survival*, Vol. XXXIII, No. 3 (May/June 1991), pp. 195–209.
7. Yigal Sheffy, "The Military Dimension of the Gulf War," in Ami Ayalon (ed.), *Middle East Contemporary Survey (MECS) 1991* (Boulder: 1993), p. 86.
8. Saudi Arabia's war-related expenses were estimated at $48 bn., while those of Kuwait were about $28 bn. Joseph Kostiner, "Saudi Arabia," in Ami Ayalon (ed.), *MECS 1991*, pp. 523, 620.
9. Haim Shemesh, *Soviet–Iraqi Relations, 1968–1988, In the Shadow of the Iraq–Iran Conflict* (Boulder: Lynne Rienner Publishers, 1992), see pp. 249–250.
10. For changing American interests in the Middle East, see Burton I. Kaufman, *The Arab Middle East and the United States* (New York: Twayne Publishers, 1996).

11. See, e.g., Amatzia Baram and Barry Rubin (eds.), *Iraq's Road to War* (New York: St. Martin's Press, 1996); Lawrence Freedman and Efraim Karsh, *The Gulf Conflict, 1990–1991* (Princeton, NJ: Princeton University Press, 1993); Majid Khadduri, *War in the Gulf, 1990–1991* (New York: Oxford University Press, 1997); Barry Rubin, *Cauldron of Turmoil* (New York: Harcourt Brace Jovanovich, 1992).

12. In mid February Bush called on the Iraqi people and the military to end the war by "taking matters into their own hands" and force Hussein to "step aside." *New York Times*, February 16, 1991.

13. *Los Angeles Times*, April 14, 1991.

14. Martin Indyk, "The Clinton Administration's Approach to the Middle East" (Washington Institute for Near East Policy, May 18, 1993) (Internet version).

15. For a discussion on imperialism, see Richard Koebner and Helmut Dan Schmidt, *Imperialism: The Study and Significance of a Political Word* (Cambridge, England: Cambridge University Press, 1964).

16. For the attacks on Kurds, see C. J. Edmonds, *Kurds, Turks and Arabs* (London: Oxford University Press, 1957). Edmonds described one such occasion thus: "I was constantly in the air... visiting Sulaimani and Halabja or accompanying bombing raids and demonstration flights," p. 392.

17. It must be stressed, though, that during the Shi'a and Kurdish uprisings in 1991, the United States did turn a blind eye on the Iraqi army's use of helicopters to attack the rioting areas, which helped decide the outcome. The no-fly zone in the south was not so helpful for the Shi'as, because Iraqi tanks and infantry could still move freely there.

18. See Fouad Ajami, *The Arab Predicament: Arab Political Thought and Practice Since 1967* (Cambridge: Cambridge University Press, 1982).

19. For the text and an analysis of the declaration, see Daniel Dishon and Bruce Maddy-Weitzman, "Inter-Arab Relations," in Colin Legum, Haim Shaked, and Daniel Dishon (eds.), *MECS 1979–80* (New York: Holmes & Meier Publishers, Inc., 1981), pp. 195–196, 224–225.

20. Ibid., p. 195.

21. An earlier example was the Arab alliance with Britain against the Ottomans in the Arab Revolt in World War I. But there the rationale was to promote Arab nationalism, and not to repulse a danger.

22. For a discussion, see Barry Rubin, "The New Middle East: Opportunities and Risks," *Security and Policy Studies*, No. 19 (Tel Aviv: BESA Center for Strategic Studies, Bar-Ilan University, 1995), pp. 47–64.

23. S. E. Ibrahim, "Management of Ethnic Issues in the Arab World," *Strategic Papers*, No. 26 (Al-Ahram Center for Strategic Studies, February 1995).

24. *The 1999 Chart of Armed Conflict*, International Institute for Strategic Studies.

25. For comparison, the fatalities of the Six Day War and border conflict of 1967–70 were 75,000. Ibid.

26. David Menashri, *Revolution at a Crossroads* (Washington, D.C.: Washington Institute for Near East Policy, 1997).

27. Samuel Huntington, "The Clash of Civilizations?" *Foreign Affairs*, Vol. 72, No. 3 (Summer 1993).

28. Ihsan Gürkan, "Turkish–Israeli Relations and the Middle East Peace Process," *Turkish Review of MES*, No. 7 (1993), p. 102. It was also maintained that at the time, Turkish Prime Minister Adnan Menderes suggested to Secretary of State John Foster Dulles that the Arabs should be left out of the defense plan. George Emanuel Gruen, *Turkey, Israel and the Palestinian Question, 1948–1960: A Study in the Diplomacy of Ambivalence* (Ph.D. dissertation, Columbia University, 1970), p. 221.

29. This was felt immediately in Israel, when Turkey decided to terminate the secret military relations.

30. Walter F. Weiker, "Turkey," in Itamar Rabinovich and Haim Shaked (eds.), *MECS 1984–85* (Tel Aviv: 1987), pp. 692–93; William M. Hale, "Turkey," in Ami Ayalon and Haim Shaked (eds.), *MECS 1988* (Boulder: 1990), pp. 768–770.

31. Sabri Sayarı, "Turkey: The Changing European Security Environment and the Gulf Crisis," *Middle East Journal*, Vol. 46, No. 4 (Winter 1992), p. 11.

32. Çevik Bir, "Turkey's Role in the New World Order: New Challenges," *National Defense University Strategic Forum Publications*, No. 135 (February 1998).

33. *Cumhuriyet*, January 1, 1991.

34. William M. Hale, "Turkey," in Ami Ayalon (ed.), *MECS 1990*, p. 683.

35. Sayarı, op. cit., p. 13.

36. *Cumhuriyet*, January 1, 1990.

37. *Cumhuriyet*, March 30, 1990.

38. *Cumhuriyet*, April 7, 1990.

39. William M. Hale, *MECS 1990*, p. 683.

40. *Cumhuriyet*, September 24, 1990.

41. David Kushner, "Turkey: Iraq's European Neighbor," in Baram and Rubin, op. cit., p. 207.

42. Kushner, op. cit., pp. 209–210.

43. Necip Torumtay, *Orgeneral Torumtay'ın Anıları* (İstanbul: Milliyet, 1993), p. 116.

44. Kushner, op. cit., pp. 207, 217.

45. Turkish losses reportedly reached $40 bn. by the year 2000. *Milliyet*, October 31, 2000.

46. Peter Galbraith, *Civil War in Iraq: A Staff Report to the Committee on Foreign Relations, United States Senate, May 1991; Time*, April 15, 1991.

47. See the remarks by Chief of Staff Necip Torumtay and Doğan Güreş's on the issue. A. Haluk Ülman, "*Turkiye'nin Yeni Güvenlik*," in Haluk Ülman (ed.), *Ortadoğu Sorunları ve Türkiye* (İstanbul: TÜSES, 1991), pp. 121–122.

48. For a detailed discussion, see Jacob Roy, "The Establishment of Relations between Israel and the Soviet Union under Gorbachev," in Benyamin Neuberger (ed.), *War and Peacemaking, Selected Issues in Israel's Foreign Relations* (H) (Tel Aviv: The Open University of Israel, 1992), pp. 402–416.

49. Ibid., Gad Barzilai, "Israel," in Ami Ayalon (ed.), *MECS 1990* (Boulder: 1992), pp. 438–439; Ministry of Immigrant Absorption, www.moia.gov.il.

50. *Al-Jumhuriyya*, January 18, February 1, 7, 12, 1994, June 8, 1996.

51. Sheffy, op. cit., pp. 84–86.

52. For the ineffectiveness of this "protection," see Aharon Levran, *Israeli Strategy after Desert Storm* (London: Frank Cass, 1997), pp. 10–16; Efraim Inbar, "Contours of Israel's New Strategic Thinking," *Security and Policy Studies No. 27* (Tel Aviv: BESA Center for Strategic Studies, June 1996), p. 58.

53. Levran, op. cit., pp. 87–96.

54. Barzilai, op. cit., pp. 455–459.

## 2  Days of Future Past—The Peripheral Alliance

1. Baruch 'Uziel, "*The Peripheral Alliance,*" *Beterem* (H), November 1948, pp. 8–11.

2. Baruch 'Uziel, *The Peripheral Alliance: A Suggestion for Israeli Policy* (H) (Tel Aviv: Hamerkaz, 1959), pp. 3–31.

3. For such hints, see the protocols of the Knesset's Foreign Affairs and Defense Committee, 7566/3, July 16, 1958.

4. Aaron S. Klieman, *Israel and the World after 40 Years* (Washington: Pergamon-Brassey's, 1990), p. 6.

5. For details on the secret track, see Aharon Klieman, *Statecraft in the Dark: Israel's Practice of Quiet Diplomacy* (Jerusalem: Jerusalem Post Press, 1988), pp. 75–113.

6. For Shiloah's personality and contributions to the state of Israel, see Haggai Eshed, *Reuven Shiloah: The Man Behind the Mossad* (London: Frank Cass, 1997).

7. Israeli State Archives (ISA), 4374/16, Reuven Shiloah to Director General, Foreign Ministry, September 11, 1957.

8. Ibid.

9. ISA, 3123/8, military attaché to Head of Military Intelligence, November 9, 1957.

10. ISA, 3125/6, Moshe Alon to Director General, Foreign Ministry, September 23, 1957.

11. For an analysis of Israeli–Iranian relations, see Samuel Segev, *The Iranian Triangle: The Secret Relations between Israel–Iran–USA* (H) (Tel Aviv: Sifriyat Ma'ariv, 1981).

12. Interview, November 28, 2000, with Moshe Sasson, Shiloah's assistant during the negotiations for the peripheral alliance and later chargé d'affaires in Turkey.

13. Segev, op. cit., p. 98.

14. R. Ankara, December 15, 1957, Summary of World Broadcasts (SWB), December 17, 1957. Baghdad's explanation was that the Iraqi mission in New York had decided on the voting and that "the government had no direct responsibility" for it. ISA, 3215/11 R. Rubek to Arab Department, December 19, 1957.

15. See, ISA, 3125/11, quoting *Vatan*, December 28, 1957; ISA, 3125/12, R. Rubek to Arab Department, August 30, 1958.

16. ISA, 3125/11, military attaché to Head of Military Intelligence, December 21, 1957; ISA, 3125/11, R. Rubek to Arab Department, December 25, 1957.

17. ISA, 3125/11, *Ulus*, March 23, 1958, quoted in memorandum No. 59, April 7, 1958.

18. ISA, 3125/5, M. Fischer to Israeli Embassy in Washington, May 12, 1958.

19. ISA, 3125/12, Rubek to Arab Department, September 2, 1958. For Nuri's tragic end, see *Majzarat Qasr al-Rihab* (Beirut, 1960).

20. For details, see George Emanuel Gruen, op. cit.

21. Even earlier, Turks expressed satisfaction with the fact that Israel had taught a lesson to the Arabs, especially to Egypt. ISA, 2329/21, E. Epstein to M. Shertok, July 20, 1948.

22. In the interview with Moshe Sasson (the chargé d'affaires to Turkey 1960–66), he described the Israeli move as a serious mistake and said that Foreign Minister Moshe Sharet came under pressure to do so from Morris Fischer, the chargé d'affaires (1953–56). Sasson assumed that the upgrading of relations would have been easier if Israel had left its representative in Ankara. Interview, November 28, 2000.

23. The Iraqi government did come under public pressure because of its policy of neutrality on the Suez War.

24. ISA, 3125/6, Israeli Ambassador in Rome to Director General, Foreign Ministry, February 5, 1957.

25. ISA, 3125/6, Yohanan Meroz to Director General, January 27, 1958.

26. See, e.g., ISA, 3125/4, W. Elyashar to Director, Arab Department, March 31, 1957; ISA, 3604/1, Algom to Arab Department, May 20, 1964.

27. See, e.g., ISA, 3125/6, Israeli Ambassador in Rome to Director General, Foreign Ministry, February 5, 1957.

28. Michael Bar Zohar, *Ben-Gurion: A Political Biography* (H), Vol. III (Tel Aviv: 'Am 'Oved, 1977), pp. 1316–1317.

29. David Ben-Gurion, *Selected Documents, Israeli State Archives (1947–1963)* (H) (Jerusalem, State Archives, 1996–97), pp. 416–417.

30. Avi Shlaim, *The Iron Wall: Israel and the Arab World* (London: Penguin, 2000), pp. 198–204.

31. Eshed, op. cit., pp. 305–311.

32. The Israeli chargé d'affaires to Ankara disclosed later that the Turks reported to the Americans about all the communications between Turkey and Israel. ISA, 3125/4, M. Alon to M. Sasson, June 9, 1959. It was also reported that the Americans praised Menderes for the cooperation between Turkey and Israel. ISA, 3750/2, Herzog to Sasson, November 3, 1959.

33. ISA, 3750/2, Middle East Division in the Israeli Foreign Office to Israeli Ambassador in Rome, December 8, 1959.

34. Segev, op. cit., p. 96.

35. ISA, 3125/5, M. Sasson to R. Shiloah, January 19, 1958.

36. Segev, p. 90; Eshed, op. cit., p. 305.

37. ISA, 3125/6, R. Rubek to Arab Department in the Foreign Ministry, July 20, 1958. Israel did provide Turkey with information on the coup.

38. For the Baghdad Pact and its ramifications, see Elie Podeh, *The Quest for Hegemony in the Arab World: The Struggle over the Baghdad Pact* (New York: E. J. Brill, 1995).

39. Interview with a Turkish official who wished to remain anonymous; Sezai Orkunt, *Türkiye ABD Askeri İlişkileri* (İstanbul: Milliyet, 1978), p. 384.

40. The existence of a written agreement was confirmed to me by Baruch Gilboa, the Israeli military attaché to Turkey (1964–67). Interview, December 5, 2000.

41. Eshed, op. cit., pp. 306–307, 314.

42. Amikam Nachmani, *Israel, Turkey and Greece: Uneasy Relations in the East Mediterranean* (London: Frank Cass, 1987), p. 75.

43. Interview with Moshe Sasson, Israeli chargé d'affaires (1960–66), November 27, 2000; interview with Baruch Gilboa, military attaché (1964–67), December 5, 2000.

44. ISA, 3750/2, Military Attaché to the Head of Military Intelligence, October 13, 1959.

45. See, e.g., ISA, 3348/26, M. Sasson to Arab Department, October 31, 1961.

46. Yossi Melman (ed.) (H), *CIA Report on the Israeli Security and Intelligence Services* (H) (Tel Aviv: Sifrei Erez, 1982), p. 56.

47. ISA, 3604/2, Sasson to Shek, December 2, 1964; interview with Sasson, November 27, 2000.

48. Anonymous interview, January 10, 2001.

49. Interview with Gilboa, December 5, 2000.

50. In one of the dispatches from the Foreign Ministry to Sasson, the need to make a clear separation between the different areas of responsibility was reaffirmed. ISA, 3604/1, Zeev Shak to chargé d'affaires, August 30, 1964.

51. It must be said, though, that in the early days of the state, and when there was still hope for peace with the Arabs, Israel was more cautious in

developing relations with "anti-Arab forces." ISA, 2536/12, Y. Shimoni to
A. Eban (Paris), October 27, 1948.

52. Gruen, op. cit., p. 170. The Communist Knesset member, Meir Vilner,
described the Turkish regime as "fascist and feudal."

53. ISA, 7566/3, Protocols of the Knesset Foreign and Security Committee,
July 16, 1958.

54. Very early Colonel Türkeş, one of the leading members of the junta,
stated Turkey's intention to develop relations on the economic, scientific,
and social levels. ISA, 2290/5, M. Alon to M. Fischer, September 14, 1960.

55. ISA, 2290/4, M. Alon to M. Fischer and the Middle East Division,
July 13, 1960.

56. ISA, 3348/24, Meeting between M. Fischer and General Gürsel,
August 15, 1960.

57. Even prior to the secret agreement, Egypt, Syria, and Jordan spoke about
the friendly relations between the two and "their secret military agreements." ISA, 3125/6, Israeli Ambassador to Rome to Director General,
Foreign Ministry, January 9, 1957. A Turkish official in the Foreign
Ministry stated clearly that even though the downgrading of relations in
1956 might have been a mistake, there was no way to upgrade relations
without publicity and without disclosing evidence to those who claimed
that there was a secret [military] agreement between the two. ISA,
3125/6, Moshe Alon to Director General, September 23, 1957.

58. ISA, 3125/4, M. Alon to Moshe Sasson, June 9, 1959.

59. Another reason put forward was that if Turkey improved relations with
Israel, Qasim might unleash the Iraqi Kurds against Turkey. In a trial in
Baghdad, the Iraq's former director of Security Services claimed that
there was a secret plot between the United States, Britain, Turkey, and
Israel against the Arabs and that Menderes's letter to Ben-Gurion of
August 1957(!) was proof of this. ISA, 3125/12, Ankara to Jerusalem,
January 11, 1959.

60. See, e.g., ISA, 3125/4, E. Sasson, Rome, to Director General Middle East
Division, June 5, 1959; ISA, 3750/2, M. Alon to General Director Middle
East Division, July 14, 1959.

61. ISA, 3750/2, Herzog (Washington) to Ministry of Foreign Affairs,
November 3, 1959.

62. ISA, 3757/2, E. Sasson to E. Cohen, March 4, 1960.

63. ISA, 3125/4, M. Alon to Moshe Sasson, June 5, 1959. See also, ISA, 3750/2,
Asher to head of Military Intelligence quoting a high-ranking Turkish officer (Sergut) who said that Zorlu had always been against the move.

64. Interview with Israeli military attaché, Baruch Gilboa, December 5, 2000.
This view was confirmed by other Israeli officials.

65. In his discussion with M. Fischer, Gürsel described the Arabs as an
"unripe" nation, and said that they did not understand reality and "lived

under illusions." ISA, 3348/24, Meeting between M. Fischer and General Gürsel, August 16, 1960.

66. ISA, 3348/26, M. Sasson to Director, Arab Department, May 17, 1961; ISA, M. Sasson to Director, Arab Department, October 11, 1961.

67. In March 1963, Ben-Gurion wrote a letter to Inönü asking for relations to be upgraded. Inönü agreed in principle, but postponed the decision to a later date (which never came). ISA, 3604/4, S. Karib (date not clear, probably) March 26, 1964.

68. ISA, 3448/20, M. Sasson to Aryeh Levavi, May 22, 1963.

69. ISA, 3448/80, Moshe Sasson to Aryeh Levavi, May 22, 1963; ibid., July 22, 1963.

70. ISA, 3604/1, Foreign Ministry to Ankara Legation, July 2, 1964; ISA, 3604/1, from Arab Department to chargé d'affaires, Ankara, June 20, 1965.

71. For a discussion of the importance of economic relations, see Gruen, op. cit., pp. 389–424. Israeli officials were given "a briefing on how to contact the Turks." Describing the Turks as a "very proud people" it warned that one should be careful not to hurt their pride or to criticize them; that one should not ask about their domestic affairs (such as the coup) but should instead praise their achievements and emphasize Atatürk's role in particular. Finally, it said, that when speaking about support for the Turks one should stress that Israelis too could learn from them. Ben-Gurion himself spoke highly of Atatürk. ISA, 3348/26, Economic Division to Ministry of Agriculture, February 7, 1961; ISA, 3448/20, Jerusalem to Istanbul, November 10, 1963.

72. ISA, 3125/6, M. Alon to Director General, September 23, 1957. Curiously, in the 1960s an Israeli company Solel Boneh (under the name of Reinolds) was building airports in Turkey, while in the 1990s a Turkish company was engaged in building an airport in Israel, although for various reasons this particular firm did not continue with the project. In 1968, Solel Boneh finished building houses in an American base near Ankara, which passed into Turkish hands in that year. ISA, 4245/4, D. Laor to Middle East Division, August 14, 1968. Interview with Baruch Gilboa, September 13, 2001.

73. ISA, 3750/4, R. Ben Eliezer to Economic Division, June 2, 1959. That Israel was taken as a model for emulation was illustrated, e.g., by the opening of a road in Nide, when the mayor called on the Israeli military attaché (who was fluent in Turkish) to speak and to compare this achievement with that of Israel. Interview, February 13, 2001, with Paul Kedar, military attaché (from the end of 1961 to mid-1964).

74. ISA, 3604/2 (Sasson?) to Shek June 30, 1964 (?) (1965?) (No date in document).

75. Interview with Sasson, November 28, 2000.

76. ISA (reference missing in original document), D. Laor to Middle East Division, October 30, 1968.

77. Baruch Gilboa, interview December 5, 2000; ISA, 3604/1, M. Sasson to Z. Shek, September 30, 1964.

78. ISA, 3604/4, *IKA* Bulletin, April 17, 1965, No. 3458.

79. For hints on this, see ISA, 3604/3, M. Sasson to W. Elyashar, December 15, 1965; ISA, 4075/26, N. Eshkol to Z. Rafiyah, June 7, 1966. It took ten years to complete the dam (1964–74).

80. ISA, 4076/24, D. Laor to Arab Department, August 23, 1967.

81. Interview with Baruch Gilboa, September 13, 2001.

82. Interview with Ehud Efrat, Head of Branch R in Military Intelligence and later Israeli military attaché in Ankara (1967–70), January 10, 2001.

83. ISA, 4075/26, Najjar to Levavi, May 18, 1966; ISA, 4075/26, military attaché to Head of Military Intelligence, June 10, 1966. The Turkish Chief of Staff who is quoted in the document uses the term "agreement" for the cooperation.

84. ISA, 4075/26, a draft letter from Rabin to the Turkish Chief of General Staff, General Cemal Tural (early June 1966). The letter was handed to Tural on June 9, 1966; interview with Meir Amit, Head of Military Intelligence and later the Mossad, March 25, 2001.

85. Interview with Baruch Gilboa, December 5, 2000.

86. Anonymous interviews with members of the Israeli security services. Cooperation on terrorism was not detailed any further.

87. Anonymous interview, February 28, 2002. My other interviewees spoke only about "expectations" that each would come to the support of the other in any contingency. Interviews, Meir Amit, March 25, 2001; Ehud Efrat, January 10, 2001, Baruch Gilboa, September 13, 2001. For the Turkish confirmation, see Orkunt, p. 384.

88. ISA, 2290/4, M. Fischer to C.[?] Yahil, June 17, 1960. For the desertion, see Nezih Tavlaş, "Türk-Israil Güvenlik ve Istihbarat Ilişkileri," *Avrasya Dosyası*, Vol. V, No. 1 (Spring 1999).

89. Anonymous interview with member of Israeli security establishment.

90. Anonymous interview. ISA, 4075/27, Military Attaché Baruch Gilboa to Jerusalem, October 5, 1965 (or 1966).

91. Meir Amit, in his role as chief of Mossad, was the mastermind behind the support to the Kurds. See Meir Amit, *Head On* (H) (Or Yehuda: Hed Arzi Publishing House, 1999), pp. 152–178.

92. ISA, 4075/26, Z. Shek to Sh. Bendor, July 18, 1966; ISA, 4075/27, Sh. Bendor to Z. Shek, February 5, 1967.

93. Interviews with Paul Kedar, February 13, 2001 and Baruch Gilboa, December 5 and 28, 2000.

94. Anonymous interview.

95. Interview with Ehud Efrat, January 10, 2001; Meir Amit, March 25, 2001.

96. ISA, 3604/1, Ankara to Arab Department, May 12, 1964. The academy was composed at the time of some dozen students.

97. ISA, 3604/2, M. Sasson to Arab Department, December 1, 1964.

98. Vamik D. Volkan and Norman Itzkowitz, *Turks and Greeks: Neighbors in Conflict* (Huntingdon: Eothen Press, 1994), p. 139; for the crisis, see pp. 129–157.

99. Salahi R. Sonyel, "New Light on the Genesis of the Conflict," in Clement H. Dodd (ed.), *Cyprus: The Need for New Perspectives* (Huntingdon: Eothen Press, 1999), p. 30. At the time, Turkey lacked military equipment such as landing craft.

100. Sonyel, op. cit., pp. 31–33.

101. R. Ankara, August 8, 9 DR, August 10, 1964; Vamik D. Volkan, *Cyprus— War and Adaptation* (Charlottesville, VA: University Press of Virginia, 1979), pp. 19–20.

102. Clement H. Dodd, "A Historical Overview," in Clement H. Dodd (ed.), op. cit., p. 8.

103. Sonyel, op. cit., p. 35. It must be stressed, however, that suspicions and fears of the USSR, especially of its penetration into Syria, continued to trouble Turkey for a long time. See, e.g., the discussion between the Israeli chargé d'affaires and the head of Turkish security services, who expressed such fears. ISA, 4245/9, chargé d'affaires to Deputy Director General, Foreign Ministry, February 7, 1968.

104. ISA, 3448/18, chargé d'affaires to Director, Arab Department, November 26, 1963.

105. ISA, 3604/1, M. Sasson to Director, Arab Department, June 10, 1964; ISA, 3604/5, M. Sasson to Director, Arab Department, October 14, 1964; ISA, 3604/4, M. Sasson to Director, Arab Department, June 30, 1965.

106. ISA, 3604/4, Arazi to Michael, July 8, 1965.

107. The George Grivas forces were being trained and armed by the United Arab Republic (Egypt). Faruk Sönmezoğlu (ed.), *ABD'nin Türkiye Politikası* (İstanbul: Der, 1995), p. 22, quoting *Facts on File*, Vol. XXV.

108. ISA, 3604/2, M. Sasson to Director, Arab Department, November 8, 1964.

109. ISA, 3604/4, M. Sasson to Director, Arab Department, June 30, 1965.

110. E.g., interview with Prof. Aryeh Shmuelevitz, a historian of the Ottoman Empire and keen observer of modern Turkey, February 12, 2001, and a number of anonymous interviewees.

111. ISA, 3604/2, Inönü's message to Eshkol, dated January 6, 1964; ISA, 3604/1, Eshkol's message to Inönü dated January 24, 1964.

112. ISA, 3604/1, M. Sasson to Z. Shek, February 19, 1964.

113. ISA, 3604/1, from Istanbul Consulate to Arab Department, May 12, 1964.

114. R. Nicosia, August 9, SWB, August 10, 1964.

115. ISA, 3604/1, Foreign Ministry to chargé d'affaires, Ankara, August 19, 1964.

116. Ibid.; ISA, 3604/1, Director, Arab Department, to chargé d'affaires, Ankara, August 30, 1964; ISA, 3604/1, Inönü's message to Eshkol (n.d.), September 1964.

117. Interview with Paul Kedar, February 13, 2001.

118. ISA, 3604/1, Abraham Shamil to the Ankara Legation, September 4, 1964.

119. ISA, 3604/1, M. Sasson to Z. Shek, September 1, 1964.

120. Nachmani, op. cit., p. 68.

121. ISA, 3604/1, Director, Arab Department, to chargé d'affaires, Ankara, August 30, 1964; ISA, 3604/1, M. Sasson to Z. Shek, September 1, 1964.

122. In an interview with Sasson on February 26, 2001, he repeated the notion that Israel was not, in fact, neutral.

123. ISA, 3604/1, M. Sasson to Z. Shek, February 19, 1964; ISA, 3604/2, M. Sasson to Z. Shek, December 2, 1964; ISA, 3604/2, Michael Tsur to M. Sasson, October 9, December 10, 1964; ISA, 3604/2, M. Sasson to Director, Arab Department, December 14, 1964; ISA, 3604/4, Golda Meir's letter to Feridun Cemal Erkin, February 7, 1965; ISA, 3604, M. Sasson to Director General, Foreign Ministry, April 28, 1965.

124. Anonymous interviews with members of Israeli security forces.

125. ISA, 3604/2, M. Sasson to Michael Tsur, December 3, 1964.

126. ISA, 3604/2, a draft letter from Israeli Prime Minister to Turkish Prime Minister; draft letter from Israeli Foreign Minister to Turkish Foreign Minister, January 31, 1965.

127. ISA, 3604/2, Ankara Legation to Foreign Ministry, October 21, November 4, 1964; interview with Zvi Rafiyah, official in the Israeli Legation in Ankara, December 27, 2000.

128. ISA, 3604/2, chargé d'affaires to Director, Arab Department, December 1, 1964.

129. Interview with Baruch Gilboa, December 5, 2000.

130. ISA, 3604/2, chargé d'affaires to Director General, Foreign Ministry, December 1, 1964.

131. ISA, 3604/2, chargé d'affaires to Director, Arab Department, November 8, 1964, January 13, 1965.

132. Demirel was reported to have courted the Islamists. ISA, 4076/24, Sasson to Arab Department, January 5, 1966.

133. On one occasion, e.g., he complained that Prime Minister Eshkol's letter to Inönü was "as dry as a visiting card." ISA, 3604/1, Sasson to Shek, September 1, 1964.

134. ISA, 3604/1, Sasson to Shek, September 1, 1964; ISA, 3604/4, Sasson to Shek, July 20, 1965; ISA, 3604/2, Director, Arab Department, to chargé d'affaires, December 13, 1964; ISA, 3604/2, Deputy Director, Arab Department, to chargé d'affaires, December 10, 1964; ISA, 3604/4, Director, Arab Department, to chargé d'affaires, June 20, July 14, 1965.

135. ISA, 3604/1, Ankara Legation to Ezra Danin, June 9, 1964.

136. ISA, 3604/2, chargé d'affaires to Director General, Foreign Ministry, December 14, 1964.

137. ISA, 3604/2, press officer to Amos Gordon, Israel Radio, December 23, 1964. For a directive to the Israel Radio Arabic Service, see ISA, 3604/2, Director General, Foreign Ministry to M. Sasson, December 11, 1964.

138. ISA, 3448/20, M. Sasson to Director, Arab Department, August 8, 1963; ISA 3604/? Sasson to Director of Arab Department, June 23, 1965, ISA, 4245/7, Zvi Rafiyah to chargé d'affaires, August 22, 1968.

139. ISA, 3604/2, chargé d'affaires to Director, Arab Department, December 30, 1964.

140. ISA, 3604/2, chargé d'affaires to Director General, Foreign Ministry, January 6, 1965.

141. ISA, 3604/2, Sasson to Foreign Ministry, December 23, 1964.

142. ISA, 3604/4, chargé d'affaires to Director General, Foreign Ministry, June 23, 1965.

143. ISA, 3604/4, chargé d'affaires to Director General, Foreign Ministry, February 12, 1965.

144. ISA, 3604/2, dispatch of Mossad representative to Foreign Ministry, January 7, 1965. ISA, 3604/4, a letter from Israeli Foreign Minister Golda Meir to Turkish Foreign Minister Feridun Cemal Erkin, February 7, 1966; ISA, 3604/4, a letter from Israeli Prime Minister Levi Eshkol to Turkish Prime Minister Suat Hayri Ürgüplü, June 10, 1965.

145. R. Nicosia, December 18, SWB, December 20, 1965.

146. After the UN vote, students in Ankara carried "a black list" of the countries that had betrayed Turkey, among which were Israel, Egypt, the United States (!), and others. ISA, 3604/2, Rapoport to Z. Shek, December 27, 1965.

147. ISA, 4075/26, a draft letter from Rabin to Tural (early June 1966); ISA, 4075/26, military attaché to the Head of Military Intelligence, June 10, 1966.

148. ISA, 4076/21 (Israeli Consul in New York to Foreign Ministry), *New York Times*, April 10, 1966; ISA, 4076/21, Sasson to Foreign Ministry, April 29, 1966.

149. ISA, 4076/21, New York (consulate) to Foreign Ministry, March 24, 1966; ISA, 4076/21, Foreign Ministry to (consulate) New York, March 25, 1966.

150. Interview with the then military attaché, December 5, 2000; ISA, 4075/26, Victor Elyashar to M. Gazit, May 13, 1966.

151. ISA, 4075/26, Levavi to the embassy in Brussels, May 11, 1966; ISA, 4075/26, Najjar to Foreign Ministry, May 18, 1966.

152. ISA, 4075/26, Military Attaché to Head of Military Intelligence, June 10, 1966. It should be noted that the decision was taken shortly after Tural had become Chief of Staff.

153. Interview with the Israeli military attaché, Baruch Gilboa, December 28, 2000.
154. ISA, 4075/27, N. Eshkal to the chargé d'affaires, Ankara, October 10, 1966.
155. ISA, 4075/26, M. Sasson to V. Elyashar, May 17, 1966.
156. ISA, 4075/27, Eshkal to chargé d'affaires, Ankara, October 10, 1966.
157. ISA, 4075/27, V. Elyashar to Director General, Foreign Ministry, December 25, 1966.
158. On one occasion when the Libyan foreign minister demanded that Turkey cut its economic relations with Israel, he was given the answer that Turkey's volume of trade with Israel was no more than the amount of Israeli goods that found their way or were smuggled into the Arab countries. ISA, 4245/16, D. Laor to Middle East Division, Jerusalem, December 22, 1969.
159. ISA, 4245/6, D. Laor to Director of Middle East Division, December 23, 1969. The planes were probably carrying ammunition to the Kurds. It must be said that this Turkish move was more than offset by the permission allegedly given to Iraq to move soldiers to the Syrian front via Turkish territory in the Yom Kippur War in 1973. Amos Gilboa, military intelligence officer, in a closed lecture, November 28, 2000.
160. ISA, 4245/8, D. Laor to Middle East Division, October 9, 1968.
161. ISA, 4075/26, Sasson to Foreign Ministry, May 5, 1966.
162. Ibid., May 11, 1966.
163. ISA, 4075/26, Victor Elyashar to Director General, Foreign Ministry, May 13, 1966.
164. ISA, 4075/26, Military Attaché to Head of General Security, June 10, 1966.
165. Interview with Baruch Gilboa, December 26, 2000.
166. ISA, 3604/1, Sasson to Shek, September 1, 1964.
167. Kleiman, *Statecraft in the Dark*, pp. 75–113.
168. For the "special relations" between Israel and Morocco that started clandestinely in the mid-1950s, see Bruce Maddy-Weitzman, "Israel and Morocco: A Special Relationship," *The Maghreb Review*, Vol. 21, No. 1–2 (1996), pp. 36–48.

## 3  The 1990s Alignment: Motives and Players

1. In an author interview on October 24, 2001 with Çevik Bir, the former deputy chief of Turkey's General Staff, he said that the two parties' share in the agreement was "50%–50%."
2. Interview with knowledgeable high-ranking Israeli officer, August 10, 2003.
3. George Gruen, *Turkey—Israel and the Palestine Question, 1948–1960.*

4. For this, see Stanford J. Shaw, *The Jews of the Ottoman Empire and the Turkish Republic* (New York: New York University Press, 1991).

5. Ibid., pp. 207–217.

6. Ibid., pp. 214–217.

7. Falih Rıfkı Atay, *Zeytin Dağı* (İstanbul: MEB. Yayınları, 1992), pp. 68–71. Interestingly, in later years he would publish pro-Israeli articles in Turkish newspapers.

8. Rifat N. Bali, *Cumhuriyet Yıllarında Türkiye Yahudileri: Bir Türkleştirme Serüveni* (1923–45) (İstanbul: İletişim, 1999), pp. 105–109, 243–254; Avner Levi, *History of the Jews in the Republic of Turkey* (H) (Jerusalem: Hamaccabi, 1992), pp. 59–76.

9. Bali, op. cit., p. 40; Shaw, op. cit., p. 289.

10. Bali, op. cit., p. 322.

11. Levi, op. cit., p. 77.

12. Lecture by Norman Stone on March 28, 2001 at the Moshe Dayan Center, Tel Aviv University. According to a new research based on Turkish archives, Turkey has opened its doors at the time not just to Jewish academics but to other Jewish refugees as well. However, its goal of assimilating them did not succeed. Information provided by Soner Cağaptay, author of an unpublished dissertation on Turkish nationalism in the interwar era.

13. Levi, op. cit., p. 77.

14. Gruen, op. cit., p. 22.

15. Çağrı Erhan and Ömer Kürkçüoğlu, "Arap Olmayan Ülkelerle İlişkiler," in Baskı Oran (ed.), *Türk Dış Politikası Kurtuluş Savaşından Bugüne Olgular, Belgeler, Yorumlar*, Vol. I (İstanbul: İletişim, 2001), p. 799; Bülent Aras, "The Palestinian–Israeli Peace Process in International Context with a Note on the Consequences for Turkish Foreign Policy"(M.A. Thesis, Boğaziçi University, 1996), p. 141.

16. Alon Liel, *Turkey: Military, Islam and Politics 1970–2000* (H) (Tel Aviv: Hakibutz Hameuhad, 1999), p. 194. The same point was made by a Turkish scholar, Hakan Yavuz, in "Turkey's Relations with Israel," *Foreign Policy 15*, No. 3 (Ankara), p. 55, quoted in Aras, op. cit., p. 146.

17. Interview with Elie Shaked, second secretary in Ankara in 1980, on September 16, 2001. Shaked reported that the Turkish move came as a shock to the Israeli Foreign Ministry and its representatives in Turkey. The quotation is from, Aryeh Shmuelevitz, "Turkey," in Colin Legun, Haim Shaked, and Daniel Dishon (eds.), *MECS 1980–81* (New York: Holmes & Meier, 1982), pp. 856–857.

18. Author interview with Türkmen, October 22, 2001.

19. For an interesting account of those who joined the PLO, see Faik Bulut, *Filistin Rüyası* (İstanbul: Bersin, 1998). On links between PKK and PLO see, Nihat Ali Özcan, *PKK, Tarihi, Ideolojisi, ve yöntemi* (Ankara: ASAM, 1999), pp. 237–247.

20. Esra Çayhan, *Dünden Bugüne Türkiye Arupa Birliği İlişkileri ve Siyasal Partilerin Konuya Bakışı* (İstanbul: Boyut, 1997), pp. 74–75.

21. Rıfat N. Bali, *Musanın Evlatları Cumhuriyet 'in Yurttaşarı* (İstanbul: İletişim, 2001), p. 345.

22. Hüseyin Nihal Atsız, "Komünist, Yahudi ve Dalkavuk," in *Bütün Eserleri-Makaleler IV* (İstanbul: Irfan, 1997), pp. 172–173. Atsız also wrote six novels with ultranationalist messages. Jacob Landau, "Ultra Nationalist Literature in the Turkish Republic: A Note on the Novels of Hüsayin Nihâl Atsız," *Middle Eastern Studies*, Vol. 39, No. 2 (April 2003), pp. 204–210.

23. Hüseyin Nihal Atsız, "Kızılelma" (?), Ibid., pp. 231–232.

24. Atsız, "Ne Zaman Savaşılır," Ibid., pp. 487–492. In spite of being influential, he remained marginal in the party and was ostracized by it in his last years.

25. Alpaslan Türkeş, *Dış Politakımız ve Kıbrıs* (İstanbul: Hamle, 1996), pp. 67–83. Türkeş was the only Turkish politician who had attended an international conference held in Antalia in November 1991 on the Prospects of Turkey's bilateral relations with Israel. This was the first conference between Turkish and Israeli academicians.

26. Şemsedin Günaltay, *Yakın Şark: Suriye ve Filistin* (Ankara: Türk Tarih Kurumu, 1987), Preface, p. XII.

27. TNA, December 19, SWB, December 19, 1991.

28. Efraim Inbar, *The Israeli–Turkish Entente* (London: King's College, University of London, 2000), pp. 16–17.

29. Anatolia, July 17; TRT TV, July 7, SWB, July 7, 1994. In an interview with the author on October 23, 2001, Çiller—by then a long time in opposition—repeated the idea that if she became prime minister she would endeavor to bring peace between Israel and the Palestinians.

30. Kenneth W. Stein, "The Arab–Israeli Peace Process," in Bruce Maddy-Weitzman (ed.), *MECS 1996* (Boulder: Westview Press, 1998), p. 56.

31. See also Ayşegül Sever, "Turkey and the Syrian–Israeli Peace Talks in the 1990s," *Middle East Review of International Affairs* (MERIA), Vol. 5, No. 3 (September 2001), pp. 2–5. Sever maintained that Turkey "suspected that US-sponsored peace talks between Israel and Syria might be detrimental to Turkish interests" (p. 4).

32. Alon Liel described this episode in an open lecture at the Moshe Dayan Center, Tel Aviv University, on December 11, 1997. Minutes of Third Annual Joint Seminar of Turkish Foreign Policy Institute, Ankara and the Moshe Dayan Center. There are, however, those who think that the ties were "a consequence of the Israeli–Arab peace process (and to a lesser degree, the end of the Cold War)." See Leon T. Hadar, "Orienting Jerusalem Toward Ankara or Cairo? Israel's New Geostrategic Debate," *Mediterranean Quarterly*, Vol. 12, No. 3 (Summer 2001), p. 18.

33. Interview, October 24, 2001.

34. See, Gencer Özcan and Ofra Bengio, "The Decade of the Military in Turkey: The case of the Alignment with Israel in the 1990s", *International Journal of Turkish Studies* vol. 7(2001) pp. 90–110.

35. Until 2002, four Chiefs of General Staff had served 15 years, an average of almost four years. They were Doğan Güreş Ismail Hakkı Karadayı, Necip Torumtay, and Hüseyin Kıvrıkoğlu.

36. For the text of the public briefings in 1997, see Hikmet Çiçek (ed.), *İrticaya Karşı Genelkurmay Belgeleri* (İstanbul: Kaynak, 1997).

37. In a briefing to the Foreign Ministry in June 1997, Deputy Chief of General Staff General Çevik Bir harshly criticized Foreign Minister Tansu Çiller for "neglecting the affairs of the ministry in such a crucial time." *Hürriyet*, June 27, 1997. Responding to her call to the military to distance themselves from politics, an unnamed military source replied that her attitude could only be explained by "her unshackled ambitions for political power." *Milliyet*, June 28, 1997.

38. Çevik Bir, "Turkey's Role in the New World Order: New Challenges," *National Defense University Strategic Forum Publications*, No. 135 (February 1998).

39. Ibid; Serhat Güvenç, "TSK'nın Sınırötesi Girişim Yetenekleri: Ulusal Güvenlik Politikasında Yeni Boyut," in Özcan and Kut (eds.), *En Uzun Onyıl*, p. 139.

40. Necip Torumtay, *Orgeneral Torumtay' ın Anıları* (İstanbul: Milliyet, 1993), p. 107.

41. Nebil İlseven, "Körfez Bunalımı ve Türkiye," in A. Haluk Ülman (ed.), *Ortadoğu Sorunları ve Türkiye* (İstanbul: TÜSES, 1991), p. 70.

42. Gülay Günlük Şenesen, "Türk Silahlı Kuvvetleri'nin Modernizasyon Programının Bir Değerlendirmesi," in Faruk Sönmezoğlu (ed.), *Türk Dış Politikasının Analizi* (İstanbul: Der, 1994), p. 199.

43. Throughout the 1980s, Israeli officials in Ankara had assiduously sought to persuade their Turkish interlocutors to differentiate between the bilateral aspects of Israeli–Turkish relations and Turkey's views of the Arab–Israeli peace process. Interview with Israeli official, July 31, 2003.

44. *Hürriyet*, June 24, 1995, *Turkish Daily News*, April 13, 1996.

45. *Türkiye'nin Gerçek Durumu Sebepleri Teşhis*, Welfare Party (n.d., possibly 1995), pp. 1–32. To turn the message easier to grasp, the pamphlet was accompanied by cartoons. See, e.g., pp. 18, 22.

46. Ismet G. Imset, *The PKK: A Report on Separatist Violence in Turkey (1973–1992)* (Ankara: Turkish Daily News, 1992), pp. 168–207. Imset was forced to leave the country following the book's publication.

47. Idris Bal, "Instability in the Middle East and the Relevant Role of the PKK," *Turkish Review of Middle East Studies, Annual 2002* (Istanbul: Foundation for Middle East and Balkan Studies (OBIV), 2003), p. 147.

48. Fatih Çekirge's interview with the Chief of General Staff, Ismail Hakkı Karadayı, *Sabah*, October 15, 1997. The solutions included the idea raised

as early as 1990 of establishing "a security buffer zone" along the Syrian and Iraqi borders. Imset, op. cit., pp. 213–219.

49. Ülman, "Türkiye'nin Yeni Güvenlik Algılamaları ve 'Bölücülük,'" in Ülman (ed.), *Ortadoğu sorunları*, op. cit., pp. 122–124.

50. *Milliyet*, December 23, 1995, February 3, 28, 1996, *Hürriyet*, February 13, 25, 1996. *Milliyet*, February 28, 1996. This was confirmed by later revelations, *Hürriyet*, February 4, 2002.

51. Çiçek, op. cit., pp. 35, 48.

52. *Milliyet*, August 11, 1996; *Sabah*, September 16, 1996. See also Philip Robins, "Turkish Foreign Policy under Erbakan," *Survival*, Vol. 39 (Summer 1997), pp. 82–100.

53. See the interview with Chief of General Staff Necip Torumtay, *Savunma ve Havacılık*, Vol. 1, No. 2 (June–July 1987), p. 5, quoted in Güvenç. "TSK'nın Sınırötesi Girişim Yetenekleri," in Özcan and Kut (eds.), p. 139.

54. Şenesen, "Türk Silahlı Kuvvetleri'nin Modernizasyon Programının Bir Değerlendirmesi," op. cit., p. 199.

55. *Cumhuriyet*, April 27, 1992; *Milliyet*, April 8, 1994.

56. *Milliyet*, April 7, 1996; *Hürriyet*, June 10, 1996; *Radikal*, December 4, 1996.

57. Nezih Tavlaş, "Türk–İsrail Güvenlik ve İstihbarat İlişkileri," *Avrasya Dosyası*, Vol. 5, No. 1 (1999), p. 93. See also, *Turkish Daily News*, July 3, 1996.

58. In 1984, the PKK established the *Hazen Rizgariya Kurdistan* ("Kurdistan Freedom Unit"), which undertook armed operations inside Turkey. Imset, op. cit., pp. 38–40.

59. *Cumhuriyet*, April 6, 1996.

60. Deputy Chief of General Staff Çevik Bir was quoted by the *Washington Post* as saying that "Turkey and Israel are the two democratic countries in the region, and we must show . . . that [they] can work together." *Turkish Daily News*, June 5, 1996.

61. Gökhan Bacik, "The Limits of an Alliance: Turkish–Israeli Relations Revisited," *Arab Studies Quarterly*, Vol. 23, No. 3 (Summer 2001), p. 52.

62. Erbakan blamed "the Zionists for inventing the concept of Islamic fundamentalism" in order to forestall the rise of Islam. See Çetin Yetkin and Uğur Özen's interview with Necmettin Erbakan, *Milliyet*, September 10, 1990. The military claimed that the Islamists put the blame on "Jewish professors" for developing the doctrine of Atatürkism. See the document entitled "Batı Harekat Konsepti," undersigned by General Çevik Bir, in Çiçek, op. cit., p. 57.

63. Shimon Peres, *The New Middle East* (H) (Bnei Braq: Steimatzki, 1993).

64. Ibid., pp. 116–119.

65. For example, a member of Peres's party, Shlomo Ben-Ami, said he was very skeptical "as to the validity of the New Middle East romanticism," Shlomo Ben-Ami, "Israel's Foreign Policy Agenda" (Friedrich Ebert Stiftung, 1999), p. 13. See also *JP*, February 11, 2000. Peres continued to be optimistic and even in 2001 still believed that the New Middle East was still possible. *Turkish Daily News* (Internet version), April 10, 2001.

66. Alon Liel, "Turkey," in Bruce Maddy-Weitzman (ed.), *MECS 1996*, p. 690.

67. It was true that Turkey participated in the Korean War in 1950–53 and invaded Cyprus in 1974, but the first was symbolic and the second short, and did not reach Turkey's borders.

68. Interview with Amnon Barzilai, a journalist from *Ha'aretz*, December 24, 2001.

69. *Ha'aretz*, April 26, 1998.

70. Leon T. Hadar, "Orienting Jerusalem Toward Ankara or Cairo?" op. cit., pp. 19–25.

71. Author interview with David Ivri former Defense Ministry Director General, June 2, 2002.

72. For example, *JP* (Internet version), December 15, 1997; October 19, 1998; July 9, 2001; *Ha'aretz*, May 12, 1998.

73. For similar opinions, see Yosef Goel, "Fostering Ties with Turkey Should be Our Highest Priority Just Now," *JP*, November 19, 1993; Barry Rubin, *JP* (Internet version), December 9, 1997; September 10, 1998; February 25, 1999; July 11, 2001.

74. Liel, op. cit.

75. For example, Minutes of the Third Annual Joint Seminar of Turkish Foreign Policy institute, Ankara and the Moshe Dayan Center, pp. 74, 83; *Ha'aretz*, December 22, 1997; September 6, 1998; *Jerusalem Post*, October 9, 1998; February 26, 1999 (Internet version). In an interview with the author on December 5, 2001, Liel suggested that he might have been wrong in his optimism regarding the development of relations with the Arabs, and that the "Turkish" trend was the correct one.

76. *JP*, October 23, 1998.

77. *JP* (Internet version), July 17, 1998; earlier, there were debates as to what Israel's stance on the Armenian issue should be. Some opined that Israel could have good relations with Ankara while recognizing "the Armenian genocide." For these debates see, e.g., *JP* (Internet version), November 7, 1994; February 22, April 24, 1995.

78. *Ma'ariv*, quoted in *Mideast Mirror*, October 7, 1998. A former head of the Israeli Foreign Ministry, Abraham Tamir, expressed as late as 2002 his reservations about the strong tilt toward Turkey, which might harm relations with the Arab countries. Author interview, February 28, 2002.

79. Hadar, op. cit., p. 19.

80. Inbar, op. cit., pp. 15–17; Alain Gresh, "Turkish–Israeli–Syrian Relations and Their Impact on the Middle East," *Middle East Journal*, Vol. 52 (1998), p. 190.

81. *JP*, March 25, 1996 (SWB).

82. For these new countries, see David Menashri (ed.), *Central Asia Meets the West* (London: Frank Cass, 1998).

83. *Ha'aretz*, October 27, 1997.

84. David Ivri said that the Foreign Ministry was not "enthusiastic" about relations with Turkey; author interview, June 2, 2002. Yossi Bar, the Israeli

military attaché between 1996 and 1999, described the Foreign Ministry as lagging behind the Defense Ministry in "years of light" in understanding the Turkish issue. Author interview, June 11, 2002.

85. *Ha'aretz*, April 26, 1998, interview with Amnon Barzilai, December 24, 2001.

86. *Ha'aretz*, December 8, 1997. *Al-Hayat*, January 10, 1998. *Al-Hayat* probably took the information from *Ha'aretz* and mistakenly gave the date of withdrawal as 1984.

87. *Ha'aretz*, December 8, 1997.

88. Interview with David Ivri, June 2, 2002.

89. Interview with Çevik Bir, October 24, 2001.

90. Interview, January 8, 2002.

91. Author interview with Alon Liel, Director General of the Ministry of Economy in Peres's cabinet, December 5, 2001. Interview with Beni Sheffer, the Israeli military attaché to Turkey during 1994–96, January 8, 2002.

92. Interview with Liel, December 5, 2001.

93. USIS, *Wireless File*, May 9, 1997.

94. Interview with David Ivri, June 2, 2002.

95. Interview with Sheffer, January 8, 2002.

96. Alpetkin Dursunoğlu, *Stratejik İttifak Türkiye–İsrail İlişkilerinin öyküsü* (İstanbul, Ankara Yayınları, 2000), pp. 51, 215, quoting the *Wall Street Journal* (undated). This author was unable to find the articles referred to. An Israeli official denied this report, saying that Jordan was brought into the alignment much later. Interview, August 24, 2003.

97. *Turkish Daily News*, July 28, 1999 (Internet version).

98. *Turkish Daily News*, June 2, 1998, April 10, 2002.

99. Interview with David Ivri, June 2, 2002. Another source mentioned that by 1997 about 60 organized Jewish delegations had visited Turkey. Robert Olson, "Turkey–Syria Relations, 1997 to 2000: Kurds, Water, Israel and 'Undeclared War,'" *Orient*, March 2001, p. 117. Olson quotes the Washington Institute but gives no further details. In all probability the pro-Turkish Jewish lobby renewed its activities in a low-keyed manner in the mid-1980s.

100. *Ha'aretz*, May 2, 1997.

101. Interview with Zvi Elpeleg, August 25, 2002.

102. *Ha'aretz*, May 17, 2001.

103. An example was the American opposition to Israel selling Falcon planes to China. Israel decided to cancel that deal in July 2000.

104. *JP*, May 11, 1997.

## 4 The Making of the Alignment

1. In this book I have chosen to use the term alignment, even though it may appear less binding than strategic partnership.

2. Amnon Barzilai, *Ha'aretz*, January 21, 2000.

3. Interview with Zvi Elpeleg, former Israeli ambassador to Turkey, November 11, 2000.
4. Interview, January 8, 2002.
5. *JP* (Internet version), July 26, 1992. Özal's declaration was not mentioned by a Turkish source, but there is no reason to doubt its authenticity.
6. *JP* (Internet version), January 30, 1994; interview with Beni Sheffer, January 8, 2002.
7. As Commander of the Air Force until the 1967 War, he prepared it for the great feats of that war.
8. Xinhua News Agency, January 25, 1994, SWB.
9. IDF Radio, January 28, 1994, SWB.
10. TRT, Ankara, January 27, 1994, SWB. Mehmet Ağar, Director General of Turkish Security Affairs, came to Israel in September 1993 to raise the level of cooperation. Saygı Öztürk, *Devletin Derinliklerinde* (Ankara: Ümit, 2002), pp. 134–135.
11. Interview, October 23, 2001.
12. *Ha'aretz*, February 17, 1999. Zvi Elpeleg, confirmed Israeli involvement in the Kurdish issue. Interview, November 11, 2000.
13. TRT, TV, October 4, 1994, SWB. This information was confirmed by an anonymous Israeli official.
14. *JP*, December 10, 1997 (Internet version); *Ha'aretz*, February 17, 1999, January 21, 2000.
15. Author interview with David Ivri, June 2, 2002.
16. *JP*, June 14, 1996.
17. David Ivri, too, described the period 1994–96 as that of a "honeymoon." Interview, June 2, 2002.
18. The agreement on mutual flights, e.g., preceded the February 1996 agreement and was put into effect in 1995. *JP*, December 11, 1995.
19. According to a public poll conducted in Turkey in May 1996, 29% supported the February 1996 agreement and 44% opposed it. A year later those opposed rose to 34% (although the question was put differently), Strateji MORI, *Siyasi Araştırmalar Bölümü*, May 1996, 1997.
20. William Safire described Ivri as "the man who has done the most" to bring about "the tectonic shift" in the relations. *International Herald Tribune*, December 11, 1997.
21. Interview with Yossi Bar, Israeli military attaché (1996–99), June 11, 2002. Güven Erkaya was commander of the destroyer *Kocatepe*, which was sunk in the 1974 Cyprus War. He was saved by an Israeli ship and taken to Israel. The captain of the Israeli boat and Erkaya met later and became friends. On the whole, as David Ivri stated in the interview (June 2, 2002), personal friendships between Israeli and Turkish officers were an important ingredient in the making of the alignment.
22. *Al-Safir* (Beirut), July 29, 1996, SWB; part of the Turkish version appeared in Ahmet Güner, "Türk–İsrail Anlaşmasının Bilinmeyenleri," *Aksiyon*,

No. 76 (May 18–24, 1996). According to David Ivri, any agreement on the transfer of high technology must include an agreement on secrecy and the safeguard of national interests. Israel had such agreements with other countries. Interview, June 2, 2002.

23. According to one Israeli source (who prefers not to be named), the Israeli side was initially interested mainly in selling arms to Turkey, and developed the rationale for a strategic alignment *ex post facto*. Interview, August 10, 2003.

24. Interview with Sheffer, January 8, 2002.

25. Greece was considered at the time to be Turkey's greatest potential enemy or rival. Interview with Sheffer, January 8, 2002. David Ivri made another differentiation, that Greece was a rival on the psychological level, meaning that it could harm Turkey in Europe and the United States, while Iran with its Islamic fundamentalism was an even bigger threat. Interview, June 2, 2002. Interestingly, a poll conducted in November 2001 about Turkey's rivals showed that Greece was considered the most unfriendly country with 34%, the United States, 21%, Iraq, 5%, Iran, 3%, Syria, 2%. Israel was not mentioned. Ali Çarkoğlu and Kemal Kirişçi, *Türkiye Dış Politikası Araştırması*, Boğaziçi Üniversitesi, March 2002.

26. Interview, David Ivri, June 2, 2002. Ivri maintained that in the 1980s as well Egypt attempted to frustrate agreements between Turkey and Israel.

27. Interview with Sheffer, January 8, 2002.

28. *Al-Safir*, July 29, 1996, SWB.

29. Interview with Sheffer on January 8, 2002. This was also confirmed by former Israeli ambassador to Turkey, Zvi Elpeleg. Interview, February 21, 2002.

30. For example, the agreement to upgrade 54 Turkish Phantoms was signed in August 1995 but made public only in March 1996. *JP*, March 25, 1996.

31. An Israeli military attaché maintained that 50% of the agreements were not made public. Interview on June 11, 2002.

32. The difference in the approach to Israel was illustrated, e.g., after the Israeli attack on Kafar Kanna in Lebanon in April 1996, when the foreign minister summoned the Israeli ambassador to protest the action, while the members of the Chief of Staff's bureau did not even mention the case. Interview with Sheffer, January 8, 2002.

33. It was the Turkish side that first published the report on the agreement. *JP*, June 14, 1996.

34. *Milli Gazete*, July 12, 1996.

35. *Milliyet*, August 10, 1996; *Turkish Daily News*, December 2, 1996.

36. *Hürriyet*, October 15, 1996.

37. *Radikal*, December 7, 1996.

38. Anonymous interview, February 28, 2002.

39. David Ivri supported this analysis. Interview, June 2, 2002.

40. *JP*, July 13, 1998. Traditionally, most Israeli attachés were from the air force.

41. *Al-Sharq al-Awsat*, February 26, 1997, quoted by *Mideast Mirror*.

42. *JP*, June 4, 9, 1996. Keeping military ties discreet was a traditional Israeli policy not only in regard to Turkey, but with any other counterpart.

43. *Ha'aretz*, August 9, 2001.

44. Ankara Türkiye Radyoları network, February 26, 1997.

45. Efraim Inbar, *The Israeli–Turkish Entente* (London: University of London, 2000), pp. 21–24.

46. Interview with David Ivri, June 2, 2002.

47. Interview with Yossi Bar, June 11, 2002. Voice of Israel, December 1, DR, December 2, 1996.

48. Interview with David Ivri, June 2, 2002.

49. For this, see Efraim Inbar, op. cit., pp. 20–25; Alpetkin Dursunoğlu, *Stratejik İttifak*, pp. 215–281; Gencer Özcan and Ofra Bengio, "The Decade of the Military in Turkey: The Case of the Alignment with Israel in the 1990s," *International Journal of Turkish Studies*, Vol. 7 (Spring 2001), pp. 90–109. By 1997, there were already 20 agreements signed. *Ha'aretz*, February 26, 1997. 30 more were signed by 2004.

50. In the period predating 1967, Israel used to ask permission to land in different European countries in order that its pilots would experience long flights. One pilot was allowed to land in Istanbul, e.g., back in 1953/54. Interview, Paul Kedar, March 6, 2002.

51. According to the International Institute for Strategic Studies, the Israeli Air Force was "almost certainly [engaged in] reconnaissance missions ... against potential adversaries." *The Military Balance 1996/97* (Oxford: Oxford University Press, 1996), p. 121.

52. *Ha'aretz*, October 24, 1999.

53. Inbar, op. cit., p. 20. According to another source, only four times annually. Ekavi Athanassopoulou, *Israeli–Turkish Security Ties: Regional Reactions* (Jerusalem: The Hebrew University, March 2001), p. 2.

54. *Hürriyet*, quoted in *Mideast Mirror*, July 14, 1998.

55. Initially, Egypt was worried about the agreement on aerial maneuvers, but once Turkey gave Mubarak the full text he stopped criticizing it. Israel TV, July 29, 1996. By the end of 2000 the Arab world as a whole stopped criticizing the maneuvers. *Ha'aretz*, January 23, 2001.

56. *Ha'aretz*, January 1, 1998; Inbar, op. cit., p. 20; *Christian Science Monitor*, July 10, 1998 (Internet version).

57. Anatolia News Agency, July 16, 1998; interview with David Ivri, June 2, 2002. The base in question, according to an anonymous source, was at Sivrihisar.

58. *Ha'aretz*, June 3, 2001; AFP, June 18, 2001.

59. Inbar, op. cit., p. 21; Athanassopoulou, op. cit., p. 2.

60. *Ha'aretz*, May 1, 1997.

61. *JP*, December 2, 1998; AFP, December 3, 2001. In an interview on October 24, 2001, Çevik Bir said that initially Egypt was furious about

the maneuvers, but when the Turks explained their aims, it dropped its opposition. The first maneuver was delayed because of Egyptian pressure. The rest went ahead smoothly, with no attempts to stop them. *Ha'aretz*, July 4, 2001.

62. *The Christian Science Monitor*, July 10, 1998.
63. *Milliyet*, April 30, 2001.
64. Athanassopoulou, op. cit., p. 3.
65. *Globes*, December 8, 1996 (Internet version).
66. Israel TV Channel 1, July 29, 1996.
67. Athanassopoulou, op. cit., p. 3.
68. *JP*, March 10, 2002. Turkey sought to be a partner in their production but the United States vetoed it.
69. *JP*, August 11, 2002. By August, Turkey had already bought 54 UCAV. The project was planned to end in two years.
70. *Ha'aretz*, May 1, 1997.
71. *Turkish Daily News*, December 10, 2001. This source reported that the trilateral talks were frozen either because of the intifada or because of a decision by President Bush.
72. *Milliyet*, January 23, 1997, DR, January 28, 1997. Netanyahu's denial however, need not be the whole truth.
73. Cooperation between the Mossad and MIT continued without interruption since the very beginning. Anonymous interview.
74. Quoted by *JP*, May 4, 1997. The Turkish Defence Minister Turhan Tayan, denied the report.
75. Athanassopoulou, op. cit., p. 4.
76. UPI Press Agency, February 13, 2002.
77. *JP*, March 10, 2002 (Internet version); *Financial Times*, March 13, 2002 (Internet version); *Turkish Daily News*, March 14, 2002 (Internet version).
78. *Hürriyet*, April 2, 3, 2002 (Internet version).
79. *Financial Times*, April 4, 2002.
80. *Hürriyet*, April 3, 2002 (Internet version).
81. Ankara Anatolia News Agency, April 2, 2002 (Internet version); *Hürriyet*, April 3, 2002 (Internet version).
82. *Milliyet*, April 2, 2002 (Internet version).
83. *Hürriyet*, April 3, 2002 (Internet version).
84. *Ankara Anatolia*, April 2, 2002 (Internet version).
85. *Globes* website, January 17, 2001.
86. *Ha'aretz*, December 2, 2001; TRT Television, March 8, 2002.
87. *Ha'aretz*, December 2, 2001.
88. *Ha'aretz*, December 2, 2001.
89. UPI, March 20, 2002.
90. *Ha'aretz*, March 19; *Turkish Daily News*, March 22, 2002.
91. *Turkish Daily News*, March 22, 2002 (Internet version).
92. *Ha'aretz*, August 7, 2002.

93. *Ha'aretz*, November 18, 2001; UPI, March 20, 2002. 67 Israeli firms were said to be involved in GAP. *Cumhuriyet*, February 21, 2002.

94. Voice of Israel, August 8, 2001, SWB.

95. *Radikal*, July 20, 2002. A Turkish company that was involved in the construction of the new Ben-Gurion airport, went bankrupt, and ceased work there.

96. Interview with Ya'acob Amidror, former personal secretary to Defense Minister Yitzhak Mordechai, April 21, 2002.

97. The Sabra and Shatila massacres of 1982 in Lebanon for which Sharon was blamed caused a stir in Turkey at the time, but did not prevent the visit now.

98. Paul Rivlin, "Economic Relations Between Turkey and Israel" (unpublished essay), p. 4.

99. TRT TV, September 24, 1998.

100. *Milliyet*, January 23, 1997, DR.

101. Interview with Zvi Elpeleg on August 25, 2002.

102. *Turkish Daily News*, September 6, 2001 (Internet version).

103. Rivlin, op. cit., p. 8; interview, June 6, 2002.

104. This information was provided by Ekrem Güvendiren, the first Turkish Ambassador to Israel and later chairman of the Turkish–Israeli Business Council. *A Concise Report on Turkish–Israeli Relations* 1999 (no further details), pp. 12–14; also Rivlin, op. cit., p. 4.

105. Anatolia News Agency, July 1, 1999.

106. www.cbs.gov.il/frtrade/td1.htm

107. Inbar, op. cit., p. 19.

108. Rivlin, op. cit., p. 3. See also Güvendiren, op. cit., p. 14.

109. Deutsche Presse-Agentur, July 3, 4, 1997.

110. Author interview with 'Amidror, April 21, 2002. The best Israeli pilots took part in the action, which cost Israel about US$500,000. Turkey's call to the United States and other countries for help did not result in such immediate reaction. Interview with Yossi Bar, June 11, 2002.

111. *JP*, October 26, 1999; *Ha'aretz*, November 21, 1999; Ecevit was quoted in *Hürriyet*, November 18, 1999. *Hürriyet*, August 17, 2000, mentioned Israel's leading role. For Israel's aid to Adapazarı after an earthquake in the 1960s, see chapter 2.

112. Anat Lewin, "Turkey and Israel: Reciprocal and Mutual Imagery in the Media 1994–1999," *Journal of International Affairs* (Fall 2000), p. 2.

113. The Israeli "connection" with Fenerbahçe started in 1950 when this soccer team came to Israel for a series of four matches. Gruen, op. cit., p. 130.

114. According to foreign publications, the Mossad helped Turkey by gathering information worldwide on Kurdish organizations and passing it to Turkish Intelligence. Regarding Öcalan, it was reported that Israeli agencies used electronic means to intercept messages and to track the aircraft in which he flew seeking asylum after he had been expelled from Syria. *Ha'aretz*, February 17, 1999.

115. *Ha'aretz*, February 18, 1999.

116. *JP*, February 21 (Internet version);Voice of Israel, March 4, 1999.
117. Anatolia News Agency, March 11, 1999, SWB.
118. Anatolia News Agency, March 4, 1999, SWB.
119. *Turkish Daily News*, April 28, 2000.
120. *Turkish Daily News*, May 12, 2000 (Internet version).
121. *JP*, April 7, 2002 (Internet version).
122. *Yeni Türkiye*, October 8, 1995; *Radikal, Milliyet*, October 5, 2001; *Milliyet*, October 2, 2001 spoke about corruption in general, not necessarily linked with Israel.

# 5 Implications and Reactions

1. For an earlier treatment of the subject see, Ofra Bengio and Gencer Özcan, "Old Grievances New Fears: Arab perceptions of Turkey and its Alignment with Israel," *Middle Eastern Studies*, April 2001. For some studies on mutual images, see Ekmeleddin Ihsanoğlu, "Qira'a li-Ta'rikh al-Dawla al-'Uthmaniyya wa-'Alaqatiha bil-'Alam al-'Arabi," *Studies on Turkish Arab Relations, Annual 1986* (Istanbul: TAIV, 1986), pp. 85–118. For a thorough discussion of this subject, see Ulrich W. Haarmann, "Ideology and History, Identity and Alterity: The Arab Image of the Turk from the Abbasids to Modern Egypt," *International Journal of Middle Eastern Studies*, No. 20 (1988), pp. 175–196. Ibrahim al-Daquqi, *Surat al-'Arab lada al-Atrak* (Beirut, Markaz al-Dirasat al-'Arabiyya, 1996).
2. Amin Shakir, Sa'id al-'Aryan, Muhammad Mustafa 'Ata, *Turkiyya wal-Siyasa al-'Arabiyya* (Cairo, Dar al-Ma'arif Bimisr, 1954), pp. 45, 71.
3. Daquqi, op. cit., pp. 74–75.
4. Oya Akgönenç Mughisuddin, "Perceptions and Misconceptions in the Making of Foreign Diplomacy: A Study of Turkish–Arab Attitudes Until the End of the 1970s," *Turkish Review of Middle East Studies*, No. 7 (1993), p. 147.
5. See, e.g., *Al-Minbar*, No. 61 (March 1991), p. 47; *Al-Mustaqbal al-'Arabi*, No. 151 (September 1991), p. 160; Muhammad al-Sammak, "Al-'Alaqat al-'Arabiyya al-Turkiyya, Hadiruha wa-Mustaqbaluha," in *al-'Arab wal-Atrak fi 'Alam Mutaghayyir* (Beirut: Markaz al-Dirasat al-Istratijyya, 1993), p. 81. Khalid Ziyada, "Al-'Arab wal-Turk fi al-Ta'rikh al-'Uthmani," in *al-'Arab wal-Atrak fi 'Alam Mutaghayyir*, p. 66.
6. For such periodization, see, e.g., Kamal al-Manufi, "Al-Tatawwurat al-Jadida fi al-Siyasa al-Kharijiyya al-Turkiyya," *Al-Siyasa al-Duwaliyya* (April 1976), pp. 144–149; Nabiyya al-Isfahani, "Turkiyya bayn al-Matalib al-Wataniyya wal-Waqi' al-Dawli," *Al-Siyasa al-Duwaliyya* (April 1978), pp. 92–107; Mustafa Muhammad 'Abd al-Hamid Thabit, "Al-'Alaqat al-'Arabiyya, al-Turkiyya ba'd Harb al-Khalij," *Al-Fikr al-Istratiji al-'Arabi* (July 1992), pp. 107–130; Mahmud 'Ali al-Dawud, "Al-'Alaqat al-'Arabiyya wal-Turkiyya wal-'Awamil al-Mu'aththira Fiha," *Al-Mustaqbal al-'Arabi* (November 1982), pp. 62–69.

7. See, Cihad Fethi Tevetoğlu, "Bugünkü Türk-Suudi Dostluğuna İlk Adım: Gazi Mustafa Kemal—Faysal bin Abdülaziz Görüşmesi," *Studies on Turkish-Arab Relations*, Annual 1986, op. cit., pp. 291–309.

8. New documents reveal that not only Iraq, but even Jordan's King 'Abdullah, was willing to consider a defense agreement between Turkey, Jordan, Iran, and Iraq as early as January 1947. Elie Podeh, *The Quest for Hegemony in the Arab World: The Struggle over the Baghdad Pact* (Leiden: Brill, 1995), p. 46. For the failed Turkish attempts to bring Jordan into the pact in 1958, see Ara Sanjian, *Turkey and Her Arab Neighbours, 1953–1958* (Wiltshire: Archive Editions, 2001), p. 218.

9. For further details on Turkish–Egyptian relations, see Muhammad wafa' Hijazi, "Al-'Alaqat al-Misriyya al-Turkiyya—Judhuruha al-Madiya wa-Ihtimalatuha al-Mustaqbala," *Al-Siyasa al-Duwaliyya* (October 1985), pp. 140–145.

10. See, e.g., *Turkiyya wal-Siyasa al-'Arabiyya* (n.d.), pp. 100–113. Mas'ud Dahir *"Nadwa al-Dinamiyya al-Jadida fi al-Sharq al-Awsat,"* *Al-Mustaqbal al-'Arabi*, No. 151 (September 1991), pp. 158–162: Sim Shakmak, Mawqi' Turkiyya fi al-Hilf al-Atlasi, *Al-Mustaqbal al-'Arabi* (November 1982), pp. 101–111.

11. Sammak, op. cit., p. 74.

12. In February 1997, the military-led National Security Council (NSC) formulated "the 28 February Decisions," which underscored that *irtica*, Islamic fundamentalism in Turkey, has become as dangerous as Kurdish separatism and should be fought by all available means. In September 1997 the NSC revised the *National Security Policy Document* in accordance with "the 28 February Decisions" and asked the government to step up its efforts to fight "*irtica*." See Gencer Özcan and Şule Kut (eds.), *Onbir Aylık Saltanat: Siyaset, Ekonomi ve Dış Politikada Refahyol Dönemi* (İstanbul: Boyut, 1998). In June 1999, the NSC, dissatisfied with the performance of the former governments, formulated new directives for fighting Islamic fundamentalism. See, *Hürriyet*, June 24, 1999.

13. Muhammad Muslih argues that the two events that have left a lasting imprint on Hafiz al-Asad and his Ba'thist comrades were the loss of Palestine to the Zionists and of Alexandretta to Turkey, although the latter was of secondary importance. He also notes that the Syrian intellectual, Zaki Arsuzi, an Alawite from the Sanjak of Alexandretta and a cofounder of the Ba'th Party, was the moving force behind the protest movement against the Turkish annexation. Muhammad Muslih, "Uneasy Relations, Syria and Turkey," in Henry J. Barkey (ed.), *Reluctant Neighbor: Turkey's Role in the Middle East* (Washington, DC: United States Institute of Peace Press, 1996), pp. 114, 116.

14. Amin Shakir, Sa'id al-'Aryan, and Muhammad Mustafa 'Ata, *Turkiyya wal-Siyasa al-'Arabiyya*, op. cit.

15. Najda Fathi Safwat, "Mawqif Turkiyya min Qadiyyat Filastin," *Al-Mustaqbal al-'Arabi*, No. 45 (November 1982), pp. 87–89, 85–100. For

further discussion of Sultan Abdül-Hamid's stance, see Tevetoğlu, op. cit., pp. 291–293.

16. Safwat, op. cit., pp. 94, 99–100. On another occasion Safwat maintained that Saudi Arabia, for example, declined to join the Baghdad Pact because of Turkey's refusal to break off relations with Israel. Sanjian, op. cit., p. 200.

17. Al-Manufi, op. cit., p. 149.

18. Safwat, op. cit., p. 99.

19. Sim Shakmak, "Mawqi' Turkiyya fi al-Hilf al-Atlasi," *Al-Mustaqbal al-'Arabi*, No. 45 (November 1982), pp. 101–111 (quote, p. 105).

20. Safwat, op. cit., p. 90; Mahmud 'Ali al-Dawud, op. cit., p. 66.

21. Muhammad Wafa' al-Hijazi, "Al-'Alaqat al-Misriyya al-Turkiyya," *Al-Siyasa al-Duwaliyya* (October 1985), pp. 140–145, Bruce Maddy-Weitzman, *The Crystallization of the Arab State System 1945–1954* (Syracuse: Syracuse University Press, 1993), pp. 143–155.

22. See also Uri Bialer, *Between East and West: Israel's Foreign Policy Orientation 1948–1956* (New York: Cambridge University Press, 1990), pp. 256–257. In 1952 the U.S. Ambassador to Turkey George McGhee, carried out a survey in Arab countries and Iran to find out their position in regard to the possibility of Turkey assuming a leading role in such an organization. The results indicated their opposition to this. George McGhee, *The US–Turkish–NATO Middle East Connection* (London: MacMillan, 1990), pp.186–207.

23. Ismail Soysal, "Political Relations between Turkey and Egypt in the Last Sixty Two Years," *Studies on Turkish Arab Relations*, No. 2 (1987), pp. 49–57.

24. Muhammad Nur al-Din, "Al-Sharq al-Awsat fi al-Siyasa al-Kharijiyya al-Turkiyya," *Al-'Arab wal-Atrak*, p. 121.

25. Shakmak, op. cit., p. 107. Common denominators mentioned: geographical neighborhood (*jiwar jughrafi*), common history and common culture, and economic interests. Rida 'Abd al-Husayn Ghali al-Quraysh and 'Abd al-Mun'im Sa'id 'Ali, "Al-'Alaqat al-Iqtisadiyya al-'Arabiyya al-Turkiyya Waqi'an wa Tawaqqu'an," *Shu'un 'Arabiyya*, No. 82 (June 1995), p. 192.

26. Al-Dawud, op. cit.

27. *Dunya al-'Arab*, No. 63 (February 1990).

28. See Ali İhsan Bağış, "The Beginning and the Development of Economic Relations Between Turkey and Middle Eastern Countries," *Foreign Policy* (Ankara), Vol. XII (1985), pp. 85–96; M. Hakan Yavuz, "İkicilik: Türk-Arap İlişkileri ve Filistin Sorunu (1947–1994)," in Faruk Sönmezoğlu (ed.), *Türk Dış Politikasının Analizi* (2nd ed.) (İstanbul: Der Yayıncılık, 1998), pp. 574–577 and Mustafa Sönmez, *Türkiye Ekonomisinde Bunalım-12 Eylül ve Sonrasının Ekonomi Politiği* (2nd ed.) (İstanbul: Belge, 1986), p. 156, p. 161; Yusuf Ziya İrbeç, *Türkiye'nin Dış Ekonomik İlişkilerinde İslam Ülkeleri* (Ankara: no publisher, 1990).

29. Butrus Labaki, "Al-'Alaqat al-Iqtisadiyya al-Turkiyya al-Rahina," *Al-Mustaqbal al-'Arabi*, No. 188 (October 1994), pp. 58, 67.

30. *Al-Shahid*, April 1990, quoting the Turkish Minister of Agriculture on "the exchange of oil for water."

31. Muhammad Nur al-Din, op. cit., p. 123.

32. See, e.g., Mahmut B. Aykan, *Turkey's Role in the Organization of the Islamic Conference: 1960–1992* (New York: Vantage Press, 1994). For a discussion on a leading group, the Aydınlar, see Anat Lapidot, "The Turkish–Islamic Synthesis: The National-Religious Narrative in the 1980s," *Hamizrah Hehadash* (H), pp. 84–96.

33. Imset, *The PKK*, p. 172; for an account of the war by two leading Israeli analysts, see Ze'ev Schiff and Ehud Ya'ari, *Israel's Lebanon War* (New York: Simon & Schuster, 1984). They make no reference to the PKK's casualties.

34. Mas'ud Dahir, *Al-Mustaqbal al-'Arabi*, No. 151 (September 1991), pp. 161–162.

35. "Turkiyya wal-Amn al-Qawmi al-'Arabi: al-Siyasa al-Ma'iyya wal-Aqalliyyat," *Al-Mustaqbal al-'Arabi*, No. 160 (June 1992), pp. 117.

36. For details of Turgut Özal's defunct proposals, see Joyce R. Starr, "Water Wars," *Foreign Policy*, No. 82 (Spring 1991), p. 31 and Ramazan Gözen, "Turgut Özal and Turkish Foreign Policy," *Foreign Policy* (Ankara), Vol. XX, No. 3–4 (1996), pp. 80–81; Kemal Kirişçi, Ali Çarkoğlu, and Mine Eder, *Türkiye ve Ortadoğu'da Bölgesel İşbirliği* (İstanbul: TESEV, 1998), pp. 180–181; interview with Tamir, February 28, 2000. Another defunct proposal, named "Peace Canal on the Golan Heights," was put forward by a New York–based consulting company, Wachtel and Associates, to Damascus in 1993.

37. Jalal 'Abdallah Mu'awwad, "Turkiyya wal-Amn al-Qawmi al-'Arabi," *Al-Mustaqbal al-'Arabi*, No. 160 (June 1992), p. 108. See also Murhaf Jouejati, "Water Politics as High Politics: The Case of Turkey and Syria," in Barkey, op. cit., p. 143.

38. *Al-Shahid*, April 25, 1990, p. 46.

39. Jalal 'Abdallah Mu'awwad, "Dawr Turkiyya fi al-Sharq al-Awsat ba'd Azmat al-Khalij," *Shu'un 'Arabiyya*, No. 69 (March 1992), p. 248.

40. Tariq al-Majzub, "Al-Ta'awun al-'Arabi wal-Turki fi Mashari' al-Bunya al-Tahtiyya," *Al-Mustaqbal al-'Arabi*, No. 188 (October 1994), p. 79.

41. Mu'awwad, "Turkiyya," op. cit., pp. 108–109.

42. Philip Robins, *Turkey and the Middle East* (London: Royal Institute of International Affairs, 1991), pp. 87–99. For the details of Turkey's "Three Staged Plan for Optimum, Equitable and Reasonable Utilization of the Transboundary Watercourses of the Euphrates-Tigris Basin," see *Water Issues Between Turkey, Syria and Iraq* (Ankara: Republic of Turkey, Ministry of Foreign Affairs' Department of Regional and Transboundary Waters, 1995), pp. 35–38.

43. 'Ali al-Sarraf, "Al-Mawt 'Atashan," *Al-Shahid*, No. 56 (April 1990), p. 45.

44. Suha Bolukbasi, "Turkey Challenges Iraq and Syria: The Euphrates Dispute," *Journal of South Asian and Middle Eastern Studies*, Vol. 16, No. 4 (Summer 1993), pp. 9–32.

45. *Dunya al-'Arab*, No. 63 (February 1990), p. 12; see also *Al-Shahid* (April 1990).

46. For a lengthy discussion of the Arab point of view on this issue, see 'Ayida al-'Ali Sari al-Din, *Al-'Arab wal-Furat bayn Turkiyya wa-Isra'il* (Beirut: Dar al-Afaq al-Jadida, 1997).

47. *Dunya al-'Arab*, op. cit.; see also *Al-Shahid*, April 1990.

48. Turki 'Ali al-Rabi'u, op. cit.; *Al-Fikr al-Istratiji al-'Arabi*, No. 38 (October 1991), pp. 145, 167.

49. *Al-Shahid*, No. 65 (January 1991), p. 79; *Al-Minbar*, No. 61 (March 1991), p. 46; Nabil Zaki, "Nahwa 'Alaqat 'Arabiyya-Turkiyya Jadida," *Awraq al-Sharq al-Awsat*, No. 18 (November 1996), pp. 15–21.

50. Hani Khalil, "Turkiyya al-Jiyubulitik," *Ma'lumat Duwaliyya*, No. 8 (November 1993), pp. 26–28.

51. For example, Husayn Ma'lum, "Al-Sira' al-Turki al-Irani wa Tada'iyatihi 'ala al-Mintaqa al-'Arabiyya," *Al-Siyasa al-Duwaliyya*, No. 114 (October 1993), pp. 217–220. For a discussion of Pan-Turkish groupings, and trends within the Turkish Ministry of Culture, see Gareth M. Winrow, "Turkey and the Newly Independent States of Central Asia and Transcaucasus," *MERIA Journal* (May 2, 1997). Winrow notes, however, that the Pan-Turkist lobby in Turkey should not be exaggerated. For a discussion of "Neo-Ottomanism" by a Turkish scholar, see Hakan Yavuz, "Turkish Identity and Foreign Policy in Flux: The Rise of Neo-Ottomanism," *Critique*, No. 12 (Spring 1998), pp. 19–43.

52. For Ankara's role in the peace process, see George E. Gruen, "Dynamic Progress in Turkish–Israeli Relations," *Israel Affairs*, Vol. I, No. 4 (Summer 1995), p. 53 and Ayşegül Sever, "The Arab–Israeli Peace Process and Turkey Since the 1995 Interim Agreement," *Turkish Review of Middle Eastern Studies*, Vol. IX (1996–97), p. 122.

53. Mu'awwad, *Shu'un 'Arabiyya*, No. 82 (September 1991), p. 64; Mas'ud Dahir, *Al-Mustaqbal al-'Arabi* (September 1991), pp. 160–162.

54. Turkiyya wal-Amn al-Qawmi al-'Arabi, *Al-Mustaqbal al-'Arabi*, No. 160 (June 1992), p. 124.

55. Mustafa Muhammad, 'Abd al-Hamid Thabit, "Al-'Alaqat al-'Arabiyya al-Turkiyya ba'd Harb al-Khalij," *Al-fikr al-Istratiji al-'Arabi*, No. 42 (July 1992), pp. 118–120.

56. *Al-Mustaqbal al-'Arabi*, No. 160 (June 1992), p. 118.

57. Thabit, op. cit., pp. 119–120; Rabi' 'Ali Ibrahim, "Tawajjuhat al-Istratijiyya al-Turkiyya," *Al-Difa'*, No. 92 (March 1994), p. 93.

58. Al-Rabi'u, *Al-fikr al-Istratiji*, p. 151.

59. *Al-Mustaqbal al-'Arabi* (June 1992), p. 119; Ma'mun Kiwan, "Al-Khilaf al-Ma'i al-Turki-al-Suri al-'Iraqi," Thabit, op. cit., pp. 117–118.

60. *Al-Mustaqbal al-'Arabi* (June 1992), p. 93.

61. 'Abdullah Salih, "Al-Ittifaq al-Turki al-Isra'ili wa-'Amaliyyat al-Salam," *Al-Siyaya al-Duwaliyya* (July 1996), p. 78; Jalal 'Abdullah Mu'awwad, " 'Awamil wa-jawanib tatawwur al-'Alaqat al-Turkiyya-al-Isra'iliyya fi al-Tis'iniyyat," *Shu'un 'Arabiyya*, No. 89 (March 1997), p. 136; Kazim

Hashim Ni'ma, "Al-Tatawwur al-Turki al-Isra'ili, Qira'a fi al-Dawafi' al-Kharijiyya," *Al-Mustaqbal al-'Arabi*, No. 220 (June 1997), p. 4. The Turkish Foreign Minister Ismail Cem, continued to stress that the alignment was not another Baghdad Pact, e.g., *Hürriyet*, March 22, 1998.

62. Israel was actually fearful of the negative implications of the Baghdad Pact for itself, including the prospect that weapons delivered to Iraq would ultimately be used against Israel. Amikam Nachmani, *Israel, Turkey and Greece—Uneasy Relations in the East Mediterranean* (London: Frank Cass, 1987), pp. 73, 75.

63. *Al-Hayat—Mideast Mirror*, April 12, 1996.

64. *Ha'aretz*, June 3, 1997; *Al-Hayat*, December 19, SWB, December 20, 1997.

65. *Al-Hayat*, January 19, SWB, January 21, 1998.

66. The idea of the role of the *dönme* became current especially in Iraqi newspapers, one of which related all Turkish policies to them, predicting sarcastically the declaration of Turkey into a Jewish state. *Al-'Iraq*, January 13, 1998. The history of the *dönme* under the Ottoman Empire was analyzed in a book by Ahmad Nuri al-Nu'aymi, *Al-Yahud wal-Dawla al-'Uthmaniyya* (Baghdad: 1990).

67. A Jordanian newspaper represented the "alliance" in a cartoon showing three men: the Turk, sucking water, the Jew, blood, and the United States, oil. *Al-Ra'y*, May 22, 1996.

68. *Mideast Mirror*, April 30, 1996; Mu'awwad, *Shu'un 'Arabiyya* (December 1996), p. 126, March 1997, p. 136. See also Mustafa Kamil Muhammad, "Turkiyya: Al-Qudra al-Tawajjuh wal-Dawr," *Kurrasat Istratijiyya*, No. 47 (1996), pp. 26–27.

69. *Mideast Mirror*, April 12, 1996; Muhammad, op. cit., p. 26; Mu'awwad, *Shu'un 'Arabiyya* (March 1997), pp. 135–137.

70. 'Abdullah Salih, *Al-Siyasa al-Duwaliyya* (July 1996), p. 78; Mu'awwad, *Shu'un 'Arabiyya* (March 1997), p. 136.

71. For the perception that the alignment was aimed against Syria, Iraq, and Egypt, see Jalal 'Abdullah Mu'awwad, "Al-Ta'awun al 'Askari al-Isra'ili," *Al-Mustaqbal al 'Arabi*, No. 237 (November 1998), pp. 10–15. Ideas raised at the end of 1980 for a military alliance between the two countries were never realized. For a discussion on their common denominators, see Ihsan Gürkan, "Reflections on Recent Perspectives in the Easten Mediterranean Security: Defense Cooperation Between Turkey and Egypt," *Studies on Turkish Arab Relations*, No. 3 (Istanbul: 1988), pp. 53–67.

72. Osama al-Baz, President Mubarak's political adviser, said in late 1998 that Egypt rejected military pacts in the region because of the damage they had caused. *Al-Nahar—Mideast Mirror*, September 28, 1998.

73. It is difficult to say that Egyptian apprehension about Turkey's new overtures to the Mediterranean and the Middle East were baseless. Indeed, there have been many official statements to that effect. For instance, the Turkish Naval Forces published in November 1997 a strategic document

entitled *Turkish Naval Strategy Towards the Open Seas*, which underscored that the Mediterranean was of "vital importance" to Turkey. Similarly, Foreign Minister Ismail Cem pointed out in an interview in late 1998 that "Turkey had returned to the stage of Middle East as an influential actor." Ismail Cem, "Türkiye, Ortadoğu Sahnesine Etkili bir Aktör Olarak Dönmüştür," *Sosyal Demokrat Değişim*, No. 11 (February 1999).

74. The Turkish Army's escalation of activities against the PKK in northern Iraq is indicated by the following numbers: the 1992 operation involved 10,000 troops, that of March 1995, 35,000, and that of 1997 about 50,000. For a detailed list of large-scale military operations within northern Iraq and their legal basis, see Sertaç H. Başeren, "Huzur Operasyonu ve Türkiye Cumhuriyeti'nin Kuzey Irak'ta Gerçekleştirdiği Harekatın Hukuki Temelleri," *Avrasya Dosyası*, Vol. II., No. 1 (Spring 1995), pp. 224–236. In Baskın Oran, "Kalkık Horoz," *Çekiç Güç ve Kürt Devleti* (Ankara: Bilgi, 1996), p. 38, footnote 25. See also *Radikal*, May 15, 26, 1997; Ümit, Özdağ, *Türkiye Kuzey Irak ve PKK* (Ankara: ASAM, 1999), pp. 62–188.

75. *Hürriyet*, July 6, 1994. Memoirs of his top military aides confirmed his interest in the plan (Yavuz Paşa, "Sayın Cumhurbaşkanım! Siz Kerkük'e Olan Mesafeyi Haritada Ölçtünüz mü?" *Yeni Yüzyıl*, February 14, 1998). For further details, see Necip Torumtay, *Orgeneral Torumtay'ın Anıları* (İstanbul: Milliyet, 1993), pp. 105–130.

76. For a discussion of Turkish–Syrian Relations, see Eyal Zisser, "Remembering the Past, Looking to the Future: Syrian–Turkish Relations and their Place in Political Discourse and the Formation of Historical Memory in Syria," paper prepared for *MESA*, November 1998.

77. A Syrian paper expressed this fear in a cartoon showing a handshake between Israel and Turkey that kills the dove of peace. *Al-Thawra* (Syria), June 27, 1996.

78. The title taken from *Mideast Mirror*, June 26, 1997.

79. *Mideast Mirror*, June 13, 1997.

80. *Al-Hayat*, May 24, 1997. For similar views, see Ibrahim al-Nafi'i, *Al-Ahram*—*Mideast Mirror*, December 4, 1998, and Salah Basyuni, "Misr wa-Turkiyya Hisabat Siyasiyya Waqi'iyya," *Awraq al-Sharq al-Awsat*, No. 23 (November 1998–March 1999), p. 56. Echoing Prince Khalid bin Sultan, Şükrü Elekdağ, an influential opinion maker and Turkey's former ambassador to Washington, wrote: "Not only had the Arab world left Turkey alone in its just cause in Cyprus, but it went as far as putting its weight on the side of Greece. Similarly, when the Bulgarian communist administration forced members of the Turkish minority there to change their names under torture and massacre and Turkey came against [this policy], it did not receive any serious support from its Arab brothers. . . What is interesting is that such sensible voices started rising only after the Turkish–Israeli rapproachement had taken place." *Milliyet*, June 30, 1997.

81. *Al-Nahar—Mideast Mirror*, September 28, 1998.

82. Ibid.

83. Nonetheless, he termed the Arab League reaction to the Turkish–Israeli alignment "pathetic." Ibid.

84. For a discussion of this period, see Özcan, op. cit.

85. One analyst blamed the Arabs of having squandered an opportunity of initiating "real cooperation" with "the pro-Arab and pro-Islamic government. *Al-Quds al-'Arabi—Mideast Mirror*, October 14, 1998. For an analysis of the Turkish military motivation for courting Israel, including embarrassing the Erbakan govenment, see M. Hakan Yavuz, "Turkish–Israeli Relations through the Lens of the Turkish Identity Debate," *Journal of Palestine Studies*, Vol. XXVII (Autumn 1997), p. 31. On Refah-Yol government see, Aryeh Shmuelevitz, *Turkey's Experiment in Islamist Government, 1996–1997* (Tel Aviv: The Moshe Dayan Center, 1999).

86. For example, Radio Monte Carlo in Arabic, January 3, 1998, DR; SANA, January 7, 1998, DR. It was reported that Jordan's participation in the alignment was discussed by the U.S. president, the king of Jordan, and the Turkish prime minister during their visit to Israel for Rabin's funeral. Sari al-Din, p. 116, quoting the *Wall Street Journal* (n.d.).

87. The Jordanian paper *al-Sabil* wrote regularly against the alignment, e.g., September 10, 1996, December 22, 1997, January 6, 1998. One of the cartoons showed Turkey and Israel squeezing an Arab, who says: "Don't hurry, we can reach an understanding," *Al-Sabil*, June 18, 1996.

88. *'Ukaz*, January 6, 1998, DR.

89. *Al-Ra'y* (Jordan), January 4, 10, 23, 1998.

90. *Al-Ra'y—Mideast Mirror*, October 5, 1998. One year later, the *Turkish Daily News* asserted that Jordan was an "active partner" in the security cooperation between Turkey and Israel, but that it attempted to draw a line between its cooperation with Turkey and that with Israel. Quoted by *Ha'aretz*, January 21, 2000. Jordan was, in fact, very sensitive to the Arab countries' reaction and sought to keep such trilateral cooperation as opaque as possible.

91. At a certain point the Turks were offended by Egypt's stance and refused to give in to these pressues. Interview with David Ivri, June 2, 2002.

92. Bruce Maddy-Weitzman, *Inter-Arab Relations*, in Bruce Maddy-Weitzman (ed.), *MECS 1996* (Boulder, CO: Westview Press, 1998), p. 78. For more on the summit and an earlier mini-summit in Damascus, see *Hürriyet*, June 9, 1996; *Turkish Daily News*, June 23, 25, 1996.

93. Eyal Zisser, "Syria," *MECS 1996*, p. 657; Alon Liel, "Turkey," *MECS 1996*, p. 705. *Al-Quds al-'Arabi—Mideast Mirror*, September 10, 1998.

94. *Al-Quds al-'Arabi—Mideast Mirror*, September 10, 1998.

95. INA, July 17, 1997, DR.

96. *Al-Jumhuriyya*, May 3, 6, 11, 1997. *Al-Jumhuriyya*, June 16, 29, 1997.

97. *Al-Jumhuriyya*, June 16, 29, 1997.

98. *Al-Thawra*, January 20, August 24, October 22, 1997.

99. The *démarche* started with harsh warnings to Syria by Army Commander General Atilla Ateş in Reyhanlı, Alexandretta. See, *Radikal*, October 2, 1998. Chief of Staff Hüseyin Kıvrıkoğlu followed suit. See "Suriye'ye Sabrımız Taşıyor" ("We Run Out of Patience with Syria"), *Hürriyet*, October 2, 1998. At the same time, military activities were intensified along the Syrian border. *Radikal*, November 3, 1998. In his opening speech to the Turkish National Assembly, President Demirel warned Syria on the same lines, *Hürriyet*, October 6, 1998. It should be noted that it was in the al-Biqa' valley in Lebanon, which was under Syrian control, that the PKK was said to have established its bases.

100. *Mideast Mirror*, September 29, 1998, quoting *Al-Sharq al-Awsat*.

101. *Mideast Mirror*, October 14, 1998, quoting an unnamed Syrian official.

102. Asked about Israel's "indifference" toward the Turkish–Syrian crisis, David Ivri pointed out that, contrary to what was written in the Turkish press, Israel had not withdrawn any troops from the Golan Heights or the Syrian frontier, but had only decreased its military activities so as to avoid provoking Syria. *Milliyet*, November 9, 1998.

103. INA, October 6, DR; *al-Thawra*, October 9, 1998, DR.

104. *Al-Majd*, October 12, 1998, DR.

105. Iraq Television, October 4, 1998, DR.

106. INA, October 7, 1998, DR.

107. *Al-'Arab, al-Quds al-'Arabi—-Mideast Mirror*, October 14, 1998.

108. *Al-Ahram—Mideast Mirror*, December 7, 1998.

109. TRT TV, October 20, SWB, October 21, 1998; *Christian Science Monitor*, June 26, 2002 (Internet version).

110. Şule Kut, "Filistin Sorunu ve Türkiye," in Haluk ülman (ed.), *Ortadoğu Sorunları ve Türkiye* (İstanbul: TÜSES, 1991), pp. 5–34.

111. Mahmut Bali Aykan, "The Palestinian Question in Turkish Foreign Policy from the 1950s to the 1990s," *International Journal of Middle Eastern Studies*, No. 25 (1993), pp. 91–110.

112. Bülent Aras, "The Impact of the Palestinian–Israeli Peace Process in Turkish Foreign Policy," *Journal of South Asian and Middle Eastern Studies*, Vol. XX, No. 2 (Winter 1997), p. 65.

113. *Radikal*, April 7, 2002.

114. AFP, November 7, 2000. Israel did not encourage such moves but accepted them when they took place.

115. Mahmut B. Aykan, *Turkey's Role in the Organization of the Islamic Conference: 1960–1992* (New York: Vantage Press, 1994), pp. 55–70.

116. Foreign Minister Emre Gönensay, who served under the Erbakan government, spoke about the Islamic model that Turkey should set before the world. Author interview with Gönensay, October 18, 2001.

117. *Radikal*, August 1, 2002; *Milliyet*, August 2, 2002.

118. AFP, April 6, 1996.

119. AFP, August 11, 1996. On the same occasion the two sides signed a gas supply agreement from Iran worth $23 bn. over 20 years.

120. Iranian Radio, August 29, SWB, August 31, 1996.

121. *Hürriyet*, February 3, 4, 1997.

122. Yeni Yüzyıl, February 21, 1997. For the ramifications of the affair, see Gencer Özcan and Ofra Bengio, "The Decade of the Military in Turkey: The Case of the Alignment with Israel in the 1990s," *International Journal of Turkish Studies*, Vol. 7, Nos. 1, 2 (Spring 2001), pp. 90–100.

123. *JP*, December 11, 1997 (Internet version); *Mideast Mirror*, December 16, 1997.

124. IRNA, December 20, 1997—SWB, December 22, 1997. Ironically, it was Erbakan himself who was behind the idea of the D-8.

125. For the historical roots of these relations, see Nachmani, op. cit., pp. 85–118.

126. Xinhua News Agency, April 16 and 17, 1996.

127. For example, *Ha'aretz*, December 9—SWB, December 11, 1996.

128. Xinhua News Agency, September 7, 1998.

129. Xinhua News Agency, November 4, 1998.

130. Info-prod Research (Middle East) Ltd., February 26, 1998.

131. See Tosun Bahçeli, "Turkish Policy Toward Greece," in Alan Makovsky and Sabrı Sayarı (eds.), *Turkey's New World* (Washington: Washington Institute for Near East Policy, 2000), pp. 131–153.

132. AFP, December 8, 1996; *JP*, January 10, 1997 (Internet version).

133. AFP, May 9, 1997.

134. AFP, December 21, 1997.

135. Net TV, December 21, 1997; *JP*, September 17, 1999 (Internet version).

136. Xinhua News Agency, April 12, 1998.

137. *JP*, September 17, October 12, 1999 (Internet version).

138. *JP*, September 17, 1999 (Internet version).

139. *Al-Ahram—Mideast Mirror*, May 2, 1996.

140. *Al-Quds al-'Arabi—Mideast Mirror*, September 10, 1998.

141. *Al-Riyadh*, December 14, 1997, DR.

142. *Strategic Comments*, IISS, Vol. 2, No. 6 (July 1996). For later talks on a possible such alliance, see Qasim Muhammad Ja'far, *Al-Wasat*, May 12, 1997. Salah al-Din Hafiz raised the possibility of a new Arab–Iranian alliance to counter the Turkish–Israeli–Western axis, but himself questioned its viability. *Al-Ahram—Mideast Mirror*, May 14, 1997.

143. 'Abd al-Malik Salman, *Akhbar al-Khalij—Mideast Mirror*, April 30, 1996.

144. For criticism of Egypt's lack of action see Ragheda Dergham, *Al-Hayat—Mideast Mirror*, May 16, 1997.

145. Greece signed a military agreement with Armenia in June 1996. *Milliyet*, June 21, 1996.

146. For further analysis of these changes, see Daniel Pipes, "The Real New Middle East," *Commentary* (November 1998).

# Conclusion: A New Regional Order?

1. A recent expression of this view is found in Bülent Aras and Hasan Koni, "Turkish–Syrian Relations Revisited," *Arab Studies Quarterly*, Vol. 24, No. 4 (Fall 2002), pp. 47–60.
2. Mark R. Parris (former U.S. ambassador to Turkey), "Starting Over: US–Turkish Relations in the Post–Iraq War Era," *Turkish Policy Quarterly* (Spring 2003), pp. 5–15.
3. Interview, July 31, 2003.
4. Interview, July 31, 2003; *Ha'aretz*, August 15, 2003.
5. *Ha'aretz*, December 22, 1997.
6. Nadav Safran, *Israel, The Embattled Ally* (Cambridge, MA: Harvard University Press, 1978), pp. 597–598.

# Postscript

1. Soner Cagaptay, "Hamas visits Ankara: The AKP shifts Turkey's role in the Middle East," *Policy Watch*, The Washington Institute for Near East Policy, February 16, 2006.
2. For the impact of 1991 Gulf war on Turkey, see Amikam Nachmani, *Turkey: Facing a New Millennium* (Manchester, Manchester University Press, 2003) pp. 16-29.
3. On the impact of the Kurdish issue on relations see, Efraim Inbar, *Israel's New Strategic Partners: Turkey and India*, Iyyunim babitahon haleumi, No.77 (in Hebrew) pp.8-9.
4. For such an example see, *Today's Zaman*, 16 March 2008.
5. Israeli general Avi Mizrahi, a veteran professional officer, called on Prime Minister Erdoğan to look in the mirror, accusing Turkey of committing genocide on the Armenians, the suppression of the Kurds and the occupation of Northern Cyprus. *Ha'aretz*, February 13, 2009. However such declaration was exception to the rule.
6. See for example, *Mideast Mirror*, January 5, 2009.
7. For example, the Turkish media hardly mentioned the Qassam missile attacks launched from Gaza on southern Israeli communities for eight years, while dwelling at length on Israeli attacks on the launchers of the missiles.
8. BBC, June 3, 2004
9. More than 100,000 copies were sold in early 2005. *The Guardian*, March 29, 2005.
10. For an in-depth discussion of relations under AKP government, see Gencer Özcan, *Türkiye- İsrail İlişkilerinde Dönüşüm: Güvenliğin Ötesi* (İstanbul, Tesev yayınları, 2005) pp. 149-167.
11. See Burak Bekdil's "The great Turkish Hypocrisy, *Turkish Daily News*, March 14, 2008.

12. Ayşe Kulin, *Nefes Nefese* (Istanbul, Everest, 2002).
13. http://www.myturkey.co.il quoting Turkey's Tourism Office
14. *Ynet* (www.ynet.co.il), 1 May 2005.
15. Crienglish.com, February 13; *Jerusalem Post*, February 12, 2008.
16. Inbar, *Israel's New Strategic Partners*, pp. 10-11.
17. Prime Minister's Office Site, May 16, 2005, http://www.pmo.gov.il
18. For a discussion of the rapprochement see, Gökhan Bacık, "An emerging friendship: Turkey and Syria" *Insight Turkey*, Vol. 9, No. 3 (2007) pp. 67-74.
19. Ministry of Industry, Trade and Labor, August 12, 2008, http://www.tamas.gov.il
20. According to a later version by Erdoğan, it was Syria which had approached him on the matter. *Washington Post*, January 31, 2009.
21. Israel Ministry of Foreign Affairs, May 21, 2005 http://www.mfa.gov.il
22. *Mideast Mirror*, May 22, 2008.
23. *Al-Jazeera*, January 6, 2009; *Cumhuriyet* as quoted in *Mideast Mirror*, January 12, 2009; *Sabah*, January 18, 2009.
24. *Today's Zaman*, December 29, 2008
25. Meanwhile prosecutors in the central Anatolian town of Eskişehir have launched a probe into those carrying such placards. *Milliyet*, January 18, 2009. *Yisrael hayyom*, February 19, 2009.
26. Private information.
27. The Turkish government denied these reports. *Hürriyet*, January 6, 2009.
28. *Today's Zaman*, December 29, 2008. Unlike in the Syrian case Israel did not accept this time the Turkish mediation possibly because of what it considered as Ankara's anti-Israeli bias.

# Selected Sources

## Archives

Ben-Gurion, David, *Selected Documents, Israeli State Archives, 1947–1963* (H), (Jerusalem: State Archives, 1996–97).

Israel State Archives (ISA), Foreign Ministry Documents (1948–1969); Protocols of the Knesset's Foreign Affairs and Defense Committee, 7566/3.

## Interviews

Amidror, Ya'acob, former secretary to Israeli Defense Minister Yitzhak Mordechai, April 21, 2002.

Amit, Meir, former Israeli head of Military Intelligence and later the Mossad, March 25, 2001.

Bar, Yossi, former Israeli military attaché to Turkey, June 11, 2002.

Barzilai, Amnon, *Ha'aretz* journalist, December 24, 2001.

Bir, Çevik, former deputy chief of Turkey's General Staff, October 24, 2001.

Çiller, Tansu, former Turkish prime minister and foreign minister, October 23, 2001.

Efrat, Ehud, former Israeli head of Branch R in the Military Intelligence and later military attaché to Turkey, January 10, 2001.

Elpeleg, Zvi, former Israeli ambassador to Turkey, November 11, 2000; February 21, 2002.

Gilboa, Baruch, former Israeli military attaché to Turkey, December 5, 28, 2000; September 13, 2001.

Gönensay, Emre, former Turkish foreign minister, October 18, 2001.

Ivri, David, former director general of Israeli Ministry of Defense, June 2, 2002.

Kedar, Paul, former Israeli military attaché to Turkey, February 13, 2001; March 6, 2002.

Liel, Alon, former Israeli chargé d'affaires in Ankara, December 5, 2001.

Rafiyah, Zvi, former Israeli official in the Ankara legation, December 27, 2000.

Sasson, Moshe, former Israeli chargé d'affaires to Turkey, November 28, 2000; February 26, 2001.

Shaked, Elie, former Israeli second secretary in Ankara, September 16, 2001.

Sheffer, Beni, fomer Israeli military attaché to Turkey, January 8, 2002.

Shmuelevitz, Aryeh, a historian of the Ottoman Empire and modern Turkey, February 12, 2001.

Tamir, Abraham, former director general of Israeli Foreign Ministry, February 28, 2000.

Türkmen, Ilter, former Turkish foreign minister, October 22, 2001.

## Radio, TV Stations, and News Agencies

Agence France Press

Anatolia News Agency

Ankara Anatolia News Agency

Ankara Türkiye Radyoları Network

Daily Report (DR)

Deutsche Presse-Agentur

Facts on File

IDF Radio

Info-prod Research (Middle East) Ltd.

Iranian Radio

Iraq Television

IRNA

Israel TV Channel 1

Mideast Mirror

Net TV

R. Ankara

R. Nicosia

Summary of World Broadcasts (SWB)

TRT TV

TRT, Ankara

UPI Press Agency

Voice of Israel

Xinhua News Agency

## Newspapers and Periodicals

*Al-Ahram*

*Al-'Arab*

*Al-Difa'*

*Al-Fikr al-Istratiji al-'Arabi*

*Al-Hayat*

*Al-'Iraq*

*Al-Jumhuriyya*

*Al-Majd*

*Al-Minbar*

*Al-Mustaqbal al-'Arabi*

*Al-Nahar*

*Al-Quds al-'Arabi*

*Al-Ra'y*

*Al-Riyadh*

*Al-Sabil*

*Al-Safir*

*Al-Shahid*

*Al-Sharq al-Awsat*

*Al-Thawra (Iraq)*

*Al-Wasat*

*Ankara Anatolia*

*Christian Science Monitor*

*Cumhuriyet*

*Dunya al-'Arab*

*Financial Times*

*Globes*

*Ha'aretz*

*Hürriyet*

*International Herald Tribune*

*Jerusalem Post*

*Los Angeles Times*

*Ma'ariv*

*Milli Gazete*

*Milliyet*

*Radikal*

*Sabah*

*The New York Times*

*Turkish Daily News*

*Yeni Türkiye*

*Yeni Yüzyıl*

# Books

*Adil Ekonomik Düzen*, Ankara, 1991.

Ajami, Fouad, *The Arab Predicament: Arab Political Thought and Practice Since 1967*, Cambridge, Cambridge University Press, 1982.

'Ali Sari al-Din, 'Ayida, *Al-'Arab wal-Furat bayn Turkiyya wa-Isra'il*, Beirut, Dar al-Afaq al-Jadida, 1997.

Amit, Meir, *Head On* (H), Or Yehuda, Hed Arzi Publishing House, 1999.

Aras, Bülent, *The Palestinian–Israeli Peace Process in International Context with a Note on the Consequences for Turkish Foreign Policy*, M.A. Thesis, Boğaziçi University, 1966.

Atay, Falih Rıfkı, *Zeytin Dağı*, İstanbul: MEB yayınları, 1992.

Athanassopoulou, Ekavi, *Israeli–Turkish Security Ties: Regional Reactions*, Jerusalem, The Hebrew University, 2001.

Atsız, Hüseyin Nihal, *Bütün Eserleri—Makaleler IV*, İstanbul, Irfan, 1997.

Aykan, Mahmut B., *Turkey's Role in the Organization of the Islamic Conference, 1960–1992*, New York, Vantage Press, 1994.

Bali Rifat N., *Cumhuriyet Yıllarında yahudileri: Bir Türkleştirme Serüveni [1923–1945]*, İstanbul, İletişim, 1999.

———, *Musanın Evlatları Cumhuriyet'in Yurttaşları*, İstanbul, İletşim, 2001.

Bar Zohar, Michael, *Ben-Gurion: A Political Biography* (H) Vol. III, Tel Aviv, 'AM 'Oved 1977.

Baram, Amatzia and Barry Rubin (eds.), *Iraq's Road to War*, New York, St. Martin's Press, 1996.

Barkey, Henry J. (ed.), *Reluctant Neighbor: Turkey's Role in the Middle East*, Washington, United States Institute of Peace Press, 1996.

Bialer, Uri, *Between East and West: Israel's Foreign Policy Orientation, 1948–1956*, New York, Cambridge University Press, 1990.

Bresheeth, Haim and Nira Yuval-Davis (eds.), *The Gulf War and the New World Order*, London, Zed Books, 1991.

Bulut, Faik, *Filistin Rüyası*, İstanbul, Bersin, 1998.

Caroz, Ya'acov, *The Man with Two Hats* (H), Tel-Aviv, Ministry of Defence, 2002.

Çayhan, Esra, *Dünden Bugüne Türkiye Avrupa Birliği İlişkileri ve Siyasal Partilerin Konuya Bakışı*, İstanbul, Boyut, 1997.

Çiçek, Hikmet (ed.), *İrticaya Karşı Genelkurmay Belgeleri*, İstanbul, Kaynak, 1997.

Daquqi, Ibrahim al-, *Surat al-'Arab lada al-Atrak*, Markaz al-Dirasat al-'Arabiyya, Beirut, 1996.

Dodd, Clement H. (ed.), *Cyprus: The Need for New Perspectives*, Huntingdon, Eothen Press, 1999.

Duru, Cenap and Mehmet Hodşer, *Milli Güvenlik Siyasetinin Oluşturulmasi*, İstanbul, Harp Akademileri yayını, 1994.

Dursunoğlu, Alpetkin, *Stratejik Ittifak: Türkiye-İsrail İlişkilerinin Öyküsü*, İstanbul, Ankara yayınları, 2000.

Edmonds, C. J., *Kurds, Turks and Arabs*, London, Oxford University Press, 1957.

Erbakan, Necmettin, *Türkiye'nin Meseleleri ve Çözümleri*, İstanbul, 1991.

Eshed, Haggai, *Reuven Shiloah: The Man Behind the Mossad*, London, Frank Cass, 1997.

Freedman, Lawrence and Efraim Karsh, *The Gulf Conflict 1990–1991*, Princeton, NJ, Princeton University Press, 1993.

Gruen, George Emanuel, *Turkey, Israel and the Palestinian Question, 1948–1960: A Study in the Diplomacy of Ambivalence*, Ph.D. dissertation, Columbia University, 1970.

Günaltay, Şemsedin, *Yakın Şark: Suriye ve Filistin*, Ankara, Türk Tarih Kurumu, 1987.

Gunter, Michael M., *The Kurds in Turkey*, Boulder, Westview Press, 1990.

Hale, William, *Turkish Politics and the Military*, London, Routledge, 1994.

Imset, G. Ismet, *The PKK: A Report on Separatist Violence in Turkey (1973–1992)*, Ankara, Turkish Daily News, 1992.

Inbar, Efraim, *The Israeli–Turkish Entente*, London, King's College, University of London, 2000.

Irbeç, Yusuf Ziya, *Türkiyeni'n Dış Ekonomik İlişkilerinde İslam Ülkeleri*, Ankara (no publisher), 1990.

Kaufman, Burton I., *The Arab Middle East and the United States*, London, Twayne Publishers, 1996.

Khadduri, Majid, *War in the Gulf, 1990–1991*, New York, Oxford University Press, 1997.

Kirişçi, Kemal Ali Çarkoğlu ve Mine Eder, *Türkiye ve Ortadoğu'da Bölgesel İşbirliği*, İstanbul, TESEV, 1998.

Klieman, Aaron S., *Israel and the World after 40 Years*, Washington, Pergamon-Brassey's, 1990.

Klieman, Aharon, *Statecraft in the Dark: Israel's Practice of Quiet Diplomacy*, Jerusalem, Jerusalem Post Press, 1988.

Koebner, Richard and Helmut Dan Schmidt, *Imperialism: The Story and Significance of a Political Word*, Cambridge, Cambridge University Press, 1964.

Lesch, David W., *The Middle East and the United States: A Historical and Political Reassessment*, Boulder, Westview Press, 1996.

Levi, Avner, *History of the Jews in the Republic of Turkey* (H), Jerusalem, Hamaccabi, 1992.

Levran, Aharon, *Israeli Strategy after Desert Storm*, London, Frank Cass, 1997.

Lewis, Bernard, *The Emergence of Modern Turkey*, 2nd ed., London, Oxford University Press, 1968.

Liel, Alon, *Turkey: Military, Islam and Politics 1970–2000* (H), Tel Aviv, Hakibutz Hameuhad, 1999.

Maddy-Weitzman, Bruce, *The Crystallization of the Arab State System, 1945–1954*, Syracuse, Syracuse University Press, 1993.

*Majzarat Qasr al-Rihab*, Beirut, 1960.

Makovsky, Alan and Sabri Sayarı (eds.), *Turkey's New World*, Washington, Washington Institute, 2000.

McGhee, George, *The US–Turkish–NATO Middle East Connection*, London, Macmillan, 1990.

Melman, Yossi (ed.), *CIA Report on the Israeli Security and Intelligence Services* (H), Tel Aviv, Sifrei Erez, 1982.

Menashri, David (ed.), *Central Asia Meets the Middle East*, London, Frank Cass, 1998.

*Milli Güvenlik Kurulu Genel Sekreterliği: 24 Nisan 1933' den 1993'e 60 Yıl*, Ankara, 1993.

Mu'awwad, Jalal 'Abdullah, *Sina'at al-Qarar fi Turkiyya wal-'Alaqat al-'Arabiyya al-Turkiyya*, Beirut, 1998.

Nachmani, Amikam, *Israel, Turkey and Greece: Uneasy Relations in the East Mediterranean*, London, Frank Cass, 1987.

Neuberger, Benyamin (ed.), *War and Peacemaking, Selected Issues in Israel's Foreign Relations* (H), Tel Aviv, The Open University of Israel, 1992.

Nu'aymi, Ahmad Nuri al-, *Al-Yahud wal-Dawla al-'Uthmaniyya*, Baghdad, 1990.

Oran, Baskı, *"Kalkık Horoz," Çekiç Güç ve Kürt Devleti*, Ankara, Bilgi, 1996.

———— (ed.), *Türk Dış Politikasi Kurtuluş Savaşından Bugüne Olgular, Belgeler, Yorumlar*, Vol. I, İstanbul, İletişim, 2001.

Orkunt, Sezai, *Türkiye ABD Askeri İlişkileri*, İstanbul, Milliyet, 1978.

Özcan, Gencer and Şule Kut (eds.), *Onbir Aylık Saltanat: Siyaset, Ekonomi ve Dış Politikada Refahyol Dönemi*, İstanbul, Boyut, 1998.

Özcan, Nihat Ali, *PKK: Tarihi, Ideolojisi ve Yöntemi*, Ankara, ASAM, 1999.

Özdağ, Ümit, *Türkiye, Kuzey Irak ve PKK*, Ankara, ASAM, 1999.

Öztürk, Saygı, *Devletin Derinliklerinde*, Ankara, Ümit, 2002.

Peres, Shimon, *The New Middle East* (H), Bnei Braq, Steimatzki, 1993.

Podeh, Elie, *The Quest for Hegemony in the Arab World: The Struggle over the Baghdad Pact*, New York, E. J. Brill, 1995.

Robins, Philip, *Turkey and the Middle East*, London, Royal Institute of International Affairs, 1991.

Rubin, Barry, *Cauldron of Turmoil*, New York, Harcourt Brace Jovanovich, 1992.

Rubin, Barry and Kemal Kirişci (eds.), *Turkey in World Politics*, Boulder, 2001.

Safran, Nadav, *Israel, The Embattled Ally*, Cambridge, Harvard University Press, 1978.

Sanjian, Ara, *Turkey and Her Arab Neighbours, 1953–1958*, Wiltshire, Archive Editions, 2001.

Schiff, Ze'ev and Ehud Ya'ari, *Israel Lebanon War*, New York, Simon & Schuster, 1984.

Segev, Samuel, *The Iranian Triangle: The Secret Relations between Israel–Iran–USA* (H), Tel Aviv, Sifriyat Ma'ariv, 1981.

Shakir, Amin, Sa'id al-'Aryan, Muhammad Mustafa 'Ata, *Turkiyya wal-Siyasa al-'Arabiyya*, Cairo, Dar al-Ma'arif bimisr, 1954.

Shaw, Stanford J., *The Jews of the Ottoman Empire and the Turkish Republic*, New York, New York University Press, 1991.

Shemesh, Haim, *Soviet–Iraqi Relations, 1968–1988—In the Shadow of the Iraq–Iran Conflict*, Boulder, Lynne Rienner Publishers, 1992.

Shlaim, Avi, *The Iron Wall: Israel and the Arab World*, London, Penguin, 2000.

Shmuelevitz, Aryeh, *Turkey's Experiment in Islamist Government, 1996–1997*, Tel Aviv, The Moshe Dayan Center, 1999.

Sönmez Mustafa, *Türkiye Ekonomisinde Bunalım 12 Eylül ve Sonrasının Ekonomi Politiği*, 2nd ed., İstanbul, Belge, 1986.

Sönmezoğlu, Faruk (ed.), *Türk Dış Politikasının Analizi*, İstanbul, Der, 1994.

————, *ABD'nin Türkiye Politikasi*, İstanbul, Der, 1995.

Soysal, Ismail, *Türk Dış Politikası İncelemleri için Kılavuz (1919–1993)*, İstanbul, Eren, 1993.

Torumtay, Necip, *Orgeneral Torumtay'ın Anıları*, İstanbul, Milliyet, 1993.

Türkeş, Alpaslan, *Dış Politikamız ve Kıbrıs*, İstanbul, Hamle, 1996.

*Türkiye'nin Gerçek Durumu Sebepleri Teşhis*, Welfare Party, n.d., possibly 1995.

*Turkiyya wal-siyasa al-'Arabiyya* (n.d.).

Ülman, Haluk A. (ed.), *Ortadoğu Sorunları ve Türkiye*, İstanbul, TÜSES, 1991.

'Uziel, Baruch, *The Peripheral Alliance: A Suggestion for Israeli Policy* (H), Tel Aviv, Hamerkaz, 1959.

Volkan, Vamik D., *Cyprus—War and Adaptation*, Charlottesville, University Press of Virginia, 1979.

Volkan, Vamik D. and Norman Itzkowitz, *Turks and Greeks: Neighbors in Conflict*, Huntingdon, Eothen Press, 1994.

*Water Issues between Turkey, Syria and Iraq*, Ankara, Republic of Turkey, Ministry of Foreign Affairs, Department of Regional and Transboundary Waters, 1995.

# Articles

Aras, Bülent, "The Impact of the Palestinian–Israeli Peace Process in Turkish Foreign Policy," *Journal of South Asian and Middle Eastern Studies*, 20 (1997): 49–72.

————, "Post–Cold War Realities: Israel's Strategy in Azerbaijan and Central Asia," *Middle East Policy*, 5 (1998): 68–81.

Aykan, Mahmut Bali, "The Palestinian Question in Turkish Foreign Policy from the 1950s to the 1990's," *International Journal of Middle Eastern Studies*, 25 (1993): 91–110.

Bacik, Gökhan, "The Limits of an Alliance: Turkish–Israeli Relations Revisited," *Arab Studies Quarterly*, 23 (2001): 49–63.

Bağış, Ali İhsan, "The Beginning and the Development of Economic Relations between Turkey and Middle Eastern Countries," *Foreign Policy*, Ankara, 12 (1985): 85–96.

Bal, Idris, "Instability in the Middle East and the Relevant Role of the PKK," *Turkish Review of Middle East Studies*, 13 (2002): 135–156.

Bali, Rifat N., "Seçimlerin Yahudi'ye Yaramasını İstemiyorsanız," *Birikim*, 86/87 (1986): 171–172.

Barzilai, Gad, "Israel" in Ami Ayalon (ed.), *Middle East Contemporary Survey (MECS) 1990* (Boulder, 1992): 424–453.

Başeren, Sertaç H., "Huzur Operasyonu ve Türkiye Cumhuriyeti'nin Kuzey Irak'ta Gerçekleştirdiği Harekatın Hukuki Temelleri," *Avrasya Dosyası*, Vol. II, No. 1 (1995).

Basyuni, Salah, "Misr wa-Turkiyya Hisabat Siyasiyya Waqi'iyya," *Awraq al-Sharq al-Awsat*, 23 (November 1998–March 1999): 54–57.

Ben-Ami, Shlomo, "Israel's Foreign Policy Agenda," *Friedrich Ebert Stiftung*, 1999.

Bengio, Ofra and Gencer Özcan, Old Grievances New Fears: "Arab Perceptions of Turkey and its Alignment with Israel", Middle Eastern Studies, 37 (2001): 50–92.

Benli Altunışık, Meliha, "Turkish-Israeli Rapprochement in the Post-cold war Era", Middle Eastern Studies, 36 (2000): 172–191.

Bir, Çevik, "Turkey's Role in the New World Order: New Challenges," National Defense University Strategic Forum Publications, 135, February 1998.

Bolukbasi, Suha, "Turkey Challenges Iraq and Syria: The Euphrates Dispute," Journal of South Asian and Middle Eastern Studies, 16 (Summer 1993): 9–32.

Çarkoğlu, Ali and Kemal Kirişçi, Türkiye Dış Politikası Araştırması, Boğaziçi Üniversitesi, March 2002.

Cem, İsmail, "Türkiye, Ortadoğu Sahnesine Etkili bir Aktör Olarak Dönmüştür," Sosyal Demokrat Değişim, 11 (1999).

Cohen, Stuart, "Israel's Three Strategic Challenges," Middle East Quarterly (December 1999): 41–49.

Dahir, Mas'ud, "Nadwa al-Dinamiyya al-Jadida fi al-Sharq al-Awsat," Al-Mustaqbal al-'Arabi (September 1991): 158–162.

Dawud, Mahmud 'Ali al-, "Al-'Alaqat al-'Arabiyya wal-Turkiyya wal-'Awamil al-Mu'aththira Fiha," Al-Mustaqbal al-'Arabi (November 1982): 62–69.

Dishon, Daniel and Bruce Maddy-Weitzman, "Inter-Arab Relations," in Colin Legun, Haim Shaked, and Daniel Dishon (eds.), MECS, 1979–80 (New York, 1981): 169–225.

Freedman, Lawrence, "The Gulf War and the New World Order," Survival, 33 (1991): 195–209.

Galbraith, Peter, Civil War in Iraq: A Staff Report to the Committee on Foreign Relations, United States Senate, May 1991.

Gözen, Ramazan, "Turgut Özal and Turkish Foreign Policy," Foreign Policy, Ankara, 20 (1996): 69–103.

Gresh, Alain, "Turkish–Israeli–Syrian Relations and Their Impact on the Middle East," Middle East Journal, 52 (1998): 188–203.

Gruen, George E., "Turkey's Relations with Israel and Its Arab Neighbors," Middle East Review (Spring 1985): 33–43.

———, "Dynamic Progress in Turkish–Israeli Relations," Israel Affairs, I (1995): 40–70.

Güner, Ahmet, "Türk–İsrail Anlaşmasının Bilinmeyenleri," Aksiyon, 76 (1996).

Gürkan, Ihsan, "Turkish–Israeli Relations and the Middle East Peace Process," Turkish Review of MES (1993): 99–135.

———, "Reflections on Recent Perspectives in the Easten Mediterranean Security: Defense Cooperation between Turkey and Egypt," Studies on Turkish Arab Relations, 3 (1988): 53–67.

Güvendiren, Ekrem, "A Concise Report on Turkish–Israeli Relations, 1999" (no further details).

Haarmann, Ulrich W., "Ideology and History, Identity and Alterity: The Arab Image of the Turk from the Abbasids to Modern Egypt," *International Journal of Middle Eastern Studies*, 20 (1988): 175–196.

Hadar, Leon T., "Orienting Jerusalem Toward Ankara or Cairo? Israel's New Geostrategic Debate," *Mediterranean Quarterly*, 12 (2001): 8–30.

Hale, William M., "Turkey," in Ami Ayalon and Haim Shaked (eds.), *MECS, 1988* (Boulder: 1990): 751–770.

Hijazi, Muhammad wafa' al-, "Al-'Alaqat al-Misriyya al-Turkiyya—Judhuruha al-Madiya wa-Ihtimalatuha al-Mustaqbala," *Al-Siyasa al-Duwaliyya* (October 1985):140–145.

Huntington, Samuel, "The Clash of Civilizations?" *Foreign Affairs*, 72 (1993): 22–49.

Ibrahim, Rabi' 'Ali, "Tawajjuhat al-Istratijiyya al-Turkiyya," *Al-Difa'*, 92 (1994): 93–97.

Ibrahim, S. E., "Management of Ethnic Issues in the Arab World," *Strategic Papers*, 26 (1995).

İhsanoğlu, Ekmeleddin, "Qira'a li-Ta'rikh al-Dawla al-'Uthmaniyya wa-'Alaqatiha bil-'Alam al-'Arabi," *Studies on Turkish Arab Relations* (Istanbul, 1986): 85–118.

Inbar, Efraim, "Contours of Israel's New Strategic Thinking," *Security and Policy Studies*, 27 (1996).

Indyk, Martin, "The Clinton Administration's Approach to the Middle East" (Washington Institute for Near East Policy, May 18, 1993) (Internet version).

Isfahani, Nabiyya al-, "Turkiyya bayn al-Matalib al-Wataniyya wal-Waqi' al-Dawli," *Al-Siyasa al-Duwaliyya* (April 1978): 92–107.

Khalil, Hani, "Turkiyya al-Jiyubulitik," *Ma'lumat Duwaliyya*, 8 (1993): 21–28.

Kostiner, Joseph, "Saudi Arabia," in Ami Ayalon (ed.), *MECS, 1991* (Boulder, 1993): 613–637.

Kutchera, Chris, "A World Apart," *The Middle East* (February 2000): 21–22.

Labaki, Butrus, "Al-'Alaqat al-Iqtisadiyya al-Turkiyya al-Rahina," *Al-Mustaqbal al-'Arabi*, 188 (October 1994): 52–70.

Landau, Jacob, "Ultra Nationalist Literature in the Turkish Republic: A Note on the Novels of Hüseyin Nihâl Atsız," *Middle Eastern Studies*, 39 (April 2003): 204–210.

Lapidot, Anat, "The Turkish–Islamic Synthesis: The National-Religious Narrative in the 1980s," *Hamizrah Hehadash* (H), XXX 19 (1997–98): 84–96.

Lewin, Anat, "Turkey and Israel: Reciprocal and Mutual Imagery in the Media 1994–1999," *Journal of International Affairs* (Fall 2000): 239–261.

Liel, Alon, "Turkey," in Bruce Maddy-Weitzman (ed.), *MECS, 1996* (Boulder, 1998): 690–715.

Lockery, Neill, "Israel and Turkey: Deepening Ties and Strategic Implications 1995–1998," *Israel Affairs*, 5 (1998): 45–62.

Maddy-Weitzman, Bruce, "Inter-Arab Relations," in Bruce Maddy-Weitzman (ed.), *MECS, 1996* (Boulder, 1998): 66–99.

———, "Israel and Morocco: A Special Relationship," *The Maghreb Review*, 21 (1996): 36–48.

Ma'lum, Husayn, "Al-Sira' al-Turki al-Irani wa Tada'iyatihi 'ala al-Mintaqa al-'Arabiyya," *Al-Siyasa al-Duwaliyya*, 114 (October 1993): 216–220.

Majzub, Tariq al-, "Al-Ta'awun al-'Arabi wal-Turki fi Mashari' al-Bunya al-Tahtiyya," *Al-Mustaqbal al-'Arabi*, 188 (October 1994): 71–95.

Manufi, Kamal al-, "Al-Tatawwurat al-Jadida fi al-Siyasa al-Kharijiyya al-Turkiyya," *Al-Siyasa al-Duwaliyya* (April 1976): 144–149.

Mua'wwad, Jalal 'Abdullah, "Dawr Turkiyya fi al-Sharq al-Awsat ba'd Azmat al-Khalij," *Shu'un 'Arabiyya*, 69 (March 1992): 233–248.

———, "Turkiyya wal-Amn al-Qawmi al-'Arabi," *Al-Mustaqbal al-'Arabi*, 160 (June 1992): 92–112

———, " 'Awamil wa-jawanib tatawwur al-'Alaqat al-Turkiyya-al-Isra'iliyya fi al-Tis'iniyyat," *Shu'un 'Arabiyya*, 89 (March 1997): 117–139.

———, "Al-Ta'awun al 'Askari al-Isra'ili," *Al-Mustaqbal al-'Arabi*, 237 (November 1998): 6–20.

Mughisuddin, Oya Akgönenç, "Perceptions and Misconceptions in the Making of Foreign Diplomacy: A Study of Turkish-Arab Attitudes Until the End of the 1970s," *Turkish Review of Middle East Studies*, 7 (1993): 147–169.

Muhammad, Mustafa Kamil, "Turkiyya: Al-Qudra al-Tawajjuh wal-Dawr," *Dirrasat Istratijiyya*, 47 (1996).

Ni'ma, Kazim Hashim, "Al-Tatawwur al-Turki al-Isra'ili, Qira'a fi al-Dawafi' al-Kharijiyya," *Al-Mustaqbal al-'Arabi*, 220 (June 1997): 4–17.

Olson, Robert, "Turkey–Syria Relations, 1997 to 2000: Kurds, Water, Israel and 'Undeclared War,' " *Orient* (March 2000): 111–129.

Özcan, Gencer and Ofra Bengio, "The Decade of the Military in Turkey: The Case of the Alignment with Israel in the 1990s," *International Journal of Turkish Studies*, 7 (2001): 90–110

Özel, Soli, "After the Tsunami," *Turkish Policy Quarterly* (Spring 2003): 17–33.

Park, Bill, "Strategic Location, Political Dislocation: Turkey, the United States and Northern Iraq," *Middle East Review of International Affairs* (MERIA), 7 (2003): 1–13.

Parris, Mark, "Starting Over: US–Turkish Relations in the Post–Iraq War Era," *Turkish Policy Quarterly* (Spring 2003): 5–15.

Pipes, Daniel, "A New Axis: The Emerging Turkish–Israeli Entente," *The National Interest* (Winter 1997/98): 31–38.

———, "The Real New Middle East," *Commentary* (November 1998): 8–11.

Quraysh, Rida 'Abd al-Husayn Ghali al- and 'Abd al-Mun'im Sa'id 'Ali, "Al-'Alaqat al-Iqtisadiyya al-'Arabiyya al-Turkiyya Waqi'an wa Tawaqqu'an," *Shu'un 'Arabiyya*, 82 (June 1995): 192–216.

Rabi'u, Turki 'Ali al-, "Turkiyya wal-Nizam al-Iqlimi al-'Arabi: al-Mu'aththirat wal-Tatawwurat 1945–1990," *Al-Fikr al-Istratiji al-'Arabi*, 38 (October 1991): 145–170.

Rivlin, Paul, "Economic Relations Between Turkey and Israel" (unpublished essay).

Robins, Philip, "Turkish Foreign Policy under Erbakan," *Survival*, 39 (1997): 82–100.

Rubin, Barry "The New Middle East: Opportunities and Risks," *Security and Policy Studies*, 19 (1995): 47–64.

Safwat, Najda Fathi, "Mawqif Turkiyya min Qadiyyat Filastin," *Al-Mustaqbal al-'Arabi*, 45 (1982): 85–100.

Salih, 'Abdullah, "Al-Ittifaq al-Turki al-Isra'ili wa-'Amaliyyat al-Salam," *Al-Siyaya al-Duwaliyya* (July 1996): 78–82.

Sammak, Muhammad al-, "Al-'Alaqat al-'Arabiyya al-Turkiyya, Hadiruha wa-Mustaqbaluha," *Al-'Arab wal-Atrak fi 'Alam Mutaghayyir* (1993).

Sarraf, 'Ali al-, "Al-Mawt 'Atashan," *Al-Shahid*, 56 (1990): 42–47.

Sayarı, Sabri, "Turkey: The Changing European Security Environment and the Gulf Crisis," *Middle East Journal*, 46 (1992): 9–21.

Sever, Ayşegül, "The Arab–Israeli Peace Process and Turkey Since the 1995 Interim Agreement," *Turkish Review of Middle Eastern Studies*, 9 (1996–97): 111–137.

———, "Turkey and the Syrian–Israeli Peace Talks in the 1990s," *Middle East Review of International Affairs* (MERIA), 5 (2001): 1–16.

Shakmak, Sim, "Mawqi' Turkiyya fi al-Hilf al-Atlasi," *Al-Mustaqbal al-'Arabi* (November 1982): 101–111.

Sheffy, Yigal, "The Military Dimension of the Gulf War," in Ami Ayalon (ed.), *MECS 1991* (Boulder, 1993): 63–87.

Shmuelevitz, Aryeh, "Turkey," in Colin Legun, Haim Shaked, and Daniel Dishon (eds.), *MECS 1980–81* (New York, 1982): 809–863.

Soysal, Ismail, "Political Relations between Turkey and Egypt in the Last Sixty Two Years," *Studies on Turkish Arab Relations*, 2 (1987): 49–57.

Starr, Joyce R., "Water Wars," *Foreign Policy*, 82 (1991): 17–37.

Stein, Kenneth W., "The Arab–Israeli Peace Process," in Bruce Maddy-Weitzman (ed.), *MECS 1996* (Boulder, 1998): 34–62.

Strategic Comments, *IISS*, 2 (July 1996).

Tavlaş, Nezih, "Türk–İsrail Güvenlik ve İstihbarat İlişkileri," *Avrasya Dosyası*, 5:1 (Spring 1999): 76–101.

Tevetoğlu, Cihad Fethi, "Bugünkü Türk-Suudi Dostluğuna İlk Adım: Gazi Mustafa Kemal–Faysal bin Abdülaziz Görüşmesi," *Studies on Turkish–Arab Relations*, Annual 1986.

Thabit, Mustafa Muhammad 'Abd al-Hamid, "Al-'Alaqat al-'Arabiyya al-Turkiyya ba'd Harb al-Khalij," *Al-fikr al-Istratiji al-'Arabi*, 41 (1992): 107–120.

Turan, Ilter, "The Military in Turkish Politics," *Mediterranean Politics*, 2 (1997).

"Turkiyya wal-Amn al-Qawmi al-'Arabi: al-Siyasa al-Ma'iyya wal-Aqalliyyat," *Al-Mustaqbal al-'Arabi* (June 1992): 113–124.

'Uziel, Baruch, "The Peripheral Alliance," *Beterem* (H) (November 1948): 8–11.

Waxman, Dov, "Turkey and Israel: A New Balance of Power in the Middle East," *The Washington Quarterly*, 22 (1999): 25–32.

Weiker, Walter F., "Turkey," in Itamar Rabinovich and Haim Shaked (eds.), *MECS, 1984–85* (Tel Aviv, 1997): 660–700.

Winrow, Gareth M., "Turkey and the Newly Independent States of Central Asia and Transcaucasus," *MERIA Journal*, 2 (July 1997).

Yavuz, Hakan, "Turkey's Relations with Israel," *Foreign Policy* 15 (Ankara): 41–68.

———, "Turkish–Israeli Relations Through the Lens of the Turkish Identity Debate," *Journal of Palestine Studies*, 27 (1997): 22–37.

———, "Turkish Identity and Foreign Policy in Flux: The Rise of Neo-Ottomanism," *Critique*, 12 (1998): 19–41.

Zaki, Nabil, "Nahwa 'Alaqat 'Arabiyya-Turkiyya Jadida," *Awraq al-Sharq al-Awsat*, 18 (1996): 15–26.

Zisser, Eyal, "Remembering the Past, Looking to the Future: Syrian–Turkish Relations and their Place in Political Discourse and the Formation of Historical Memory in Syria," paper prepared for MESA, November 1998.

———, "Syria," *MECS, 1996* (Boulder, 1998): 630–668.

Ziyada, Khalid, "Al-'Arab wal-Turk fi al-Ta'rikh al-'Uthmani," in *Al-'Arab wal-Atrak fi 'Alam Mutaghayyir*, Beirut, 1993.

# Index

Breinigsville, PA USA
16 November 2009
227631BV00003B/2/P